C000136139

STUDYING RELIGION AND SOCIETY

How do you study religion and society? In this fascinating book, some of the most famous names in the field explain how they go about their everyday work of studying religions in the field. They explain how the ideas for their projects and books have come together, how their understanding of religion has changed over the years, and how their own beliefs have affected their work. They also comment on the changing nature of the field, the ideas which they regard as most important, and those which have not stood the test of time. Lastly they offer advice to young scholars, and suggest what needs to be done to enable the field to grow and develop further.

Contributions by Nancy T. Ammerman, William Sims Bainbridge, Eileen Barker, James A. Beckford, Peter Beyer, Irena Borowik, Steve Bruce, Mark Chaves, Grace Davie, Karel Dobbelaere, Barry A. Kosmin, Robert A. Orsi, Wade Clark Roof, Jean-Paul Willaime, Robert Wuthnow.

Titus Hjelm is Lecturer in Finnish Society and Culture at University College London, UK. He is editor of *Religion and Social Problems* (Routledge, 2011).

Phil Zuckerman is Professor of Sociology at Pitzer College, USA. His books include *Invitation to the Sociology of Religion* (Routledge, 2003).

STUDYING RELIGION AND SOCIETY

Sociological Self-Portraits

Edited by
Titus Hjelm and Phil Zuckerman

Routledge
Taylor & Francis Group

LONDON AND NEW YORK

First published in 2013
by Routledge
2 Park Square, Milton Park, Abingdon, Oxon OX14 4RN

Simultaneously published in the USA and Canada
by Routledge
711 Third Avenue, New York, NY 10017

Routledge is an imprint of the Taylor & Francis Group, an informa business

British Library Cataloguing in Publication Data
A catalogue record for this book is available from the British Library

Library of Congress Cataloging in Publication Data
Studying religion and society : sociological self-portraits / edited by Titus Hjelm
and Phil Zuckerman.
p. cm.
Includes index.
1. Religion and sociology – Study and teaching. I. Hjelm, Titus.
II. Zuckerman, Phil.
BL60.S833 2013
306.6071 – dc23
2012025184

ISBN: 978-0-415-66797-5 (hbk)
ISBN: 978-0-415-66798-2 (pbk)
ISBN: 978-0-203-07568-5 (ebk)

Typeset in Bembo
by Taylor and Francis Books

MIX
Paper from
responsible sources
FSC
www.fsc.org   FSC® C004839

Printed and bound in Great Britain by the MPG Books Group

CONTENTS

CONTRIBUTORS

Nancy T. Ammerman is Professor of Sociology of Religion at Boston University's School of Theology, and Chair of the Department of Sociology in the College of Arts and Sciences. She has spent much of her career studying American religious organizations, especially congregations and denominations. Her book *Pillars of Faith: American Congregations and their Partners* (2005) describes the common organizational patterns that shape the work of America's diverse communities of faith. She has also written extensively on conservative religious movements, including *Bible Believers: Fundamentalists in the Modern World* (1987) and *Baptist Battles: Social Change and Religious Conflict in the Southern Baptist Convention* (1990). Currently she is completing *Sacred Stories: Religion and Spirituality in Everyday Life* (forthcoming 2013) a book that analyzes how and when religion is present in the everyday worlds of ordinary Americans.

William Sims Bainbridge earned his sociology doctorate in 1975 from Harvard, with a dissertation about space exploration. After 20 years in universities, he joined the National Science Foundation, where he is a program director in Human-Centered Computing. His most recent book, *eGods* (forthcoming), is his ninth about religion and his fifth about virtual worlds, arguing that the supernatural fantasies in 41 computer games are no less realistic than conventional faiths. His most recent edited project, *Leadership in Science and Technology*, is a 725,000-word reference work intended to strengthen the ability of scientists and engineers to play leading roles in society. His current research focuses on information technology responses to death – artificial intelligence based on real individuals and ancestor veneration avatars – to replace a function traditionally served by religion. He is a theoretician in two radical movements seeking to transform society: the World Transhumanist Association and Pirate Parties International.

Eileen Barker, PhD, PhD h.c., OBE, FBA, is Professor Emerita of Sociology with Special Reference to the Study of Religion at the London School of Economics. Her main research interest is "cults," "sects," and new religious movements, and the social reactions to which they give rise. She has over 250 publications (translated into 27 different languages), which include the award-winning *The Making of a Moonie: Brainwashing or Choice?* (1989) and *New Religious Movements: A Practical Introduction* (1989). In the late 1980s she founded INFORM, a charity based at the LSE, which provides information about the new religions that is as accurate, objective, and up-to-date as possible.

James A. Beckford, a Fellow of the British Academy, is Professor Emeritus of Sociology at the University of Warwick. His main fields of research are the sociology of religions and social theory. His publications include *The Trumpet of Prophecy. A Sociological Analysis of Jehovah's Witnesses* (1975), *Cult Controversies* (1985), *Religion and Advanced Industrial Society* (1989), *Religion in Prison. Equal Rites in a Multi-Faith Society* (1998, with Sophie Gilliat), *Social Theory and Religion* (2003), and *Muslims in Prison: Challenge and Change in Britain and France* (2005, with D. Joly and F. Khosrokhavar).

Peter Beyer is Professor of Religious Studies at the University of Ottawa, Canada. His work has focused primarily on religion in Canada and on developing sociological theory concerning religion and globalization. His publications include *Religion and Globalization* (1994), *Religion in the Process of Globalization* (ed., 2001), and *Religions in Global Society* (2006), *Religion, Globalization, and Culture* (ed. with Lori Beaman, 2007), *Religion and Diversity in Canada* (ed. with Lori Beaman, 2008), as well as around 60 articles and chapters in scholarly journals and edited volumes. Since 2001 he has been conducting research on religious diversity in Canada and specifically on the religious expression of second-generation immigrant young adults in that country. From this research, he is principal author of the forthcoming volume, *Growing Up Canadian: Muslims, Hindus, Buddhists.*

Irena Borowik is Professor of Sociology at Jagiellonian University, Krakow, Poland. She has been President of Nomos Publishing House since 1991. She is interested in theoretical and methodological problems in the sociology of religion, religious change in post-communist countries, and the religiosity of European societies. She teaches courses related to the social aspects of religion, and her latest empirical research concerns the relation between religion and identity in the Crimea among Orthodox, Muslim, and Catholic populations. Her recent publications include "The Religious Landscape of Central and Eastern Europe after Communism" in *The Sage Handbook of the Sociology of Religion* (2007), (with Małgorzata Zawiła) *Religions and Identities in Transition* (2010), and "The Changing Meanings of Religion: Sociological Theories of Religion in the Perspective of the Last 100 Years," *International Review of Sociology* (2011).

Steve Bruce was born in Edinburgh and educated at the Queen Victoria School, Dunblane, Perthshire. He studied sociology and religious studies at the University of Stirling and taught at The Queen's University, Belfast, from 1978 to 1991 when he became Professor of Sociology at the University of Aberdeen. In 2003 he was elected a Fellow of the British Academy and in 2005 he was elected a Fellow of the Royal Society of Edinburgh. His published work in the sociology of religion includes: *God Save Ulster: The Religion and Politics of Paisleyism* (1986); *Religion in the Modern World: From Cathedrals to Cults* (1996); *Conservative Protestant Politics* (1998); *Choice and Religion: A Critique of Rational Choice Theory* (2000); *Fundamentalism* (2001); *God is Dead: Secularization in the West* (2002); *Politics and Religion* (2003); *Paisley* (2007); and *Secularization: In Defence of an Unfashionable Theory* (2011).

Mark Chaves is Professor of Sociology, Religion, and Divinity at Duke University. Among other projects, he directs the National Congregations Study (NCS), a wide-ranging survey of a nationally representative sample of religious congregations. The NCS was first conducted in 1998, a second wave occurred in 2006, and a third wave is happening in 2012. Professor Chaves is the author of *American Religion: Contemporary Trends* (2011), *Congregations in America* (2004), *Ordaining Women: Culture and Conflict in Religious Organizations* (1997), and many articles, mainly on the social organization of religion in the United States. He has chaired the General Social Survey's Board of Overseers, and has been President of the Society for the Scientific Study of Religion.

Grace Davie is Professor Emerita in the Sociology of Religion in the University of Exeter. She is a past president of the American Association for the Sociology of Religion (2003) and of the Research Committee 22 (Sociology of Religion) of the International Sociological Association (2002–2006). In 2000–2001 she was the Kerstin-Hesselgren Professor in the University of Uppsala, where she returned for the 2006–2007 academic session and again in 2010. In January 2008, she received an honorary degree from Uppsala. In addition to numerous chapters and articles, she is the author of *Religion in Britain since 1945* (1994), *Religion in Modern Europe* (2000), *Europe: The Exceptional Case* (2002) and *The Sociology of Religion* (2007); she is co-author of *Religious America, Secular Europe* (2008), and co-editor of *Predicting Religion* (2003) and *Welfare and Religion in 21st Century Europe* (2 vols) (2010 and 2011).

Karel Dobbelaere is Emeritus Professor at the University of Leuven and the University of Antwerp (Belgium), where he taught sociology, sociology of religion and culture, and sociological research. He is an elected member of the Royal Flemish Academy of Belgium for Sciences and Fine Arts and of the Academia Europaea. He was president and secretary general of the International Society for Sociology of Religion; a Visiting Fellow of All Souls College (Oxford, UK), the Nanzan Institute for Religion and Culture (Nagoya, Japan), Sofia University (Tokyo, Japan), and the *Institut de Recherche sur les Sociétés Contemporaines* (CNRS, France), and Visiting Professor in Germany, Italy, the Netherlands, Scandinavia, and the USA. He has more than 250 publications, including 25 books, mostly in Dutch, English, and French. Some of his publications have also been translated into Danish, German, Italian, Japanese, Polish, and Spanish. His main fields of interest are religious and church involvement, pillarization, New Religious and Sectarian Movements, and secularization.

Titus Hjelm is Lecturer in Finnish Society and Culture at University College London, UK. His main areas of expertise are sociology of religion, social problems, social theory, media, and popular culture. His recent publications include *Religion and Social Problems* (ed., 2011), a special issue of the *Journal of Religion in Europe* on Islam in European news media (2012), and a special issue of *Popular Music History* on heavy metal music (ed. with Keith Kahn-Harris and Mark LeVine, 2012). In addition, he has published several books in Finnish, and articles in journals such as *Social Compass* and *Journal of Contemporary Religion*. He is co-editor of the *Journal of Religion in Europe* (published by Brill) and the founding Chair of the American Academy of Religion's Sociology of Religion Group.

Barry A. Kosmin is Founding Director of the Institute for the Study of Secularism in Society and Culture (ISSSC) and Research Professor, Public Policy and Law, at Trinity College, Hartford, Connecticut. He is a Senior Associate at Oxford Centre for Hebrew and Jewish Studies, University of Oxford, UK. Dr. Kosmin is also joint editor of *Secularism & Nonreligion* and has been Principal Investigator since 1990 of the American Religious Identification Survey (ARIS). He is co-author (with Seymour P. Lachman) of *One Nation Under God* (1993) and (with Ariela Keysar) of *Religion in a Free Market* (2006), and co-editor (with Ariela Keysar) of *Secularism and Secularity: Contemporary International Perspectives* (2007), *Secularism and Science in the 21st Century* (2008), and *Secularism, Women and the State* (2009). An internationally known expert in Jewish demography, he was Founding Director of the Mandell L. Berman Institute – North American Jewish Data Bank 1986–1996 and directed the 1990 US National Jewish Population Survey.

Robert A. Orsi is Professor of Religious Studies and History at Northwestern University and Grace Craddock Nagel Chair in Catholic Studies. His publications include *The Madonna of 115th Street: Faith and Community in Italian Harlem, 1880–1959* (3rd edn, 2010); *Thank You, Saint Jude: Women's Devotions to the Patron Saint of Hopeless Cases* (1996); and *Between Heaven and Earth: The Religious Worlds People Make and the Scholars Who Study Them* (2005). He is also editor of *The Cambridge Companion to Religious Studies* (2012). Professor Orsi has held fellowships from the National Endowment for the Humanities and the Guggenheim Foundation and a member of the American Academy of Arts and Sciences. He is currently at work on a history of Catholic childhoods in the United States in the 20th century.

Wade Clark Roof is J.F. Rowny Professor of Religion and Society at the University of California, Santa Barbara. He is Director of the Walter H. Capps Center for the Study of Ethics, Religion, and Public Life and author (with William McKinney) of *American Mainline Religion: Its Changing Shape and Future* (1987), *A Generation of Seekers: The Spiritual Journeys of the Baby Boom Generation* (1993), *Spiritual Marketplace: Baby Boomers and the Remaking of American Religion* (1999), and (with Jackson W. Carroll) *Bridging Divided Worlds: Generational Cultures in Congregations* (2002). Each year for the past ten years he has directed a "Study of the United States Summer Seminar" for

18 scholars from other countries, a program funded by Fulbright/US Department of State. Currently, he is conducting a research project on "Progressive Religion in Southern California" funded by the Ford Foundation.

Jean-Paul Willaime is Professor of the History and Sociology of Protestantism at the Ecole Pratique des Hautes Etudes, Department of Religious Studies, Sorbonne, Paris. He is a member of the Group Societies, Religion, Laïcite Research Centre (EPHE/CNRS) and of the European Institute for Religious Sciences. His research interests include sociology of religion (history, methodology, and theory), mainline and evangelical Protestantism, religions and school education, and European religion. His main publications include *Profession: pasteur* (1986); *La précarité protestante: Sociologie du protestantisme contemporain* (1992); *Sociologie des Religions* (3rd edn, 2004); with Danièle Hervieu-Léger, *Sociologies et religion: Approches classiques* (2001); *Europe et religions. Les enjeux du XXIe siècle* (2004); *Sociologie du Protestantisme* (2005); with Robert Jackson, Siebren Miedema, Wolfram Weisse (eds), *Religion and Education in Europe* (2007); *Le retour de la religion dans la sphère publique. Vers une laïcité de reconnaissance et de dialogue* (2008); with Matthias Koenig Hg, *Religionskontroversen in Frankreich und Deutschland* (2008); with Céline Béraud (eds), *Les jeunes, l'école et la religion* (2009); with Micheline Milot, Philippe Portier (eds), *Pluralisme religieux et citoyenneté* (2010); and with Sébastien Fath (eds), *La nouvelle France protestante. Essor et recomposition au XXIe siècle* (2011).

Robert Wuthnow teaches sociology and directs the Center for the Study of Religion at Princeton University where he recently spent six years in department chair purgatory. He is the author of more than two dozen books on American culture and religion, including *The Restructuring of American Religion: Society and Faith since World War II* (1988); *Red State Religion: Faith and Politics in America's Heartland* (2011); and *Small Town America: Finding Community, Shaping the Future* (2013).

Phil Zuckerman is Professor of Sociology at Pitzer College in Claremont, California. His main areas of expertise are the sociology of religion, sociology of secularity, and Scandinavian society. He has published several books, including *Faith No More: How and Why People Reject Religion* (2011), *Society without God* (2008), and *Invitation to the Sociology of Religion* (2003). He has edited several books, including *Sex and Religion* (2005), and has served on the editorial board of the journal *Sociology of Religion* and currently serves on the editorial board of the journal *Secularism & Nonreligion*.

1

INTRODUCTION

On sociological self-reflection

Titus Hjelm and Phil Zuckerman

This is a book we have always wanted to read. We are both sociologists hovering somewhere in the grey area between early and mid-career, and our main area of interest for the past several years has been religion. We have read the theories, we have grappled with the methodologies, and we have learned from numerous case studies. But we have never had a chance to read about how the most famous and influential names in the field went about their everyday work of studying religion and society. True, we have been lucky enough to have met and worked with many of them personally – and have gained unique insights from such associations – but there is so much more we wanted to know. In addition, we feel – no, we *know* – that there are many others like us who would like to know more about the *craft* of sociology of religion.

Sociology is very much a human endeavor. We engage our subjects not as passive observers, but as thinking and feeling human beings. While most sociologists nowadays would acknowledge the reflexive nature of our work, very little has been written about the issue – except in abstract, normative terms. It is with this in mind that we set out to edit this book. What we had in mind was an "informal methodology textbook,"[1] a collection of narratives that are not normative, like usual methods literature, but illustrative of how the craft of sociology of religion is *actually* practiced. We have taken the words of one sociological giant, Robert K. Merton, seriously. Speaking of scientific methods literature, he commented that "this literature is concerned with [...] ways in which scientists ought to think, feel, and act. It does not necessarily describe, in needed detail, the ways in which scientists actually do think, feel, and act."[2]

Why, for example, do scholars undertake particular research projects or identify with a particular theoretical perspective?[3] This is something we only rarely get to read from the published monographs or articles. We agree with Richard Jenkins, who notes that:

> [T]he role of individual history and experience – which includes political and ethical conviction – in shaping our curiosity, in deciding *which* research gets done and by *whom*, shouldn't be underestimated. If there is a cumulative logic to scientific discovery – and I'm not wholly convinced that this notion applies to science, let alone sociology – then it's probably no more important than the biographies and idiosyncrasies of the human beings who plan and execute it.[4]

In a scholarly self-portrait of his own, prominent American sociologist Seymour Martin Lipset questions whether "an author or scholar is the best person to properly evaluate or explain the logic contained in the work which he [*sic*] has done."[5] Certainly, posthumous biographies of sociology's classic figures – even when written by sociologists or other academics – make connections between the classics' personal lives and their work that few autobiographers like to admit to. No wonder that Joachim Radkau's psychoanalytically tinged biography of Max Weber, for example, caused such a stir in the field.[6]

Nevertheless, looking at the history of sociology, the intersections of personal biography and scholarship are everywhere to be found: Marx and especially Engels (although firmly bourgeois themselves) found inspiration from their observations of the injustices suffered by the working classes in 19th-century Manchester and London. Weber grappled with the simultaneous urge to analyze the world scientifically and change it by being active in politics. Perhaps most acutely, Georg Simmel observed the micro interactions of people in order to understand the forms of sociability. His essay on the "outsider," for example, gets much of its power in the context of Simmel's ancestry as a Jew barred from employment in German academia for most of his life.[7]

The classic sociologists were not always explicit about the connection between biography and scholarly interests – indeed none wrote autobiography as such – and post-WWII sociology, especially in the USA, tended to downplay the role of the individual in the pursuit of social scientific knowledge. It was C. Wright Mills, the "deviant academic,"[8] who "rehistoricized" sociology as an academic endeavor. For Mills the (now ubiquitous) "sociological imagination" meant bringing together and recognizing "history and biography and the relations between the two within society."[9] Although sociologists were somewhat slow to turn this sociological gaze reflexively towards their own profession, several publications in the past 40 or so years have taken the challenge of sociological autobiography seriously. At the one end of the autobiographical spectrum is Phillip Hammond's *Sociologists at Work*, a collection of research project "chronicles" which discuss the social context of sociological research – but less so the biography of the individual researcher.[10] At the other end is Arthur Shostak's *Private Sociology*, which aims to go beyond the autobiographical, to be "the study of what we hesitate to tell,"[11] and the impact of these experiences – interracial relationships, abortion, and being religious, for example – on sociological work. In between are collections that take the middle road between the personal and the contextual, most notably Horowitz's *Sociological Self-Images: A Collective Portrait*,[12] Riley's *Sociological Lives*,[13] Berger's *Authors of their Own Lives: Intellectual Autobiographies of Twenty American Sociologists*,[14] Glassner and Hertz's *Our Studies, Ourselves: Sociologists' Lives and Work*,[15] and Deflem's *Sociologists in a Global Age: Biographical Perspectives*.[16] These books concur on the point that where people come from, who they interact with, and the institutional contexts of their work all influence socio-logical research. Even Pierre Bourdieu, who begins his book *Sketch for Self-Analysis*[17] with the words "this is not an autobiography," spends a significant amount of space describing the intellectual framework (the "field" of academia) that shaped his career.

What is lacking in almost all of the above examples, however, is the sociology of religion. With the exception of Robert Bellah, Andrew Greeley, Philip Hammond, and Edward Tiryakian, none of the sociologists in the above works can be char-acterized as sociologists of religion. True, Bourdieu has written about religion, but he is hardly known as a sociologist of religion. This lacuna is most likely an effect of the marginal status of the sociology of religion in the broader field, bemoaned by many of its proponents – some of them featured in this book.[18] Thus, although Peter Berger, one of the most influential sociologists of religion ever, recently published an autobiography,[19] there is a gap in the literature that this book seeks to address.

With the above idea about an "informal methodology textbook" in mind, we sent out an invitation with the following guidelines.

> The form/style of the essay is free and open, but would hopefully include discussion of the "nuts and bolts" of your way of doing sociology of religion and thoughts on some of the following questions:
>
> - How has your identity as a sociologist of religion developed?
> - How have the ideas for your research projects and books come together? (Perhaps focus on one project in particular.)
> - Are there particular events in your personal and/or professional life that have shaped your scholarship?
> - How has your understanding of religion changed over the years? Do you still think about religion in the same way as when you started your career?
> - Looking back on your work, are there any regrets? Things you could have done better or differently?
> - Are there any ideas or theories that you no longer espouse or hold to be true?
> - In the past 40 years, what do you think have been the greatest/most important insights, theories, answers, etc. generated by sociologists of religion?
> - What do you think are the greatest strengths and weaknesses of the sociological perspective when applied to religion?
> - In what ways have your own personal religious beliefs (or lack thereof) been an advantage or disadvantage in your work? How have they affected what you study and how you study it?

- What advice would you give to young scholars? If the sociology of religion is to remain relevant and strong in the decades ahead, what should we be mindful of? What might we do differently than previous generations?

Although we wanted to give broad guidelines, the authors in this volume address the above questions in different ways, of course. In terms of coverage, while we acknowledge serious gaps in gender, ethnic, and geographical representation, we believe we have succeeded in capturing a wonderful variety of important insights from people whose work we have always admired – even when we have disagreed with them.

Thus, while (auto)biography may indeed be the "illusion" Bourdieu claims it to be,[20] it can – when reflexively engaged – give us insights into influences, patterns, and styles that might otherwise remain unacknowledged or implicit. True to form, we will give you a glimpse of our own sociological trajectories before summarizing some insights from the contributions.

Phil: Studying the religious and the secular

When it comes to knowing about a sociologist's personal background, I am quite conflicted. On the one hand, I think such information should be deemed irrelevant. On the other hand, I find it downright fascinating.

Let me explain.

I strongly believe that scholarship should be assessed, critiqued, or appreciated by its contents alone: the parsimoniousness of its theoretical assertions, the empirical strength of its data, and the clarity of its articulation. The author's background shouldn't be taken into account. In fact, I once became rather worked up about this very issue, arguing with a graduate student during a class discussion. We were having a back-and-forth about the week's assigned reading (a book on rational choice theory and religion), when the student wanted to know the personal details about the author: What was his race? His age? His religious background? His political persuasion? I replied that such information was irrelevant, and that to refer to or draw upon such matters was inappropriately *ad hominem*. "Imagine if we didn't even know who the author was," I vehemently exhorted. "Suppose we found the book with its cover torn off. No name attached. We would still be faced with the content of the book: the arguments and the data. What do you think of *them*?" The student wasn't convinced, demanding that one cannot separate scholarly arguments from their author. But I remained firm. And I know that many share the point of view I was holding to: a scholar's background, upbringing, religious beliefs, demographics, or educational experiences should remain immaterial. Indeed, one very prominent sociologist of religion whom we invited to contribute to this volume declined, stating succinctly: "I prefer to let my work speak for itself." I am sympathetic to that position.

However, in flagrant contradiction to what I have just expressed above, I must admit that I find learning about the personal backgrounds, worldviews, and formative experiences of various sociologists to be intrinsically compelling. Undeniably illuminating. To know, for instance, about Max Weber's personal history – the relationship he had with his mother and father, the social milieu within which he grew up, his professional arc, his own self-designation as being "religiously unmusical" – such background information sheds an undeniable ray of light upon his scholarly output, and makes it all the richer. And I am certain that Emile Durkheim's status as a non-believing Jew in fin-de-siècle France affected, influenced, and perhaps even made possible the unique way in which he was able to theorize about religion and society. The same may be said of any of the pioneers of the sociology of religion, from W.E.B. Du Bois to Charlotte Perkins Gilman: their family upbringing, personal worldviews, and the significant influences in their development as scholars helped to shape their published work, and the more we learn of the former, the better we can enjoy and appreciate the latter. And so it goes for the top sociologists of religion today: knowing a little about who they are is undeniably illuminating. So it is this latter personal compulsion – to learn something about the influential scholars whose work has been so important to me in my own attempt to study and make sense of religion within society – which has won out, and propelled me to be a co-editor of this volume. And the next time a graduate student wants to bring an author's background into the discussion, I will be a little more open and sympathetic, to be sure.

So, in the spirit of this volume, I'll just say a little about myself.

Although brought up in a very Jewish home (my father was a Yiddish professor and my mother's parents just narrowly escaped the Holocaust), I was not raised to believe in God or anything supernatural. My father was an atheist and my mother was simply indifferent to such matters. Yes, we celebrated major Jewish holidays with our extended family, I went to Hebrew school two days a week after school; I also went to Yiddish school for a spell, I had a bar mitzvah, I attended Jewish summer camps, and I even lived for a year in Israel—and yet my entire Jewish existence was devoid of any theological convictions or supernatural assumptions. Being Jewish was about culture, politics, family, books, history, heritage, food, klezmer music, and hanging out with other Jews with similar orientations. It wasn't about God – *at all*. Indeed, since all liturgy was in Hebrew, I didn't even know what I was saying as I learned to recite this or that prayer. Given my background, I have always had a very easy time understanding the communal aspects of religious life, and empathizing with those who find it nurturing or enjoyable. And it helped guide the ethnographic research for my first book, *Strife in the Sanctuary*,[21] which was about contemporary Jewish congregations in the Pacific Northwest. I have also had a very easy time understanding the ritual aspects of religion, and can readily see their appeal and function as ways to infuse life with a bit of specialness, sacredness. But as for belief in God – or anything supernatural – this has always dumbfounded me, which I made clear in my second book, *Invitation to the Sociology of Religion*.[22] To this day, and even though I am familiar with all the standard sociological and psychological explanations, I still find it very hard to understand how so many people can believe in gods, demons, angels, heaven, hell, and the like. Clearly, my own atheistic background has greatly shaped the way I approach and theorize about religion, and the kinds of questions I seek to explore. It has also meant that I simply don't "get" faith, which perhaps limits my ability to truly understand that aspect of religion. Or maybe, some might argue, it *enhances* my ability to do so. Either way, nothing confounds, baffles, and frustrates me more than encountering intelligent, well-read, articulate, thoughtful men and women who are strong religious believers; the mystery of how they can believe what is – to me – so obviously nonsensical will gnaw at me until I die.

After many years of trying to understand how and why it is that people can believe what I cannot, I grew a little weary. I thus decided to change my focus. I realized that no one was studying the millions of people like me and those I grew up with: non-believers. Atheists, agnostics, humanists, and various other secular folk had simply not received any substantial attention from sociologists, anthropologists, or psychologists. And so, about eight years ago, I began to look at secularity in the contemporary world; I have studied secular culture in Scandinavia, which resulted in my book *Society without God,*[23] and also apostates in America, which resulted in my book *Faith No More.*[24] Fortunately, many other scholars – both here in the USA and in Europe – recognized the same lacuna that I did, and now there are dozens of social scientists studying various aspects of irreligion. We have even founded a new journal, *Secularism & Nonreligion* – the first peer-reviewed journal of its kind. I am excited to be a part of this new enterprise.

In my study of religion and secularity, sociology has been my main lens, my unyielding flashlight. I love the sociological approach to religion and secularity because it focuses on how religion and secularity are actually lived, on the ground, in everyday life. Sociology studies religious and secular *people*, not just ancient texts, religious scriptures, or philosophical thought. The sociology of religion/secularity always links a given religious/secular individual, group, or movement to broader societal trends and historical developments. It recognizes the degree to which religion/secularity are shaped and influenced by various other elements in society, and conversely, how such elements in society can in turn be shaped and influenced by religion/secularism. And finally, for me, the sociological stress on socialization is key. I am fairly convinced that most people are religious or secular because they have been socialized to be so. Indeed, socialization helps me to understand and explain belief in God specifically; people tend to believe what they have been taught to believe as children, and when one's social world is infused with certain religious beliefs – when those beliefs are espoused by one's parents, family, neighbors, teachers, media, government, and so on – most people will successfully internalize them. And non-believers, such as me, are certainly not exempt from this dynamic.

Titus: Religion, sociology, and being critical

When I was born in the mid-1970s, more than 90 percent of the population of Finland were members of the Lutheran state church. And so was I. Yet, early on I realized that this meant very little. We went to church for baptisms, weddings, and funerals, but other than that, religion played little part in everyday life. In school we had to attend mass at the end of the year and the religion teacher would say a morning prayer once or twice a week on the PA system, but these were occasions to be endured rather than enjoyed. A student of mine remarked – much later – that Finnish Lutheranism could be best described as "lukewarm" and I think she had a point. Certainly that was how I personally felt about it.

Considering the above – and the fact that my mother was firmly part of the 1968 generation and an admirer of Marx, Engels, and Lenin – it is perhaps somewhat surprising that I found religion fascinating. Admittedly, for a long time I didn't. But when an upper secondary school teacher showed me that religion can be examined "objectively" without subscribing to religious beliefs, I became interested. Although music was my first choice, I thought I needed a "backup" just in case playing in a rock band didn't quite work out professionally. The Department of Religious Studies at the University of Helsinki seemed to offer a good backup solution. And here I am.

The good thing about religious studies in the Finnish context was that, although to an extent embedded in the "world religions" tradition, there was disciplinary variety as well. We were told that history, phenomenology, anthropology, psychology, and sociology were the main approaches to studying religion and that we should specialize in one of them. Although initially historically attuned, I became interested in sociology quite early on because I was always more interested in studying people than traditions as such. Pursuing a PhD in the sociology of religion required some creative thinking, though. The effects of the post-1968 radicalization meant, as I have argued elsewhere,[25] that sociology departments in Finland had no expertise in religion. I was not interested in "church and social studies" offered by the practical theology department, so religious studies was the only realistic place to study for a PhD. This meant, however, that most of the actual sociology I had to learn by myself. Although my supervisor organized a vibrant seminar on discursive and rhetorical approaches to the study of religion, which led to my first publications (and continues to influence my work),[26] I didn't really have the kind of mentor that most contributors to this volume mention as key people in their formative stages. On the one hand, a mentor is something that I have missed in retrospect. On the other hand, however, I was free to choose my topic, my theoretical framework, and methods, which suited me more than well. I soon became interested in whatever people thought of as "bad religion," especially New Religious Movements and the dynamics of how these groups became pejoratively labeled as "cults."[27] I found my "mentors" in Jim Beckford's and Eileen Barker's fantastic books[28] in that early stage. Needless to say, it has been a great honor to work with them in later years.[29]

Sociology fitted my profile also in the sense that I soon realized religion wasn't the only thing I was interested in academically. True, in terms of empirical research, religion has been a steady feature of my work, but it has often overlapped with sociological approaches to the media, popular culture, social movements, and social problems, for example. I have also always had a keen interest in social theory and social research methods.[30] I find it therefore unfortunate that those who pass for sociologists are still defined primarily by their degrees rather than what they do. I sympathize – to a degree – with Steve Bruce's view that sociological "borrowings" in religion research can be problematic especially in terms of unfamiliarity with sociological theory and practice[31] (p. 100), but again, I would like to think that sociology is something people *do* rather than something they simply qualify in by virtue of their degree. Some just do it better than others. I absolutely do agree with Bruce and Beckford in thinking that *religion is not special*. For me at least, sociology provides the perspectives and tools with which to study religion just like I would any other form of collective human action. My disciplinary identification with sociology has been guided by this idea – which perhaps also explains why I have found many of the key debates in religious studies just not very interesting.

Finally, an increasingly important theme in my work arises from another intersection of the personal and the professional. Although social critique was in some ways ingrained in me from early on – my mother did, after all, think that hanging a poster of Lenin at the foot of my bed when I was five was terribly funny – it was easy to avoid seeing blatant inequality in the Finland of my youth and student days. Not only has the world changed since, but moving to London for work has opened my eyes in many ways. Class and ethnic boundaries are not only visible but actively reproduced in politics, media, and everyday life. Not that London is unique – news from the "old country" point to similar developments, if on a smaller scale.

This personal interest in inequality and injustice led me to explore how these issues were tackled in the sociology of religion. While critical approaches to religion and ethnicity (and/or race) have been quite well established in the field, there is little research on religion and class.[32] Most importantly in my opinion: regardless of individual "critical" studies, *critical sociology of religion as a sub-field or a coherent perspective does not currently exist.*[33] To me, critical sociology of religion means taking boundaries as a starting point and analyzing the reproduction and transformation of those boundaries, both in the sense of (1) the religious legitimation of social inequality, and (2) the social legitimation (and de-legitimation) of religious groups. To this end I have found going back to Marx revitalizing (as have many economists in the wake of the current crisis), but I have never found a knee-jerk Marxist approach helpful. Hence (among other things), "being critical" does not in my case equal atheism— unlike what some religious people like to think whenever they hear the name of Marx. I have, however, in the spirit of "criticalizing" the sociology of religion, become increasingly critical of the privileged positions of state churches in countries such as Finland—and of scholarship that insists on denying the inequality of religious communities in such countries.[34] Perhaps that makes me a "secularist," even if otherwise I am simply indifferent to the truth claims of religion.

In many ways this critical perspective follows from and expands my earlier fascination with "bad religion" and "cults." A recent special issue of the *Journal of Religion in Europe*,[35] for example, looked at the ways in which Islam and Muslims are constructed in the media, and how those constructions reproduce ideas of "us" versus "them" in the European public sphere. What I see as the critical function of research such as this (even if the individual contributors to the above issue don't necessarily) is to employ social scientific methods to recognize the processes that reproduce inequality and hamper intercultural dialogue and peaceful coexistence. I do think that as sociologists we need to talk to a broader audience than other academics. At the same time – as someone equally inspired by Weber and Marx – I think our choice of topics can (and should perhaps) be inspired by our interests, but interests can never dictate our results. Obviously, this is a rather simplistic take on a perennial problem, but something that is beyond the scope of this reflection. I hope that in the future this "critical sociology of religion" finds a place in the broader field. Certainly the contributions to this volume show that many of the leading names today found their research topics by identifying a gap in the field, and have consequently carved a niche for themselves by filling that gap. It is easy to be inspired by that.

At the crossroads of the personal and the professional: first impressions

Among these assembled essays, written by the leading sociologists of religion of the past half century, one finds numerous commonalities, while also many differences. Which ones are significant and which ones are not will, of course, vary according to each reader. That said, we shall proceed here to highlight and discuss those similarities which provide this collection with some underlying, unifying themes. We will also highlight some of the more overt idiosyncrasies.

In terms of distinctions among the contributions, we first note that it is the female scholars who tend to include details about their own immediate family life – being a parent and/or a spouse – and the effect and influence this had on their careers, as well as their sociological imaginations, both positively and negatively. For example, Irena Borowik writes about the important influence of her husband in opening up the doors of academia to her. Eileen Barker writes about the time when her daughter became severely ill – a trying period which put her career on hold. Grace Davie writes about the ways in which she too had to put her career on hold in order to raise her children, and the various moves she had to make as a result of her husband's career. As she says in her chapter, these experiences caused her to remain deeply sympathetic to women who must juggle the simultaneously hefty undertakings of family responsibilities and career building. Interestingly, not a single one of the male contributors discusses the impact of family life, or raising children, or spousal connections had on his life or career.

Another notable difference among the various contributions is the extent and degree to which individual authors discuss their own childhoods, parents, grandparents, family backgrounds, ethnicities, communities, and/or other early non-academic influences. Some, like Robert Orsi, Wade Clark Roof, and Irena Borowik, include rich, extensive details about such things – starting their essays by situating themselves within the familial, ethnic, and communal contexts from which they sprang. Yet others do not.

As for commonalities, interestingly, few contributors discuss their own personal faith or spirituality. Some – like ourselves – identify with Weber in being religiously "unmusical" or "tone-deaf." But one might think that – for people who study such matters – they would feel compelled, if not expected, to shed some light on their own souls. Do they believe in God? An afterlife? Karma? The power of prayer? And yet, contrary to possible expectations, we don't find much in the way of answers here. Aside from a distinct minority of overt non-believers who make their atheism clear, such as William Sims Bainbridge, the vast majority of contributors leave the question of their own faith/spirituality a mystery. One can only wonder: do they lack personal religious faith, but don't feel like saying so? And if that is the case, why not? Or conversely, do they in fact possess personal religious faith, but don't feel like saying so? And if that is the case, why not? The actual extent of the spirituality, personal faith, and/or religious beliefs of nearly all of the contributors is left notably opaque. One can only speculate as to why that is so.

As for other overriding themes that appear in almost every chapter, the prominence of intellectual/academic mentors is most apparent. Nearly every contributor stresses the key role a specific individual – or sometimes individuals – played in their scholarly development. As Peter Beyer bluntly declares, "mentors are crucial" (p. 69). For Nancy Ammerman, there was Barbara Hargrove. For James Beckford, there was Bryan Wilson. For Grace Davie, there was Margaret Hewitt. For Wade Clark Roof, there was Gerhard E. Lenski. For Robert Wuthnow, there was Charles Glock. And so on. In some instances, it was a specific mentor who first exposed them to the very possibility of studying sociology to begin with. For others, it was a specific mentor who turned them on to the option of studying religion sociologically. And yet for others, it was a specific mentor who prodded them to focus on a certain research topic or investigative undertaking – a prodding that would change their lives, change their academic trajectories, and ultimately, change the way they thought about religion.

Another common thread is the emphasis on the importance of data and real-world research concerning the study of religion. If there is anything which unites sociologists of religion, it is this: we always base our speculations and assertions concerning religion on the best empirical evidence we can muster. As Karel Dobbelaere clearly argues in his essay, "sociology is an empirical science, not a philosophy; its theoretical insights are based on empirical research" (p. 136). Whether it be survey responses, multivariate analysis, demographic information, in-depth interviews, participant observation, or an impressive combination thereof, we cannot and must not seek to understand the complex and colorful world of religion without doing actual research that generates verifiable data. Without some form of actual evidence, we simply aren't doing sociology. As Steve Bruce emphasizes towards the conclusion of his chapter, the most important question we can ask, as we navigate various debates or theories, is: To what extent does the evidence support this or that explanation?

Another commonality – which is not too surprising, given people's similar religious backgrounds, their geographical location, as well as the limited resources available in academic research – is the fact that nearly all of the contributors to this volume have studied Western religions, and more specifically, some version(s) of Christianity. Indeed, one of Jean-Paul Willaime's main points is to discuss how "sociology of Protestantism" (in the French context) can inform broader sociology of religion. To be sure, there are some exceptions to the dominance of Christianity, here and there. For example, Barry Kosmin has spent a considerable amount of time studying the secular and non-religious. James Beckford and Eileen Barker have studied Eastern-inspired new religious movements. Karel Dobbelaere has done work in Africa and Japan. And Peter Beyer characteristically talks about religion on a global scale. But despite these admirable exceptions, the fact remains that the bulk of the most important sociology of religion of the past half century has largely been the sociology of Western religion, or perhaps even more specifically, sociology of Christianities. Judaisms, Islams, Buddhisms, Shintos, Hinduisms, Chinese religions, Jainisms, Sikhisms, Zoroastrianisms, Indigenous South American and African religions – these have received far less attention by beacons of the field.

Finally, prominent throughout this collection is the tangible joy one feels in each chapter. Theses authors have clearly enjoyed what they have done for a living. They clearly love sociology. And they are overtly fascinated by religion, in all of its varied manifestations. And they have clearly found the sociological study of religion to be a deeply rewarding, satisfying intellectual enterprise. But it isn't just the joy for their life's work or their chosen discipline that comes across in these essays – it is also the joy they seemed to have experienced in the very writing of these autobiographical pieces. One senses an engaged, almost delighted vibe throughout each chapter. From the very tangible tone of each essay, it is clear that these esteemed scholars appreciated the chance to reflect upon themselves, their lives, their careers, their motivations, their research, and the various serendipities – as James Beckford or Mark Chaves would surely say – that permeated them all.

In this book, men and women who have spent their lives examining other people have had a unique opportunity to examine themselves – and they clearly relished that opportunity. Which makes for some great reading.

Notes

1 Cf. Irving Louis Horowitz, "Introduction," in *Sociological Self-Images: A Collective Portrait*, ed. Irving Louis Horowitz (Beverly Hills, CA: Sage, 1969), 9.

2 Quoted in Phillip E. Hammond, "Introduction," in *Sociologists at Work: The Craft of Social Research* (Garden City, NY: Anchor Books, 1967 [1964]), 3.

3 Cf. Seymour Martin Lipset, "Socialism and Sociology," in *Sociological Self-Images: A Collective Portrait*, ed. Irving Louis Horowitz (Beverly Hills, CA: Sage, 1969), 172.

4 Richard Jenkins, *Foundations of Sociology: Towards a Better Understanding of the Human World* (Basingstoke: Palgrave, 2002), 86. Italics in original.

5 Martin Lipset, "Socialism," 172.

6 Joachim Radkau, *Max Weber: A Biography* (Cambridge: Polity Press, 2009). For other good examples of sociological biography, see Steven Lukes, *Emile Durkheim: His Life and His Work: A Historical and Critical Study* (Harmondsworth: Penguin, 1973); Irving Louis Horowitz, *C. Wright Mills: An American Utopian* (New York: The Free Press, 1983); Helmut R. Wagner, *Alfred Schutz: An Intellectual Biography* (Chicago, IL: University of Chicago Press, 1983).

7 Georg Simmel, *Soziologie: Untersuchungen über die Forme der Vergesellschaftung* (Leipzig: Verlag von Duncker und Humblot, 1908), 685–691.

8 Horowitz, *Mills*, 4.

9 C. Wright Mills, *The Sociological Imagination* (New York: Oxford University Press, 1959), 6.

10 Phillip E. Hammond, *Sociologists at Work: The Craft of Social Research* (Garden City, NY: Anchor Books, 1967 [1964]).

11 Arthur B. Shostak, "Preface: On Getting Personal," in *Private Sociology: Unsparing Reflections, Uncommon Gains* (Dix Hills, NY: General Hall, 1996).

12 Irving Louis Horowitz (ed.), *Sociological Self-Images: A Collective Portrait* (Beverly Hills, CA: Sage, 1969).

13 Matilda White Riley (ed.), *Sociological Lives* (Newbury Park, CA: Sage, 1988).

14 Bennet M. Berger (ed.), *Authors of Their Own Lives: Intellectual Autobiographies of Twenty American Sociologists* (Berkeley: University of California Press, 1990).

15 Barry Glassner and Rosanna Hertz (eds), *Our Studies, Ourselves: Sociologists' Lives and Work* (Oxford: Oxford University Press, 2003).

16 Matthieu Deflem (ed.), *Sociologists in a Global Age: Biographical Perspectives* (Aldershot: Ashgate, 2007).

17 Pierre Bourdieu, *Sketch for Self-Analysis* (Cambridge: Polity Press, 2007 [2004]).

18 E.g., James A. Beckford, "The Sociology of Religion 1945–89," *Social Compass* 37(1/ 1990): 45–64; Malcolm B. Hamilton, *The Sociology of Religion: Theoretical and Comparative Perspectives*, 2nd edn (London: Routledge, 2001), vii; Helen Rose Ebaugh, "Return of the Sacred: Reintegrating Religion in the Social Sciences," *Journal for the Scientific Study of Religion* 41/3(2002): 385–395. It seems that despite the increasing public interest in religion, the subdiscipline's place in academic hierarchies has not changed. The attention of sociological luminaries such as Jürgen Habermas and Ulrich Beck attests to the fact that even if *religion* is back on the sociological agenda, the *sociology of religion* is still mostly absent. Beck's *God of One's Own* (Cambridge: Polity Press, 2010), for example, does not contain a single reference to insights from the sociology of religion, past or present.

19 Peter L. Berger, *Adventures of an Accidental Sociologist: How to Explain the World without Becoming a Bore* (Amherst, NY: Prometheus Books, 2011). Berger declined an invitation to contribute to this volume because he was just working on the above book – one of the few times that an editor can be genuinely happy about a declined invitation!

20 Bourdieu, *Sketch*, 1.

21 Phil Zuckerman, *Strife in the Sanctuary: Religious Schism in a Jewish Community* (Walnut Creek, CA: Alta Mira, 1999).

22 Phil Zuckerman, *Invitation to the Sociology of Religion* (New York: Routledge, 2003).

23 Phil Zuckerman, *Society without God: What the Least Religious Nations Can Tell us About Contentment* (New York: New York University Press, 2008).

24 Phil Zuckerman, *Faith No More: Why People Reject Religion* (New York: Oxford University Press, 2011).

25 Titus Hjelm, "To Study or Not to Study Religion and Society: The Institutionalization, Fragmentation, and Marginalization of Sociology of Religion in Finland," *Acta Sociologica* 51/2 (2008): 91–102.

26 E.g., Titus Hjelm, "Discourse Analysis," in *The Routledge Handbook of Methods in the Study of Religion*, ed. Michael Stausberg and Steven Engler (London and New York: Routledge, 2011).

27 E.g., Titus Hjelm, Henrik Bogdan, Asbjorn Dyrendal and Jesper Petersen, "Nordic Satanism and Satanism Scares: The Dark Side of the Secular Welfare State," *Social Compass* 56/4 (2009): 515–529; Titus Hjelm, "Between Satan and Harry Potter: Legitimating Wicca in Finland," *Journal of Contemporary Religion* 21/1 (2006): 33–48.

28 James A. Beckford, *Cult Controversies: The Societal Response to the New Religious Movements* (London: Tavistock, 1985); Eileen Barker, *The Making of a Moonie: Choice or Brainwashing?* (Oxford: Blackwell, 1984).

29 See Titus Hjelm (ed.), *Religion and Social Problems* (New York: Routledge, 2011).

30 E.g., Titus Hjelm, *Perspectives on Social Constructionism* (Basingstoke: Palgrave, forthcoming 2013)

31 As the Founding Chair of the Sociology of Religion Group at the Annual Meeting of the American Academy of Religion – a society for religious studies and theology professionals – I have come across this problem more than once. It is very difficult to attract good-quality submissions for themes that explore the more theoretical aspects of the field.

32 With some brilliant exceptions such as Sean McCloud, *Divine Hierarchies: Class in American Religion and Religious Studies* (Chapel Hill, NC: University of North Carolina Press, 2007); Sean McCloud and William A. Mirola (eds), *Religion and Class in America: Culture, History, and Politics* (Leiden, and Boston, MA: Brill, 2009).

33 Some headway is being made: e.g., Warren Goldstein (ed.), *Marx, Critical Theory, and Religion: A Critique of Rational Choice* (Chicago, IL: Haymarket Books, 2006). My take on the critical sociology of religion does not, however, draw from the "critical theory" of the Frankfurt School, but rather from Marx and Marxists such as Gramsci and Kautsky, and the critical tradition in empirical sociology.

34 In the case of Finland, for example, this of course begins with denying that there is a state church in the first place.

35 Titus Hjelm (ed.), "Islam and Muslims in the European Media." A special issue of the *Journal of Religion in Europe* 5/2 (2012).

2

A LIFE IN RELIGIOUS COMMUNITIES

Nancy T. Ammerman

I have been an observer of religious communities for as long as I can remember. It wasn't just that I went to church a lot when I was growing up. What made the difference was the particular vantage point from which I experienced the worship services and Sunday school classes and church meetings. As the daughter of the pastor, I was peculiarly both an insider and an outsider, someone with the intimate access of dinner-table conversations, but someone who would be gone again in a few years. During my growing up, my father took on a new pastoral challenge roughly every three years, so I became adept at reading the culture of each new congregation. It certainly never occurred to me at the time that I was learning to be a sociologist, but the skills and perspectives of those childhood experiences stayed with me.

Given that I was a girl, it also never occurred to me that I might follow in my father's footsteps. Baptist girls didn't become preachers. Not until I was well into my first professorial job did it suddenly hit me that if I had been a male child I almost certainly would have been groomed for the pastorate. But I wasn't, so my aspirations were shaped more by my mother's occasional career as a teacher. When I lined up my dolls, it was in a pretend classroom, not in pretend pews. When I went to college, I enrolled in the secondary education program so that I could get a teaching certificate to teach high school social studies. I double majored in history and sociology, but I still imagined myself in a very conventional public school classroom. How ironically fortunate for me that there were no high school social studies teaching jobs in Louisville, Kentucky, in the year I graduated and moved there to put my husband through seminary. (And how doubly fortunate that his career has been very unlike the track of a traditional Baptist pastor. He is now a university librarian.) Had there been a high school job that fall, I might still be trying to persuade 15-year-olds to care about Reconstruction.

My childhood and college education, then, had provided raw ingredients for a sociological career, but those ingredients were by no means arranged into a recognizable career track. When I started a sociology Master's program at the University of Louisville I knew little more than that I needed to go back to school, I had always been drawn to sociology, and I still wanted to be a teacher. It was there that I met Tony Blasi, Jon Rieger, Pam Oliver, and Tom Keil – professors who began to teach me what it is to be a sociologist. Tony introduced me to the sociology of religion in a whirlwind directed study. *Elementary Forms* one week; *Protestant Ethic* the next; *Sacred Canopy* the next – not excerpts, but the whole thing vigorously discussed each week.[1] I still have the typed (yes typed) notes I banged out in those heady weeks. I was being equally challenged in classes on urban life and on deviance, and Blasi's theory seminar ranged from Marx to Husserl. But turning a sociological eye on religion fascinated me the most. I still had little notion of how a sociological career was structured, but I knew more about what I wanted to study – and that a Master's degree would not be enough.

It still seems completely absurd and amazing to me that my fairly random application to Yale's PhD program was successful. Mine was not the usual Yale profile. But they took a chance, and so did we. Living in the northeast was a far cry from the midwestern and mid-south regions where we had been at home. While I had experience outside the midwest (having spent half my childhood in Arizona and southern California), New Haven, Connecticut, was definitely new territory. As we learned the terrain of our Jewish and Puerto Rican and Jamaican neighborhood, I was also learning the academic terrain of the field. From Rosabeth Kanter, I learned the intricacies of power in organizations. From Albert Reiss, I learned that one could do systematic statistical analysis of data gathered from direct observations. From Hillel Levine, I learned to think about how our moral categories – like the notion of evil – are constructed, maintained, and hidden from view. But most of all, the mentorship of Kai Erikson and Barbara Hargrove helped to shape me into the sociologist of religion I was becoming.

Erikson was fresh from the experience of being immersed in the culture of the West Virginia mountains of Buffalo Creek and, thankfully for me, fascinated by the religious communities and worldviews he found there.[2] When I said I might want to do a dissertation on fundamentalism, he was a willing co-conspirator.[3] Kai taught me to think about the social shape of the stories I was hearing and about how to survive in the field. But he also taught me (and a generation of my cohorts in his famous professional workshop) how to write about what I observed in a way that was shaped by the discipline, but true to the stories.

Hargrove, on the other hand, had been deeply engaged in the sociology of religion for more than a decade,[4] and she made sure that I knew the current literature in the field. Then when I first started to attend professional meetings, she was unrelenting in introducing me to the people who had produced that literature. In the late 1970s, it was truly remarkable to have a female mentor of this stature. When the women attending the meetings of the Association for the Sociology of Religion (ASR) gathered for lunch (probably in 1978), perhaps half a dozen senior women – Ruth Wallace, Helen Rose Ebaugh, Barbara, Meredith McGuire – were joined by an equal number of neophytes like me – Mary Jo Neitz and Lynn Davidman among them.

ASR was not many years past its evolution from the American Catholic Sociological Society, and the priestly presence was still there (as was the formidable Sr. Maria Augusta Neal). Women were scarce, and gender was not on the agenda.[5]

Thriving organizations not sheltering enclaves

In those years, the field was turning its attention to a much broader range of religious phenomena and slowly discovering, in spite of itself, that its primary theoretical paradigm – secularization – was inadequate to the task. My own work in the 1980s, however, seemed to move squarely with the old tides. Fundamentalism had been interesting to sociologists in large measure because it still seemed to fit the old model. As the modern world advanced, religion would either disappear or retreat into sheltering enclaves. These were the sheltering enclaves.[6] And nowhere in the US was the advance of the modern world more visible than in the transformation of the American South in the post-World War II period. A fundamentalist movement attempting to wrest control of the Southern Baptist Convention from the modernizing forces of its progressive-leaning leadership fit the script rather perfectly.

That the fundamentalists won, and that their leaders now have ready access to the highest levels of political power in the nation, did not fit the script. Their movement, as I discovered, could only partly be explained by macro-level cultural forces of change. One also had to employ the analytical tools of social movement theory and a sociology of organizations.[7] The long-term cultural trend might not have been on the side of the fundamentalists, but their ability to mobilize a movement easily overcame that liability. And their subsequent ability to utilize the organizational resources they captured paved the way for the cultural influence they now wield.[8]

If sociologists were to understand religion, then, we not only needed a wider range of vision, we also needed more than our macro theories of change and our micro theories of belief and identity. Religion is neither an amorphous cultural force nor a private "worldview." It takes shape in organizations that have a life of their own. My instinct in studying fundamentalism had been to study it in a single local congregation. When my Yale professors had asked, "How can those people believe those things?" my answer was, "They are enmeshed in a supportive community where 'those things' are normal." Now when asked to explain how a minority movement with a minority worldview could take over the largest Protestant denomination in the country, my answer was similar: They created a successful organization that could get out the vote. In the midst of trying to study "big things," I had discovered that those big things happen in communities and in organizations that embody and sustain them.

Having created a multi-layered analysis of a denomination, I began to think much more systematically about the nature of organized religious life, especially as it has taken shape in the United States. Through the 1990s and well into the first decade of the 21st century, I charted the webs of organizational life that continue to thrive and expand in this country. At about the time Stephen Warner[9] was writing about this country's "de facto congregationalism," I was documenting the usefulness of that perspective. There is indeed a remarkable structural similarity in the way different religious groups organize here, at the same time that our constitutional separation of church and state has opened the door to unprecedented religious variety.

Two things had sent me back from the large-scale denominational system to the local face-to-face gatherings Americans call congregations. I had joined an informal peer network called the Congregational Studies Project Team and had been introduced to their passionate advocacy for the importance of these local gatherings, as well as to the wealth of scholarship that was beginning to develop in a field they were essentially inventing – congregational studies.[10] And in the early 1990s I faced a remarkable challenge that allowed me to take those tools on a robust outing. Peter Berger suggested that I devise a plan for studying key social trends that were affecting American religion, and my answer was that we should look at local communities where those trends were especially visible and examine the work of the congregations in those communities. The Lilly Endowment funded the proposal, we fielded a stellar group of researchers in nine local communities around the country, and the resulting book, *Congregation and Community*, was among the first attempts to provide a systematic mapping of the relationships between religious institutions and the geographic and social places in which they were located.[11]

Exploring growing religious diversities

Each new project was stretching me further and further from the parochial world in which I grew up, even as it continued to build on what I had learned in moving from church to church and region to region. The "Congregations in Changing Communities" project (CCCP) took me from a gay-friendly Catholic parish in Long Beach, California, to black churches that were thriving pillars of the civil rights community in nearby West Adams. I worshiped in Lutheran, Jewish, Church of God, and country Methodist services. Some were independent and nondenominational; others, like the Existentialists, invented their own traditions.

The "Organizing Religious Work" project, undertaken in the late 1990s, stretched the boundaries even further, identifying 91 distinct religious traditions among the 549 congregations we studied. Reflecting back on the diversity I experienced in visiting the sites for that project, I wrote the following in an essay for *The American Interest*.[12]

> One weekend several years ago, when I was in Chicago doing research on American congregational life, I managed to attend six religious services in the space of a little over 24 hours. ... These services took me from the north suburbs to the south side and from Episcopal and Catholic to four distinct versions of American evangelicalism. My first stop, on Saturday afternoon, was a small Assemblies of God mission on the edge of one of Chicago's most notorious public housing projects. A group of young adults on mission, white and black, had moved their families from more comfortable locations into the neighborhood, rented a gym, and gathered kids and a few parents for sports, tutoring, bible study, and worship. The kids themselves led in lively singing, performed in skits, showed off their Bible memorization, and generally took responsibility for themselves and each other. While this is a "Pentecostal"

denomination, the service was absent any faith healing or speaking in tongues. Just a message about salvation and a plea to live a godly life in the midst of temptations that were only too apparent to everyone in the room.

Later that evening, I joined 3000 or so suburbanites on the campus of the famous Willow Creek Community Church for their "seeker service." As I entered, a multi-screen, multi-media presentation reminded me that "This is my Father's world," and as I took in the rolling fields and lake outside the floor-to-ceiling windows, the beauty and peacefulness was undeniable – and a far cry from the scene on the south side. But there were hints of the common culture of evangelicalism nonetheless – "I Lift My Voice," a Maranatha Music praise chorus, was sung in both places. The service here was led by a host of trained professionals, and the troubles to be avoided were loneliness and hypocrisy, rather than drugs and guns – but sin and salvation were still the theme. People need to recognize that they can't do it alone. They need God, and they need the support of a congregation.

Sunday morning found me at the early Mass in one of Chicago's myriad ethnic Catholic churches – this one Polish by heritage, but on a block where Spanish signs competed with the Polish and English ones, and Our Lady of Guadalupe had taken her place in the sanctuary along with Our Lady of Czestochowa. At this Mass, it was the elderly Polish population that came to visit with each other and experience the familiar rhythms of the service. Just being there was their way of expressing their religious devotion; it was hard to imagine them marching in anything more militant than a saint's day procession.

Catholics now constitute about a quarter of the American population, and many of them represent immigrant national communities, new and old – there are now roughly 25 million Latino/a Catholics, one-third of the total. They join an American Church transformed by Vatican II and shaped by members who are nearly as educated, middle class, and suburban as the well-heeled Episcopalians I met at the 10:00 service I attended that day in Hyde Park. Such "mainline" Protestants represent slightly less than a quarter of Americans, and most are decidedly non-evangelical in their piety. The accomplishments to be celebrated here were the beautifully renovated gothic building, the church's contributions to neighborhood activities, and their involvement in a peace and justice ministry. Doing good in the world is the chief mission to which these Christians feel called.

From Hyde Park, it was not such a long drive to the Baptist church that was next on my list, but I was afraid that my 11:45 arrival would make me unconscionably late. Not to worry. The African American evangelical traditions share none of their white counterparts' obsession with the clock. There was still a good three hours to go, hours that encompassed music and preaching that took the congregation from deep joy to solemn repentance, announcements that offered tips on job openings and recognition for students who had done exceptionally well, and a range of spiritual encounters from speaking in tongues to full immersion baptism to intense prayers for the deliverance of a young man from the demons that possessed him. This, too, is American evangelicalism – relatively small in numbers (about 5 percent of the population), but large in visibility and influence.

After the full-bodied engagement of that service, the last event of the day was much more serene and cerebral. The Sunday evening service held at a suburban, Dutch-heritage, Reformed Church in America was as traditionally evangelical as it gets. There were turn-of-the-century gospel hymns from the denominational hymnal, a sermon intended to encourage faithful church workers in their efforts, lots of references to missionaries and bible study and church programs. This is the well-oiled institutional machinery that has served evangelicals well for a century. As surely as they know that Jesus saves, they also know how to organize to proclaim that message.

The weekend was ending, but if I had started 24 hours sooner, I could easily have added Friday jumah prayers at any of Chicago's more than three dozen mosques and Sabbath services at one of the five dozen synagogues and perhaps even a service or two with a Buddhist, Hindu, Baha'i, or African indigenous community. About 5 percent of the active religious attenders in the U.S.A. go to something besides a church. And, of course, nearly 20 percent never go anywhere at all.

Expanding methods of study

This marathon 24 hours took place in the context of the research which my colleagues at Hartford Seminary and I were undertaking (again with the support of the Lilly Endowment). We were asking about the changing institutional shape of American religion — what do religious groups attempt to accomplish, and how do they organize themselves to do it? In exploring local congregations, I had been struck by the ubiquitous local service organizations that were woven, along with the congregations, into the fabric of those communities, but the organizational field is more expansive than that. In the United States, the voluntary principle has left the field open for religious people of all sorts to organize an enormous range of special purpose groups, publishers, mission societies, homeless shelters, and food pantries, in addition to the congregations, dioceses, and denominations we recognize as the backbone of the religious organizational world.[13] My task in this new project was to explore the connections through which congregations do their work.

The project started out with a design similar to the CCCP design. We would define a set of instructively varied geographic areas; and because the areas were bigger this time, we would select a random sample of the congregations in each. The plan then was to gather basic information from that whole sample, focusing finally on a small group of case study congregations for in-depth study. What we discovered quickly, however, was that the "basic" information we needed was significant enough that our primary activity would be gathering key informant interviews from that whole random sample. The local partner organizations they named then allowed us to create a sampling frame of organizations from which we could also select groups to interview about their work in the community and how congregations were a part of that work. In addition, the detailed questions we asked about congregations' relationship with their denomination allowed us to map those network ties, as well.

As a result, I was able to specify further the nature of the ties between congregations and their local communities, while expanding the focus beyond the local community. Looking for the flows both in and out of the congregation, we probed for the cultural, human, and financial resources which congregations draw on. What work do they do, with what partners? The base from which I would work in answering those questions was a much larger group of congregations than I had worked with before – 549 – which meant that much of what I learned was summarized in statistical tables, in addition to the stories that emerged in the interviews.[14] The analysis was both quantitative and qualitative.

It led me, among other conclusions, to argue against the received wisdom that denominations are a thing of the past. Many of them are formidable organizations. But, more importantly, they also have ways of telling their stories that can perpetuate and rejuvenate their traditions. We could also see new religious communities recognizing the cultural and institutional pressures to adopt denomination-like structures: national, state, and regional bodies, publishing houses, public spokespeople, and – above all – youth camps. There is work which local congregations cannot do alone, and they turn to these denominational partners, as well as to the local voluntary organizations that serve and enrich their local communities.

For me, observing religious communities had come to mean observing a very diverse and expansive organizational network, alongside careful on-the-ground attention to detail and nuance. Those details, along with the work of dozens of others who had been observing congregational life, helped to inform the ground-breaking work Mark Chaves was able to do in the National Congregations Study (NCS).[15] His brilliant sampling strategy helped to create a national base of organizational-level data on congregations, and our projects fed each other. Years of fieldwork – mine and many others' – found its way into questions that could, in the NCS, be asked of key informants in a representative national sample. In turn, his results provided a check on what I was finding. Sometimes he and I were asking exactly the same thing of our respondents, and the similar distributions of answers we got were somewhat awe-inspiring reminders that we can trust the scientific principles on which our research is built. Methods for the study of congregations had now expanded from the single ethnographic case studies with which most of us began into analysis based on a broad array of tools and comparisons.

In the midst of those new tools, many of my old skills and instincts were still there; but they, too, were being expanded and defined in new ways. As I observed religious communities, I watched for how people gathered, forming and reinforcing the connections I was learning to call "social capital."[16] I listened for what they said, not just in the sermons, but also in the announcements and prayer requests. And I tried in each place to tune my body and spirit to the rhythms of emotional engagement evoked by each community in its gathering. I had also learned to pay attention; that is, to the embodied and emotional character of congregational life, as well as to its material manifestations in buildings and furniture, signs and technology. A growing number of sociologists of religion were making a "cultural turn" that focused attention on more than belief and belonging.[17] At the same time I was publishing a book

that depended heavily on numbers, generalizations, and the importance of organizations, I was also becoming attuned to these material, emotional, and experiential
dimensions of religious life. That is a focus to which I would return in my early
Boston years.

Engaging larger publics

Meanwhile, the national context in which *Pillars of Faith* was published was a far cry
from the cultural and scholarly climate in which I had first begun my work. In the
early 1980s, religion was to be found and studied in big cultural movements and
small individual beliefs. By the mid-1990s, religious organizations were widely
recognized as worthy of sociological attention. This was especially true in the wake of
the Welfare Reform Act of 1996. Although religious organizations had been conduits
of state social service funds for more than a century, this legislation highlighted that
partnership and expanded its legal boundaries. As a result, suddenly everyone wanted
to know about what congregations and religious voluntary organizations were doing.
It was a time in my scholarly life when I spent a great deal of energy producing
articles and talks for non-scholarly audiences. It was frankly gratifying to remind
groups of religious leaders that the work they do makes a difference. At the same
time, I worried about the consequences of a society that depends so much on
private religious communities to deliver on our common public obligation to people
in need.

The level of public engagement I had in those years was miniscule compared to
the odd episode in the mid-1990s when I became a "cult expert."[18] In April 1993, the
FBI and the ATF had bungled a deadly encounter with the Branch Davidians, a small
sectarian religious group living communally outside Waco, Texas. The study of new
religious movements has never been my specialty, but I did teach courses on the
subject a few times, so I knew the literature. On the day the Davidian compound
burned, I talked with a couple of Atlanta television stations about the story and was
dubbed, for the first time, a cult expert. When I received a call from the Justice
Department a few months later, I tried to suggest that they call any of several of my
friends who were more legitimately experts on new religious movements, but their
choice of me for their review panel seemed to be set. In a matter of weeks, my
fellow panelists and I reviewed piles of transcripts and interviewed all the major
(living) players, producing a report that was immediately "spun" to suit the people in
office and relegated to collecting dust. Still, I gave yet more television interviews and
testimony before the Senate Judiciary Committee. Because I took a relatively sympathetic view of the plight of the Davidians, I became a "cult apologist" in the eyes
of those who make opposing new religious movements their full-time business.
Indeed, they have routinely edited and re-edited my Wikipedia entry to make sure
that the world sees this episode as the defining moment in my career.

For me, however, this was a blip. It did grow out of two decades of research on
the dynamics of religious community life, but my usual interests were with much
more conventional groups. It was not, however, a blip in a growing commitment to

make my scholarship as broadly accessible as possible and to talk with the press when they asked. Interpreting American religious life was something I felt increasingly competent to do.

Redefining religious identity

Interpreting American religious life was, however, leading me to new questions, and those questions grew out of a nagging suspicion that all the theoretical noise being generated around whether or not secularization theory could survive was irrelevant to understanding how religion was actually lived on a day-to-day basis. I had been thinking a great deal about how "religious identity" is understood,[19] and I was increasingly struck by the contrast between the static categories in which religion was described and how the study of other identities – gender, race, ethnicity, sexual orientation – routinely acknowledged situational and fluid presentations of the self. There were arguments about how "essential" each of these identity frameworks might be, but even essentialists acknowledged that identities mean different things at different times in one's life and in different cultural and institutional settings. So why then was religion still being treated as a yes/no, more/less essence that was either present or absent? Why were everyday settings treated as *either* secular or sacred, rather than looking for the ways both secular and sacred definitions are at play?

I came to think that it would be useful to follow the lead of Margaret Somers in defining identity in narrative terms,[20] looking for the intertwining of auto-biographical and public stories, and that called for gathering stories of everyday life that would capture the ways in which sacred and secular co-mingle. An exciting and generative weekend gathering in Boston, in the fall of 2003, brought together a baker's dozen scholars whose work seemed to me to be breaking the ground that needed to be broken. The result was both the edited collection, *Everyday Religion*,[21] and a proposal to the Templeton Foundation for a research project that would ask new questions with methods designed to elicit everyday stories. Not only did we design an initial interview that was intentionally narrative in structure, but we asked participants to take pictures of the important places in their lives and tell us stories about what happens there. We also gave them digital recorders and asked them to record oral diary entries about what was going on in their everyday world.[22]

The result was an astonishing array of intimate narratives that took the listener from a grandmother's lap in childhood to an intense argument with a spouse over birth control, from the anguished account of a friend's brain tumor diagnosis to reflections from an ER resident over a long weekend on call. And in between there were the mundane accounts of jobs gained and lost, daily commutes and parent-teacher conferences, and the beauty of a spring day – literally thousands of stories from the 95 people who participated in the study, people whose range of religious and non-religious identifications mirror those of the American population, from utterly disinterested to devoutly committed to an array of Christian, Jewish, and neo-pagan ways of life.

As I have analyzed the stories, I have been asking when and where the story turns spiritual. What parts of life are seen through a spiritual lens? What religious and spiritual practices are and are not present? Yes, many people do say grace at home, but what else do they do in their households that expresses or draws on their faith? Do people doing some kinds of work think of their workplace in sacred terms, while others do not? How do religious and spiritual sensibilities shape what people do in their communities and their participation in political life? The answers to those questions are painting a complex picture of the intermingling of sacred and secular in American life.

They are also, ironically, returning me once again to the importance of religious communities themselves. As I have looked for the presence and absence of spiritual dimensions in the everyday stories we heard, one conclusion is inescapable. Everyday expressions of spirituality are present in direct proportion to the engagement of the person in the life of an organized religious community. The more often they participate, and the more intimately they are involved in friendships and conversations with other members, the more likely it is that the stories they tell about work, family, politics, and neighborhood will be inflected with a spiritual sensibility. For all the talk about Americans becoming "spiritual but not religious," the reality seems to be that sustaining spiritual practices and a sense of life as spiritual is something that is still primarily fostered in religious communities.

Having ventured deeply into the individual everyday worlds of this disparate collection of Americans, then, I have come back once again to the importance of religious communities. There is clearly a gap between those communities and the growing "unaffiliated" population of people who reject them, but it might be better to call most of those people spiritually open than spiritual. The critics are right to resist labeling them as atheist or secular. That designation is far more accurate (although not wholly so) in Europe than in the US. Continuing to explore this territory along the margins of organized religious life is well worth doing, but sociologists who wish to understand religion in the US would do well to continue observing religious communities themselves.

My own fascinations continue to be in just that task, but the communities that will demand my attention in the coming years will, I hope, allow the kinds of comparisons outside the US that will further expand our understanding of how religion is lived in the widely varied legal and organizational contexts in which it is shaped around the world. Whether in Johannesburg or Helsinki, Shanghai or Padua, I have never stopped observing religious communities. That is the sociological life for which I seemed destined and the life I hope to continue to lead.

Notes

1 The references, of course, are to Emile Durkheim, *The Elementary Forms of the Religious Life*, trans. Joseph Ward Swain (New York: Free Press, 1964); Max Weber, *The Protestant Ethic and the Spirit of Capitalism*, trans. Talcott Parsons (New York: Scribner, 1958); and Peter L. Berger, *The Sacred Canopy* (Garden City, NY: Anchor Doubleday, 1969).

2 His account of that experience is Kai Erikson, *Everything in Its Path: Destruction of Community in the Buffalo Creek Flood* (New York: Simon & Schuster, 1976).

3 That dissertation was eventually published as Nancy Tatom Ammerman, *Bible Believers: Fundamentalists in the Modern World* (New Brunswick, NJ: Rutgers University Press, 1987).

4 See, e.g., Barbara Hargrove, *The Sociology of Religion: Classical and Contemporary Approaches* (Arlington Heights: Harlan Davidson, 1979).

5 Thanks in no small measure to one of those priests, Fr. Joseph Fichter, that would begin to change. Research on gender began to be supported through the ASR's Fichter fund.

6 This is an argument made especially eloquently by Berger in *Sacred Canopy*.

7 See Nancy Tatom Ammerman, *Baptist Battles: Social Change and Religious Conflict in the Southern Baptist Convention* (New Brunswick, NJ: Rutgers University Press, 1990).

8 See, e.g., D. Michael Lindsay, *Faith in the Halls of Power: How Evangelicals Joined the American Elite* (New York: Oxford University Press, 2007).

9 R. Stephen Warner, "Work in Progress Toward a New Paradigm for the Sociological Study of Religion in the United States," *American Journal of Sociology* 98.5 (1993).

10 Among the early definitive statements of this group's work is Jackson W. Carroll, Carl S. Dudley and William McKinney, *Handbook for Congregational Studies* (Nashville, TS: Abingdon Press, 1986).

11 Nancy Tatom Ammerman, *Congregation and Community* (New Brunswick, NJ: Rutgers University Press, 1997).

12 Nancy T. Ammerman, "Deep and Wide: The Real Evangelicals," *The American Interest* 2.1 (2006).

13 James Luther Adams, "The Voluntary Principle in the Forming of American Religion," in *Voluntary Associations: Socio-Cultural Analyses and Theological Interpretation*, ed. J. Ronald Engel (Chicago, IL: Exploration Press, 1986); and Peter Dobkin Hall, "Religion and the Organizational Revolution in the United States," in *Sacred Companies*, ed. N. Jay Demerath III, Peter Dobkin Hall, Terry Schmitt and Rhys Williams (New York: Oxford University Press, 1998).

14 Nancy Tatom Ammerman, *Pillars of Faith: American Congregations and Their Partners* (Berkeley: University of California Press, 2005).

15 Mark Chaves, *Congregations in America* (Cambridge, MA: Harvard University Press, 2004).

16 This is thanks in large measure to the work of Robert D. Putnam, *Bowling Alone: The Collapse and Revival of American Community* (New York: Simon & Schuster, 2000).

17 Among the growing literature that exemplifies this turn is Colleen McDannell, *Material Christianity* (New Haven, CT: Yale University Press, 1995), Meredith B. McGuire, *Lived Religion: Faith and Practice in Everyday Life* (New York: Oxford University Press, 2008); Omar Maurice McRoberts, *Streets of Glory: Church and Community in a Black Urban Neighborhood* (Chicago, IL: University of Chicago Press, 2003); Mary Jo Neitz, "Queering the Dragonfest: Changing Sexualities in a Post-Patriarchal Religion," *Sociology of Religion* 61.4 (2000); Timothy J. Nelson, "Sacrifice of Praise: Emotion and Collective Participation in an African-American Worship Service," *Sociology of Religion* 57.4 (1996); R. Stephen Warner, "2007 Presidential Address: Singing and Solidarity," *Journal for the Scientific Study of Religion* 47.2 (2008); and Courtney Bender, *The New Metaphysicals: Spirituality and the American Religious Imagination* (Chicago, IL: University of Chicago Press, 2010).

18 I have provided a more extensive account of this episode in Nancy T. Ammerman, "Forum: Interpreting Waco," *Religion and American Culture* 8.1 (1998).

19 Nancy T. Ammerman, "Religious Identities and Religious Institutions," in *Handbook of the Sociology of Religion*, ed. Michele Dillon (Cambridge: Cambridge University Press, 2003).

20 Margaret R. Somers, "The Narrative Constitution of Identity: A Relational and Network Approach," *Theory and Society* 23 (1994).

21 Nancy T Ammerman (ed.), *Everyday Religion: Observing Modern Religious Lives* (New York: Oxford University Press, 2006).

22 A fuller description of the project's methods may be found in Nancy T. Ammerman and Roman R. Williams, "Speaking of Methods: Eliciting Religious Narratives through Interviews, Photos, and Oral Diaries," in *Annual Review of the Sociology of Religion: New Methods in Sociology of Religion*, ed. Luigi Berzano and Ole Riis (Leiden: Brill, 2012).

3

STRANGER IN A STRANGE LAND

William Sims Bainbridge

> I have been a stranger in a strange land.
>
> (Exodus 2:22)

It may seem odd that a lifelong atheist like myself would invest so many years in studying religion, and yet my motivation is clear. I have always been surrounded by people who believed many things that were utterly incredible to me, so I needed to understand their psychopathology in order to survive in their world. I am like an anthropologist studying the rituals of a "primitive tribe," with no possibility whatsoever of believing in the premises on which they are based, but nonetheless dedicated to unraveling their mysteries. To the extent that students should emulate my professional life at all, it would be by living their own lives, true both to their own personal values and to whatever heritage they possess. The social science of religion needs people who feel passionately, and who use that emotion to energize their research under the disciplines of the facts, of logic, and of the duty to think things through from multiple viewpoints.

Psychohistory is an appropriate scholarly approach to autobiography,[1] although no particular school of depth psychology has a monopoly on it, and frankly my family is unusual in both intellect and personality.[2] In tracing the origins of my work in my family history and my own childhood, I seek the factors that inspired exploration along certain intellectual directions. The results of my labors can stand on their own merits. As advice for students and colleagues who undertake research projects, this chapter will suggest that preparation to undertake research is often more important than the doing of the research. In the social science of religion, preparation requires deep and early soul searching.

Religious roots

Samuel McMath Bainbridge (1816–1865), my great-great-grandfather, was the son of a printer, entered Hamilton Theological Seminary in 1836, and was ordained the pastor of a church in Stockbridge, New York, in 1841. In the great Removal Controversy he took the side who wanted Hamilton to secularize to a significant degree, the ultimate result of which was the foundation of not one but two modern universities, Rochester and Colgate.[3] The high point of Samuel's intellectual career came in 1856, when he gave a sermon that so moved his listeners they had it printed. "The Last Great Shaking"[4] drew its text from the twelfth chapter of Paul's epistle to the Hebrews, where the Lord said, "Yet once more I shake not the earth only, but also heaven." This was a prophecy. All that could be shaken would be swept away, and all that would remain was unshakable. Samuel explained that this epistle showed the superiority of the Christian dispensation over the Jewish, and the shaking of heaven removed Judaism from God's favor. But now, a second upheaval was imminent that would establish Protestantism as the religion of the whole world, sweep tyrannical regimes from Europe and Asia, and end slavery in the United States.

Samuel named his first son William, presumably after his great-grandfather's grandson, Commodore William Bainbridge, who had the dubious distinction of sinking both British and American battleships, and spending two years in captivity by the Barbary Pirates.[5] William Folwell Bainbridge (1843–1915) sought to surpass his father in the ministry, and also as a man of letters. He served the spiritual needs of the northern troops near the battlefront in Virginia in 1864, where he met his future bride, Lucy Seaman (1842–1928), a volunteer nurse from Ohio who grandiosely thought of herself as "Sister Ohio."[6] Their wedding trip in 1867 took them to Europe, Russia, and the Middle East, including a tenting expedition throughout Palestine that provided material for many popular sermons. In the pharaoh's burial chamber deep inside the great pyramid on the Nile, William fired his revolver into the darkness, just to hear the ancient reverberations, not realizing that the shock would cause the native guides to drop their torches and run away. On their trip, William and Lucy established a family tradition of scholarly adventures in exotic realms where the deepest intellectual issues arise during bizarre exploits.

During 1879–1880, William and Lucy, accompanied by their boy William Seaman Bainbridge (1870–1947), traveled 50,000 miles through Japan, China, India, and Burma, visiting American Protestant outposts so that William could develop what he called "a science of missions." Two books that resulted are classics of social science,[7] although the third landed him in a great deal of trouble because he used the novel form to criticize the foibles of missionaries, apparently not realizing how easily particular leaders of the missionary movement would find themselves in its pages.[8] Lucy published a very insightful travelogue that revealed her love of attending alien funerals in exotic lands, and lambasting Asian religions for their mistreatment of women.[9] Among the highlights of their world tour was their stay in China with William's missionary cousin John Livingston Nevius (1829–1893), the person whose plan for missionary work was proven in the success Christianity later achieved in Korea,[10] and William inspired John to do his pathbreaking questionnaire study of spirit possession in China.[11] Near the end of the voyage, William adventured by horseback through Mesopotamia, sending his wife and son ahead by boat, and even stayed for a while with the Yezidis, whom he thought were the nicest Satan-worshipers he had met.

Around 1890, William abandoned his ministry and his family to write a great book tracing the origins of all the names of places and tribes in the Bible. In abject despair, on January 2, 1891, Lucy knelt to pray. "I was in great perplexity what the Lord wanted me to do. One day I was alone on my knees, and I fancied – strange fancy, you may think – I saw our personal Savior standing before me. 'Wait,' he said to me, 'wait and you shall know what to do'."[12] At that instant, many miles away, the Superintendent of the Women's Branch of the New York City Mission dropped dead, and shortly after Lucy was offered the job.[13] Her husband's great intellectual project monopolized the remaining quarter century of his life, perplexing his family greatly, because on the one hand they thoroughly respected biblical scholarship, but on the other hand his obsession seemed insane. Their son was a world-famous surgeon when his father died, and my grandfather responded in classic Bainbridge fashion. He dissected his own father's brain, looking for a medical explanation. He found none, and after a discouraging attempt to get his father's fourth book published, he destroyed it.

My own father, William Wheeler Bainbridge (1914–1965), was not an intellectual, but ended his career as a First Vice President of the Equitable Life Insurance Company, which at that time was to some extent a secular analog of religion, deeply rooted both in American history and social science.[14] Life insurance was initially a "new form of ritual with which to face death,"[15] and my father privately described it as "death insurance." Prior to his own death, the Equitable was a mutual insurance company, which meant that it was not really a capitalist enterprise, but a cooperative serving the policy holders alone. While not himself an adventurer, my father had been an instructor in the horse cavalry during World War II and admired his uncle, Consuelo Andrew Seoane, who was a model of horseback warrior. "Uncle Con" gained a Mauser bullet in his shoulder in the Spanish-American War, served as a map expert in putting down the Philippine Insurrection, and carried out a daring spy mission for two years around 1910 inside Japan, in partnership with Joseph "Snake" Thompson whose later friendship with L. Ron Hubbard contributed greatly to the creation of Scientology.[16]

My mother, Barbara Elizabeth Sims Bainbridge (1914–1965), was the daughter of a Wall Street attorney, William E. Sims (1886–1959). His greatest joys were reading vast works of history, playing chess, collecting stamps, savoring European classical music, and gardening. All branches of the family were remarkably cultivated, and each house was like a museum filled with antique furniture, hundreds of exotic artifacts, and historical art. Many walls of many rooms were covered with bookshelves. We lived history, and in fact the Bethel, Connecticut, house I grew up in had been built in 1743. We believed the house we moved to in Old Greenwich, Connecticut, in 1950, had been designed early in the century by Stanford White, the flamboyant architect who was shot dead by a millionaire who resented White having an affair with his wife.

Religion cast long but complex shadows over our lives. My father was sentimental about his family's tradition, but not personally devout. My mother was a complete skeptic, but maintained the illusion that she was religious because she thought it earned social respect. Her sister, Audrey (1923–2010), married an Episcopal priest, Max Rohn, who was something of an adventurer and once taught me a wrestling hold that could break a man's arm. My father's brother, John Seaman Bainbridge (1915–2006), was an idealistic attorney who for ten years ran a project to build law schools in Africa, a secular form of missionary work.[17] Their sister, Barbara Bainbridge (1917–88), married a professor of historical linguistics, Angus McIntosh (1914–2005), who had been a student and close friend of J.R.R. Tolkien and worked at the Bletchley Park cryptography center during the war.[18] One of their three children, Christopher McIntosh, has published extensively on the history of esoteric spiritual groups.[19]

I feel closest to my paternal grandfather, William Seaman Bainbridge, who died when I was just 7 years old. His close friend, Norman Vincent Peale, described his passing as the ideal Christian death.[20] On his deathbed, he gave me a little purse in the form of a turtle with $5 in it, a fortune for a child at that time. I fully understood that he was dying, so I wisely spent the money on a toy machine-gun, the kind that spins a wheel against flint when you squeeze the trigger to shoot off sparks. It successfully defended me from danger for four years, until, in one of the great shocks of my life, another child stole it.

My paternal grandfather was an extremely ambitious surgeon, whose friends called him "Will" in tribute to his willpower, and whose children called him "Dr. Dad." He considered himself a scientist and hungered for honor from the leaders of the Western world, publishing 100 journal articles and 11 books. Most prominent among them was a vast 1914 monograph, *The Cancer Problem*, translated into French, Spanish, Italian, Polish, and Arabic, and *Report on Medical and Surgical Developments of the War* published in 1919, based on extensive ethnographic research on both sides of the Western front.[21] In this latter study he was probably influenced by his older cousin, Louis Livingston Seaman (1851–1932), who had attached himself to the Japanese army in Manchuria to study their medical practices and experience the adventure of the Russo-Japanese War.[22] However, Will's personal adventures had begun before Seaman's exploits, when he escorted an insane financier named John Sinclair on an expedition to observe Kitchener's army on its way to defeat the Mahdi at Khartoum in what Winston Churchill called "The River War."[23] We still have a Sudanese broadsword he brought back, inscribed with "Allahu Akbar" in Arabic. Well, sorry, that time Allah lost and British technology won.

Beginnings

I still possess exceedingly detailed recollections of my own early life, already about 20 episodic memories from the age of 4, readily dated by the fact that they centered on a train trip in the summer of 1945, to retrieve my father from Fort Riley, Kansas. Given such memories, I can say with complete confidence that I have never for a moment imagined that any of the supernatural beliefs of the Judeo-Christian-Islamic tradition could possibly be true. I recall being taken to Sunday schools in early childhood, several different ones because I was always repelled by the experience, and refused to return. The little statues of biblical characters and camels in the children's sandbox did not look at all like my own ancestors, who rode horses rather than camels and did not wear bathrobes during the day. I have always been perplexed about why Europe exchanged its own rich, Pagan religious traditions for the narrow-minded superstitions of the people of the Middle East – not the most obvious choice I would have thought if one were seeking a tribe to anoint as one's spiritual advisors.

By the age of 10 I was an avid reader of science fiction, and my conception of faith was very much shaped by novels like *The Gods of Mars* by Edgar Rice Burroughs,[24] and the Flash Gordon movie serials of the 1930s inspired by Burroughs, that portray organized religion as a conscious fraud. Yet I also found the exotic religions of science fiction rather attractive. I greatly admired the Babylonian tablets and Egyptian scarabs owned by my grandfather Sims, who was a science fiction fan and had the issue of *Astounding Science Fiction* where I first read about Dianetics (Scientology). My mother preferred supernatural fantasies like those written by A. Merritt,[25] which like Scientology had no connection whatsoever to Christianity. I think she always regretted settling down, rather than voyaging off to the South Seas with Margaret Mead, which once had been a real possibility when she was working prior to her marriage at the American Museum of Natural History.

I was exceedingly unhealthy as a child, and was sick in bed for the whole second half of second grade, thereby becoming an avid reader. By the age of 12 my reading speed with perfect comprehension was tested at 600 words per minute. But I was not at all interested in the material taught in school. My first scholarly studies were at age 12 when I constructed card catalogs of every invented word and place name in the novels of Edgar Rice Burroughs, while drawing maps and making calculations about both the geography and the cultures of his invented worlds. When I studied the Children of God many years later, they were kind enough to channel a personal letter from his departed spirit to me; I was grateful for their gesture, but did not for a minute believe he wrote it.[26]

In eighth grade, my atheism cost me all my friendships. The teacher, Miss Lyons, was talking about how America was the land of the free, but I objected that we were not in fact free. In a tone that I recall as serious and respectful, she asked what I meant. I said one example was the fact that we were required to begin each day with a prayer, even though this was a public school. I did not believe, I said, so making me pray was an act of oppression. She said I did not need to pray if I did not want to. One of my best friends actually leapt to his feet and denounced me from his Roman Catholic dogma, waving his arms dramatically. My very best friend, a Congregationalist, simply stopped talking to me. Only decades later, when I reconnected with both of them, did I discover that each had found his own path to atheism. Every school day for the rest of that year began with all the other children bowed in prayer, and me sitting straight up and feeling very isolated.

At the beginning of that school year, my unconventional beliefs had found a different expression, one that also contributed to my sociological mentality. The school held an election for safety patrol captain, putting up as candidates four students the teachers trusted. I argued that we students should nominate the candidates, not the teachers. So I founded a political party, called the Caprocialists, and nominated the only non-Caucasian student, but the teachers refused to count his votes. Although the fellow who won did a good job, I am pleased to report that my boyhood confidence in my candidate was proved right by the fact that he later became a college dean. The name of my party, Caprocialist, was a combination of Capitalist-Progressive-Socialist, a union of the interesting extremes against the dull moderates, and I published a mimeographed newspaper called *The Caprocialist Worker* (in imitation of a communist newspaper), until the teachers prevailed upon me to stop. Recall, these were the 1950s when we were required to "drop-and-cover" under our desks in case the communists attacked us, and I was only 13 years old. To this day, my political views are a combination of the far right and far left, and thus incompatible with our current political institutions.

My three years at the Choate boarding-school were really the end of my formal education, and traumatic in their own way. It was an Episcopal school, and I was threatened with expulsion when I failed to pray in daily chapel. My classmate Paul Cowan has described this Christian environment from his Jewish perspective,[27] but he did not seem to recognize that atheists and doubters may have suffered as much as he.

My immediate family was nominally Episcopalian, because my mother felt it was the most respectable denomination, but I saw no evidence that the church offered anything except social status, especially troublesome in the case of my sister, Barbara Constance Bainbridge (Connie) (1943–1965), a sweet and faithful child who was betrayed by her religion. Connie sometimes exhibited "sleep-walking" (somnambulism) in the middle of the night, which I thought was remarkable, pushing her dolly carriage down the hallway without being fully conscious. At age 11 she began exhibiting symptoms of epilepsy, although remarkably she herself never knew that *epilepsy* was the name of her condition, something I knew perfectly well, because my mother thought she would be too ashamed if she knew.

I often observed Connie's *petit mals* as we were sitting together at dinner. Her eyes would gaze out into space and she would stop eating, perhaps aimlessly scraping her fork around the plate, for as much as a minute, not responding to anything in her environment but neither slumping down nor falling over. I once observed a *grand mal* seizure, as she convulsed on the floor of the upstairs hall while the rest of us rushed around frantically trying to prevent her from injuring herself. After junior high school, Connie was unable to continue her education, because she needed more support than the public schools could then provide. My mother attempted unsuccessfully to find a boarding-school that would take her, and I recall the anger she expressed when an Episcopal school that ought to have been doing God's work refused to take Connie. Later, she expressed gratitude that the local Episcopal minister was willing to perform a marriage ceremony for my sister, despite the fact that the outdated laws of Connecticut at the time technically forbade marriage for epileptics. Frankly, that seems like a rather small mercy for the church to perform, considering how badly my sister needed help. I saw absolutely no evidence that my sister's religious faith consoled her at all, nor provided guidance to either of her nominally religious parents.

I have before me her medical records, which I obtained in 1983. A letter written by neurologist Charles G. McKendree to our family doctor, Francis A. "Frank" Read, dated September 21, 1957, notes that Connie may have suffered *petit mal* episodes for three years, but had just experienced her first *grand mal* seizure, in which her skull was slightly injured. He noted how Connie's medical condition may have affected her personality, through her struggle to react to problems she could neither understand nor control: "There has been considerable rebelliousness to parental guidance and there had probably been more self-consciousness in regard to the petit mal episodes than had been recognized." He explained that her two problems were related, and his letter uses the term "paroxysmal cortical dysrhythmia" rather than epilepsy. "She was apparently relieved to learn that she could not be blamed for her day dreams or fainting spell." This painfully illustrates a long-lasting but usually suppressed debate between religion and science, which has two facets. First, it is problematic to give moral significance to any human behavior, if it is conditioned by physical factors such as brain functions. Second, it is problematic to believe that a person has an immortal soul, if in fact every thought and feeling depends upon the survival of a fragile network of neurons.

In December 1959, Connie's kidneys ceased functioning, and she entered the Greenwich hospital in a serious condition. Dr. Frederick Christie searched the literature, and found reference to a half-dozen cases of a potentially lethal side effect of Paradione, so that medication was discontinued, and she survived. Paradione is still in use today, although the mechanism by which it is effective is unknown, and sad to say treatments available for epilepsy have improved little in the half century since my sister suffered. Around 1964, a friend of my sister committed suicide by swallowing an entire bottle of her pills. Then, in 1965, Connie was killed in a home fire, along with both our parents, most likely caused by the failure of antiquated wiring. The general sense of horror surrounding my sister's condition and the failure of both religion and science to help her was a continuing burden, that ended only with her meaningless death. I am glad I did not believe in God, because he would have become my enemy after allowing such senseless suffering.

The influential writer of supernatural horror stories, H.P. Lovecraft, once admitted: "All my tales are based on the fundamental premise that common human laws and interests and emotions have no validity or significance in the vast cosmos at large."[28] Lovecraft also asserted:

> The most merciful thing in the world, I think, is the inability of the human mind to correlate all its contents. We live on a placid island of ignorance in the midst of black seas of infinity, and it was not meant that we should voyage far. The sciences, each straining in its own direction, have hitherto harmed us little; but some day the piecing together of dissociated knowledge will open up such terrifying vistas of reality, and of our frightful position therein, that we shall

either go mad from the revelation or flee from the light into the peace and safety of a new dark age.[29]

Lovecraft's words plague me even today. Religion became untenable following the emergence of the science of human behavior; any comfort it provided was limited to earlier eras of human history, and to people unable to accept the true nature of the human condition. Yet science may not offer anything better. In the soaring 1960s, after having briefly majored in physics at Yale, and philosophy at Oberlin, I found myself outside academia observing two of the most interesting atheist movements of the decade: Ayn Rand's Objectivists[30] and the Twin Oaks commune in Louisa, Virginia, based on B.F. Skinner's *Walden Two*.[31] By the time I enrolled at Boston University in the summer of 1969, I was already a practicing sociologist; I just needed to gather up footnotes.

From the Process to the new paradigm

I was greatly perplexed by the sociology of religion course I took from T. Scott Miyakawa at Boston University. It was an extremely demanding and well-organized course, with voluminous reading requirements including the professor's own book *Protestants and Pioneers: Individualism and Conformity on the American Frontier*.[32] Yet it presented an extremely bland vision of the field, shying away from many of the most important issues, such as the truth claims of various competing religions. An exception, although other students did not seem to notice, was Durkheim's *Elementary Forms of the Religious Life*.[33] If God is a representation of the unified society, sanctifying societal norms and values, then religion is a collectivist lie. Or, to put the point more mildly, what happens to Durkheim's conceptualization if in fact society is not a unity, or indeed if social life is highly chaotic despite a veneer of unity?

The dominant culture in the sociology department at the time was phenomenological, because a group of ethnomethodologists had fled the chaos at Washington University in St. Louis,[34] notably George Psathas who encouraged me greatly. I also learned much that would be useful in future from a seminar taught by Maren Lockwood Carden, who had written a book on the Oneida community.[35] Most courses I took required term papers, and I did several that combined library scholarship with fieldwork; for example, on the John Birch Society and the 1968 Columbia University student uprising. For one term paper, I had groups of students come to my apartment to do Ouija board sessions which I observed, notably one in which a Vietnam veteran collapsed after communicating with "the departed spirit" of a comrade he had abandoned to die. My 1971 senior honors thesis was based on six months inside Scientology as a covert participant observer, and led to some early publications.[36] Immediately afterward, I began studying an offshoot of Scientology, the Process Church of the Final Judgment, performing two years of covert participant observation, eventually leading to my second book.[37]

At Harvard, I continued my research on the Process, and the origins of both Scientology and the Process in the Psychoanalytic Movement suggested to me that many apparently secular organizations in modern society are "really" religious cults that have avoided labeling as such. For my doctoral oral exams in ethnopsychiatry, in which I earned distinction, I read widely in psychiatry, anthropology of personality, and the sociology of deviance. My doctoral dissertation, which was a social history of space exploration, was published as my first book.[38] My dissertation chairman was Seymour Martin Lipset, but I was closest to behaviorist George Homans, who was department chair and for whom I was a teaching assistant. After a quick four years in graduate school, with material for two books in my car, I drove from Boston to Seattle to take a position at the University of Washington. My third book, *The Future of Religion*, was written in collaboration with Rodney Stark who was already at that institution, and my sixth book, also with Stark, was *A Theory of Religion*.[39]

Homans liked to say that social science should be reductionist, but he was not convinced that there were any general laws of society worthy of reduction.[40] In his own work, Homans tried to show how regularities of social behavior could be logically derived from axiom-like propositions about the cognition and motivation of individuals in interaction with each other.[41] In a series of publications, Stark and I showed how this strategy for theorizing could be applied to religion, generating hypotheses that received some significant empirical support.[42]

The human brain evolved over millions of years to solve practical problems related to survival and reproduction in a complex environment where humans compensated for their lack of physical specializations like fangs and claws by developing technology. Problems are recurrent situations in which people seek rewards and endeavor to avoid costs. In solving problems, people follow abstract instructions which might be called *recipes* or *algorithms*, but which Stark and I called *explanations*.

Individuals gain their explanations both from their own personal experimentation and through communication with other people. In the absence of a verified explanation for how to obtain a highly desired reward, people will provisionally accept unverified explanations, especially when the explanations come from other people who are trusted and who endorse them. But some of the most desired rewards – such as justice and eternal life – are difficult or even impossible to obtain. In such stressful situations, humans tend to accept *compensators* which substitute for empirically verified explanations. Religious beliefs are compensators based on supernatural assumptions, giving people hope that they can obtain the highly desired rewards, but in an unverifiable context.

In my own part of the theorizing and research, I was especially interested in how compensators are invented in small social groups and often by single individuals, and then are sold to a wider public through social interaction. Coherent doctrines can consolidate in cohesive small groups, which can then use the doctrines to recruit additional members. It seems that the very large world-religious traditions also went through a phase of consolidation on a much larger scale, through alliances with the governments of ancient and medieval nations. Holy books, such as the Bible and Koran, help to anchor doctrines, but their effectiveness in doing so seems limited among educated populations. After the historical separation of church and state, family tradition and formal churches can sustain faith for a long time, but it remains for future researchers to determine if any particular faith would eventually become extinct through extreme fragmentations, if not supported by a societal authority.

After collaborating with Stark, I have often returned to our work, to build upon it. One essay introduced the concept of secondary compensation, in which one individual engages in a religious ritual to satisfy an obligation to another individual which cannot be satisfied in a direct and practical manner.[43] In one series of publications, I showed how aspects of our theory could be simulated in computers through the use of artificial intelligence multi-agent systems.[44] And very recently, I connected our theory to the atheistic theories of religion that have been arising in cognitive science, with a focus on the dynamics of cognitive errors.[45] Stark, in contrast, has seemed to abandon our joint work, and ironically I have come to the conclusion that he may have had good reasons for doing so. He has often argued in recent years that Christianity is good for humanity,[46] but this could be true even if its chief beliefs are false. Perhaps he has chosen the side of human benefit in this debate, while I choose the side of scientific accuracy.[47] What a tragedy if science and mercy are in fact enemies!

Conclusion

What advice can I offer students and colleagues? They should be true to their principles, whatever those principles are, but at the same time challenge them with ideas and intense experiences which they find alien. Without drinking so deeply from the wells of pessimism to become poisoned, they should read not only the standard European classics, but also others opposed to them.[48] They should turn their eyes away from the tired question of God's nature, and read cognitive science exposing the questionable nature of the human soul. Other sources not only of inspiration but also specific topics for research are the modern quasi-religions, like psychoanalysis,[49] transhumanism, and the still unrecognized supernatural dimension of massively multiplayer online role-playing games.[50] If, as some believe, the world is descending into yet another century-long clash between Islam and Christendom, then some of the most interesting developments may be taking place far from that grim battlefield.

At the risk of being impolite, I must say that progress in the social science of religion is greatly impeded by the piety of most of its practitioners, and indeed by the politeness of the few non-believers in the field who do not wish to offend the majority who are believers. One of my role models is Snorri Sturluson, the Icelandic scholar who 900 years ago sought to preserve the Pagan legends of his people, despite himself being a Christian, arguing that these legends had a basis in historical fact, despite having been mythologized into supernatural narratives. I wonder if any of his colleagues were still Pagans, and if so, how well they got along. Emotionally, I would have sided with the Pagans, but intellectually I believe we must move beyond Christianity, Islam, and the other ancient monotheist fictions, to see the real human meaning that lies beneath all the exaggeration and fabrication. Only if we study the ways in which humans construct fantasies like religion, can we fully understand the human spirit.

Notes

1 Erik H. Erikson, *Young Man Luther: A Study in Psychoanalysis and History* (New York: Norton, 1958).
2 Louis Effingham De Forest, *Ancestry of William Seaman Bainbridge* (Oxford: The Scrivener Press, 1950).
3 Colgate University, *The First Half Century of Madison University, 1819–1869* (New York: Sheldon, 1872), 53–80; Jesse Leonard Rosenberger, *Rochester and Colgate: Historical Backgrounds of the Two Universities* (Chicago, IL: University of Chicago Press, 1925), 51; Howard D. Williams, *A History of Colgate University, 1819–1969* (New York: Van Nostrand, 1969), 106–139.
4 Samuel McMath Bainbridge, "The Last Great Shaking" (Penn Yan, New York: S.C. Cleveland, 1856).
5 David F. Long, *Ready to Hazard: A Biography of Commodore William Bainbridge, 1774–1833* (Hanover, NH: University Press of New England, 1981).
6 Lucy Seaman Bainbridge, "Sister Ohio," *The Outlook* 122(4) (1919): 155–157; Lucy Seaman Bainbridge, *Yesterdays* (New York: Fleming H. Revell, 1924); Alexander H. McKinney, *Triumphant Christianity: The Life and Work of Lucy Seaman Bainbridge* (New York: Fleming H. Revell, 1932).
7 William Folwell Bainbridge, *Along the Lines at the Front: A General Survey of Baptist Home and Foreign Missions* (Philadelphia, PA: American Baptist Publication Society, 1882a); William Folwell Bainbridge, *Around the World Tour of Christian Missions* (New York: C.R. Blackall, 1882b).
8 William Folwell Bainbridge, *Self-Giving* (Boston, MA: D. Lothrop, 1883).
9 Lucy Seaman Bainbridge, *Round the World Letters* (Boston, MA: Lothrop, 1882); cf. Lucy Seaman Bainbridge, *Jewels from the Orient* (New York: Fleming H. Revell, 1920).
10 John L. Nevius, *China and the Chinese* (New York: Harper, 1869); Helen S. Coan Nevius, *Our Life in China* (New York: Robert Carter, 1869); Helen S. Coan Nevius, *The Life of John Livingston Nevius* (New York: Fleming H. Revell, 1895).
11 John L. Nevius, *Demon Possession and Allied Themes, Being an Inductive Study of Phenomena of Our Own Times* (New York: Fleming H. Revell, 1896).
12 Anonymous. "Work for the Downtown Poor," *New York Times*, November 9, 1895: 5.
13 Lucy Seaman Bainbridge, *Helping the Helpless in Lower New York* (New York: Fleming H. Revell, 1917); William Sims Bainbridge, *The Sociology of Religious Movements* (New York: Routledge, 1997), 300–332.
14 T.R. Jencks, "Life Insurance in the United States," *Hunt's Merchants' Magazine* 8 (1843):109–131, 227–240; John W. Riley, Jr., "Basic Social Research and the Institution of Life Insurance," *American Behavioral Scientist* 6(9) (1963): 6–9.
15 Viviana A. Zelizer, "Human Values and the Market: The Case of Life Insurance and Death in 19th-Century America," *American Journal of Sociology* 84 (1978): 591–609.
16 Consuelo Andrew Seoane, *Beyond the Ranges* (New York: Robert Spellar, 1960); Rhoda Low Seoane, *Uttermost East and the Longest War* (New York: Vantage, 1968); William Sims Bainbridge, "The Cultural Context of Scientology," in *Scientology*, ed. James R. Lewis (New York: Oxford University Press, 2009b).
17 John Seaman Bainbridge, *The Study and Teaching of Law in Africa* (South Hackensack, NJ: F.B. Rothman, 1972).
18 John Anderson (ed.), *Language Form and Linguistic Variation: Papers Dedicated to Angus McIntosh* (Amsterdam: J. Benjamins, 1982); Angus McIntosh, M. L. Samuels and Michael Benskin, *A Linguistic Atlas of Late Mediaeval English* (Aberdeen: Aberdeen University Press, 1986).
19 Christopher McIntosh, *The Astrologers and their Creed* (London: Hutchinson, 1969); Christopher McIntosh, *Eliphas Lévi and the French Occult Revival* (London: Rider, 1972); Christopher McIntosh, *Gardens of the Gods: Myth, Magic and Meaning* (New York: Palgrave Macmillan, 2005); Christopher McIntosh, *The Rose Cross and the Age of*

Reason: Eighteenth-century Rosicrucianism in Central Europe and its Relationship to the Enlightenment (Albany, NY: State University of New York Press, 2011).

20 Norman Vincent Peale and Smiley Blanton, *The Art of Real Happiness* (Englewood Cliffs, NJ: Prentice-Hall, 1950).

21 William Seaman Bainbridge, *The Cancer Problem* (New York: Macmillan, 1914); William Seaman Bainbridge, *Report on Medical and Surgical Developments of the War* (Washington, DC: U. S. Government Printing Office, 1919).

22 Louis Livingston Seaman, *From Tokio through Manchuria with the Japanese* (New York: Appleton, 1905); Louis Livingston Seaman, *The Real Triumph of Japan: The Conquest of the Silent Foe* (New York: Appleton, 1906).

23 Winston Churchill, *The River War* (London: Longmans, Green, 1899).

24 Edgar Rice Burroughs, *The Gods of Mars* (Chicago, IL: A.C. McClurg, 1918); Richard A. Lupoff, *Edgar Rice Burroughs and the Martian Vision* (Westminster, MD: Mirage Press, 1976).

25 A. Merritt, *The Ship of Ishtar* (New York: G.P. Putnam's Sons, 1926).

26 William Sims Bainbridge, *The Endtime Family: Children of God* (Albany, NY: State University of New York Press, 2002b).

27 Paul Cowan, *An Orphan in History: Retrieving a Jewish Legacy* (Garden City, NY: Doubleday, 1982).

28 Paul A. Carter, *The Creation of Tomorrow* (New York: Columbia University Press, 1977).

29 H.P. Lovecraft, "The Call of Cthulhu," in *The Call of Cthulhu and Other Weird Stories* (New York: Penguin, 1999 [1926]), 139–169.

30 Ayn Rand, *Atlas Shrugged* (New York: Random House, 1957); Barbara Branden, *The Passion of Ayn Rand* (Garden City, NY: Doubleday, 1986).

31 B.F. Skinner, *Walden Two* (New York: Macmillan, 1948); Kathleen Kinkade, *A Walden Two Experiment: The First Five Years of Twin Oaks Community* (New York: Morrow, 1973).

32 T. Scott Miyakawa, *Protestants and Pioneers: Individualism and Conformity on the American Frontier* (Chicago, IL: University of Chicago Press, 1964).

33 Emile Durkheim, *Elementary Forms of the Religious Life* (London: Allen & Unwin, 1915).

34 Henry Etzkowitz, "The Brief Rise and Early Decline of Radical Sociology at Washington University: 1969–72," *American Sociologist* 20(4) (1989): 346–352.

35 Maren Lockwood Carden, *Oneida: Utopian Community to Modern Corporation* (Baltimore, MD: Johns Hopkins University Press, 1969).

36 William Sims Bainbridge and Rodney Stark, "Scientology: To Be Perfectly Clear," *Sociological Analysis* 41 (1980): 128–136; William Sims Bainbridge, "Science and Religion: The Case of Scientology," in *The Future of New Religious Movements*, ed. David. G. Bromley and Phillip. E. Hammond (Macon, GA: Mercer University Press, 1987a), 59–79.

37 William Sims Bainbridge, *Satan's Power: A Deviant Psychotherapy Cult* (Berkeley: University of California Press, 1978).

38 William Sims Bainbridge, *The Spaceflight Revolution* (New York: Wiley Interscience, 1976).

39 Rodney Stark and William Sims Bainbridge, *The Future of Religion* (Berkeley: University of California Press, 1985); Rodney Stark and William Sims Bainbridge, *A Theory of Religion* (New York and Toronto: Lang, 1987).

40 George C. Homans, *The Nature of Social Science* (New York: Harcourt, Brace & World, 1967).

41 George C. Homans, *Social Behavior: Its Elementary Forms* (New York: Harcourt, Brace, Jovanovich, 1974).

42 Rodney Stark and William Sims Bainbridge, "Of Churches, Sects, and Cults: Preliminary Concepts for a Theory of Religious Movements," *Journal for the Scientific Study of Religion* 18 (1979): 117–131; Rodney Stark and William Sims Bainbridge, "Towards a Theory of Religion: Religious Commitment," *Journal for the Scientific Study of Religion* 19 (1980): 114–128; Rodney Stark and William Sims Bainbridge, *Future*;

Rodney Stark and William Sims Bainbridge, *A Theory*; Rodney Stark and William Sims Bainbridge, *Religion, Deviance and Social Control* (New York: Routledge, 1996).

43 William Sims Bainbridge, "A Prophet's Reward: Dynamics of Religious Exchange," in *Sacred Markets, Sacred Canopies*, ed. Ted. G. Jelen (Lanham, MD: Rowman & Littlefield, 2002a); William Sims Bainbridge, "Sacred Algorithms: Exchange Theory of Religious Claims," in *Defining Religion*, ed. David Bromley and Larry Greil (Amsterdam: JAI Elsevier, 2003).

44 William Sims Bainbridge, *Sociology Laboratory* (Belmont, CA: Wadsworth, 1987); William Sims Bainbridge, "Neural Network Models of Religious Belief," *Sociological Perspective* 38 (1995a): 483–495; William Sims Bainbridge, "Minimum Intelligent Neural Device: A Tool for Social Simulation," *Mathematical Sociology* 20 (1995b): 179–192; William Sims Bainbridge, *God from the Machine: Artificial Intelligence Models of Religious Cognition* (Walnut Grove, CA: AltaMira, 2006).

45 William Sims Bainbridge, "Atheism," in *The Oxford Handbook of the Sociology of Religion*, ed. Peter B. Clarke (Oxford: Oxford University Press, 2009); William Sims Bainbridge, "Cognitive Science and the New Atheism," in *Religion and the New Atheism*, ed. Amarnath Amarasingam (Leiden: Brill, 2010); William Sims Bainbridge, "The Future of an Illusion: Cognitive Theories," in *Science and the World's Religions*, ed. Patrick McNamara and Wesley Wildman (Santa Barbara, CA: Praeger, in press).

46 Rodney Stark, *The Rise of Christianity* (Princeton, NJ: Princeton University Press, 1996); Rodney Stark, *The Victory of Reason* (New York: Random House, 2005).

47 William Sims Bainbridge, *Across the Secular Abyss* (Lanham, MD: Lexington, 2007).

48 Mary Wollstonecraft Shelley, *Frankenstein; or, The Modern Prometheus* (London: Lackington, Hughes, Harding, Mavor, and Jones, 1818); Friedrich Nietzsche, *Die Geburt der Tragödie* (Munich: Goldmann, 1872); Friedrich Nietzsche, *Also Sprach Zarathustra* (Stuttgart: Kroner, 1885); Oswald Spengler, *The Decline of the West* (New York: A.A. Knopf, 1926–1928); Pitirim A. Sorokin, *Social and Cultural Dynamics* (New York: American Book Company, 1937); Georg Büchner, *Dantons Tod, and Woyzeck* (Manchester, England: Manchester University Press, 1954); Samuel Beckett, *Malone Dies* (New York: Grove Press, 1956).

49 David Bakan, *Sigmund Freud and the Jewish Mystical Tradition* (Princeton, NJ: Van Nostrand, 1958); William Sims Bainbridge, "The Psychoanalytic Movement," in *Leadership in Science and Technology*, ed. William Sims Bainbridge (Thousand Oaks, CA: Sage, 2011).

50 Catullus (pseudonym for William Sims Bainbridge), "Letter to a Supernatural Being," in *Human Futures: Art in an Age of Uncertainty*, ed. Andy Miah (Liverpool: Liverpool University Press, 2008), 247–255; Williams Sims Bainbridge, *The Warcraft Civilization* (Cambridge, MA: MIT Press, 2010b).

4

DOING SOCIOLOGY

Confessions of a professional stranger

Eileen Barker

> All the world's a stage,
> And all the men and women merely players:
> They have their exits and their entrances;
> And one man in his time plays many parts.
>
> (Shakespeare (1623) *As You Like It,* Act II Scene VII)

I never planned to be a sociologist of religion – indeed, I never planned to be an academic. I didn't get an undergraduate degree until I was 32. My desire had always been to go on the stage and at school I studied for A levels in zoology, physics, and chemistry because my parents said they would pay for me to go to drama school only if I had something to fall back on when I realized my mistake. They assumed that, like the rest of my family, I would want to study medicine.

During two happy years at drama school we learnt "the Method," avidly reading Stanislavski[1] and delving into our psyches to unearth the passions of tragic heroines and murderous villains. But we also learnt how to master a number of basic techniques: how to speak in a variety of accents and dialects; how to sit gracefully in a crinoline; how to project our voices to the back of the "gods";[2] how to fire guns – and how to breathe in, then exhale on a laugh. We took classes in ballet, fencing, make-up, falling without hurting ourselves, and slapping faces without hurting the slappee.

I then spent the next five years playing a variety of roles in theaters throughout Britain and, occasionally, overseas. There was, for example, a delightful season in Valetta where I played "sweet little Cicely" in *The Importance of being Earnest* and Frankie Howerd's girlfriend in *Charlie's Aunt*. I little thought that nearly half a century later I would return to give a lecture attended by Malta's President on the topic of "Cults, Sects and New Religious Movements."

My career came to what I thought would be a temporary halt when my daughter became severely ill. I became a suburban housewife discussing how to make marrow and ginger jam at Presbyterian coffee mornings. Frustrated, I looked around for a little more stimulation and noticed that the local technical college was offering evening classes in lampshade making and social history. We had enough lampshades so I chose social history. A series of chance encounters, a growing interest in sociology, and getting enveloped by a students' demo while buying tickets at the Aldwych Theatre, resulted in my enrolling for an undergraduate course at the London School of Economics – but still expecting to return to the theater. By the end of three years I was, however, pretty well hooked, and when, a couple of days after the final results came out, I was offered a temporary lectureship, I accepted – and that was the start of a career that was to continue until and beyond my retirement as an emeritus "Professor of Sociology with Special Reference to the Study of Religion" at the LSE.

When people find out about my theatrical past they often assume that I must have undergone some dramatic conversion between two very different worldviews. In fact, the driving forces in my life have not really changed that much. I have always possessed a vulgar curiosity – I enjoyed doing my science A levels because I was interested in how the natural world worked, but I was also interested in how people worked. As an actress not only did I have to search within myself for the emotions that would help me to understand what the character I was portraying might be experiencing, I also had to recognize how the situation in which she found herself would push her one way rather than another. Yet, at the same time, I had to be "in control," employing the techniques of the trade and constantly aware of what was going on around me, both on stage and in the audience. I had to be both inside and outside the character.

In many ways, this somewhat schizophrenic approach has been replicated throughout my career as a sociologist.[3] An important difference when I became an academic researcher was that I did not have to follow a written script,[4] but I did have to discover how the "actors" I was observing came to play the roles in which society cast them. While engaged in participant observation, I have had to learn how to "pass," as the ethnomethodologists would say, as a member of the group I am studying – learning the correct vocabulary, and what clothes and body language are appropriate.[5] Yet, at the same time, like the actor, the sociologist has to be wary of "going native" and becoming completely immersed in the situation. She has to stay alert to what is going on around her.

The analysis and the techniques employed by the social scientist do, of course, differ from those of the thespian, but they should (in my kind of sociology at least) involve both *Verstehen* and a more positivistic approach. As well as trying to develop an empathic understanding of what is going on, the sociologist is likely to want to make generalizations about groups and to assess the probability that certain variables are related to each other in certain ways. To do this, questionnaires, control groups, and statistical manipulation are among the tools of the trade. Just as actors who mumble their lines or distract the audience's attention at an inappropriate moment are not good actors, questionnaires that are designed by someone without both an understanding of the subject and an awareness of the potential pitfalls of ambiguous questions can elicit misleading or even totally incorrect results.

Influences

I have already mentioned that I come from a family of doctors (brother, nephew, aunt, uncle, and stepfather), but, back a generation, my grandfather and great-grandfather were medical missionaries, and before them there was a long line of fiercely devout ministers in the Church of Scotland and some of its sectarian groupings. As a child I was close to my maternal grandfather who had devoted his life to serving the spiritual and physical well-being of others. In particular, he had worked among lepers in India and Africa (my mother was born in a leper colony). Not only had he developed one of the first effective cures for the disease, but he had also fought against the social discrimination that the lepers faced – a challenge far greater, he claimed, than healing their bodies.

I did not share my grandfather's faith, but I did respect him and the life that he had led. He in turn gently acknowledged my agnosticism, while suggesting books I might read and engaging me in conversations about thinkers such as Teilhard de Chardin and Mahatma Gandhi, whom he had known and greatly admired. All that was against a background of ten years' incarceration in boarding-schools where I had to attend prayers twice a day and learn the week's collect on Fridays. Originally I attended Church of Scotland services, but I found the Minister, whose sermon always lasted at least an hour, incredibly boring, and when I found out from my Anglican friends that their priest never spoke for more than ten minutes I expressed an interest in the Church of England, and Sunday mornings became more bearable. Thus, by the time I left school, I had become well versed in the Bible and the Book of Common Prayer, and I had learnt to appreciate the beauty of liturgical music.

When we had to choose our options for the undergraduate course, the sociology of religion, which was taught by David Martin, seemed more interesting than some of the other courses on offer. I was tutored by Ernest Gellner in my final year and he, more than anyone, introduced me to the enormous variety of religious beliefs that had been held throughout the world and throughout history. Gabriel Newfield opened my eyes to the delights of social and moral philosophy, a course that I was later to teach alongside both undergraduate and postgraduate courses on the sociology of religion.[6] So far as my reading was concerned, among the scholars who excited me most, and continue to do so, were Max Weber, Georg Simmel, and Mary Douglas. I was also greatly influenced by Berger and Luckmann's *Social Construction of Reality*, and would still, if pushed, call myself a social constructionist.[7] Another sociologist of religion who played an important role in my intellectual development, and who was to become a close friend until his death in 2004, was Bryan Wilson.

How could they?

Despite the fact that I was given a horrific teaching load, I was expected to conduct research and publish if I wanted to achieve tenure at the LSE – and I did. The debate that was dominating the sociology of religion scene at that time (1970) was over the secularization thesis. While it seemed obvious that aspects of secularization had clearly gone hand-in-hand with the development of European society, I had been intrigued to learn that approximately half the US population still disavowed the theory of evolution and believed that the world was created pretty well as it is now within the past 10,000 years. I discovered that there were some "creationists" in Britain and decided to investigate. One thing led to another, and soon I found myself studying a wide range of fully accredited scientists who were proclaiming that science proved (or disproved) a wide range of beliefs about the Bible and God. I immersed myself in the writings of these scientists and visited the numerous movements to which they belonged. These ranged from strictly fundamentalist groups proclaiming the literal truth of Genesis, through new age groups pushing the boundaries of science to embrace such phenomena as psychokinesis, telepathy, and dousing, to Marxist groups whose members vehemently eschewed bourgeois science in favor of Science for the People.[8]

When I had been an actress I had not been as interested in playing "straight" roles as I was in taking on "character" parts. This was largely because I relished posing the question "How could they?", the challenge being to try to understand how another human being could believe things and do things that I would be unlikely to believe and do myself. The scientists I was studying certainly presented me with such a challenge, but I was going to find myself facing even greater challenges as I entered "the cult scene." This started with an invitation to talk at the Second International Conference on the Unity of the Sciences, which was to be held in London in 1974. My husband, who worked at the BBC, looked up the file on the man who was promoting the conference and discovered that the Reverend Sun Myung Moon was a Korean Messiah who had amassed a vast fortune, had been imprisoned more than once, was reputedly connected with the Korean CIA, and, it was alleged, brainwashed his followers. "You can't go now!" said my husband. "I can't *not* go now!" I replied.

The conference was almost disappointingly respectable. There were, however, these smiling young helpers who hovered around us, attending to our every need, and who Ninian Smart and I decided must be the brainwashed "moonbeams" – the term "Moonies" had not yet been coined for Unificationists. A few weeks later, Ninian and I were invited to the Unification London headquarters for a weekend round table on science and religion. Our curiosity having been ignited, we accepted. On their home ground, the members seemed far more "ordinary." They no longer smilingly agreed with everything we said, and several of them were obviously intelligent and, apparently, in full command of their senses. This was even more intriguing. How could they have come to join the movement when, it seemed, they were expected to give up their university studies and sacrifice excellent career prospects in order to sell flowers and religious tracts for up to 18 hours a day, cut themselves off from family and friends, and marry someone who might not speak the same language but had been selected for them by this Korean Messiah? How could they? An obvious answer, and one that was vociferously promoted in increasingly lurid and sensational media reports, was that this was not their choice – they had been subjected to some sorts of irresistible and irreversible mind-control techniques.

During breaks in the round table discussions, I spent some time talking with a young Unificationist, whom I shall call Andrew. It turned out that he had gained an excellent history degree from Cambridge and was the son of a London University professor whom I knew slightly. Some weeks later, I learned that Andrew had been asking for me at the LSE. I immediately jumped to the conclusion that he might be wanting to escape from the movement and was seeking me out for help. I was wrong. When he eventually found me, he told me that a sociologist of religion, whose only information came from former members and the "anti-cult movement," was going to deliver a paper on the Unification Church at an international conference. Was there, Andrew wanted to know, any way that I would be prepared to rebut this sociologist's one-sided accusations?

I told him that the sociologist, who happened to be Jim Beckford, was a highly respected academic and that, as the Unification Church was so secretive, it was their fault rather than his that his material would be limited. At that point Andrew asked whether I would like to study the movement. He would approach the leadership and ask for permission for me to have access to the members. He didn't know what my feelings were about his church, but he did know that I listened – and that, it seemed, he didn't think any other outsider was prepared to do.

It took some time to reach an agreement to do research on my own terms, with independent funding and a complete list of the membership so that I could conduct interviews on a random sample basis.[9] Before long it was evident that what I had originally thought would be an article was going to be a book, and then it became obvious that the entire monograph would address only what I had thought would be the first chapter – how people came to join the movement.

Individual choice and social determinism

By now it was becoming clear to me that this research directly addressed some of the more challenging theoretical and philosophical issues I have faced as a sociologist of religion – and as a citizen. The explanation that people joined the Unification Church only because they had been "brainwashed" had provided "deprogrammers" with an excuse to convince worried parents that they should pay tens of thousands of pounds in order to have their adult children captured and held against their will until they managed to escape or convince their captors that they had renounced their faith. Although there were undoubtedly gross exaggerations from many of the parties concerned, there was ample evidence that the deprogramming process was involving some very unpleasant procedures with, in some cases, tragic consequences, including both rape and suicide.[10]

Part of my undergraduate training had convinced me that value neutrality was an important requirement for any sociological study. Of course, it was never fully attainable, but it was a goal towards which we should strive, taking every precaution to ensure that we were gaining information about the object of our study rather than disseminating information about our own subjective values. At the same time, I had fully taken on board Weber's distinction between value neutrality and value relevance[11] so that, it seemed to me as a "concerned citizen," if the Unification Church did indeed employ irresistible and irreversible recruitment techniques, these should be exposed and something done about it – but whatever was done should be done by accountable professionals with proper training, and not by some of those who were employing the dubious deprogramming techniques about which I was learning. If, on the other hand, Unificationists had, as they insisted, freely chosen to join and stay in the movement, then there were good arguments (not least those promoted by the United Nations Universal Declaration of Human Rights)[12] why they should be allowed to follow their new-found faith – so long, of course, as they were adults and did not transgress the laws of a democratic country.

Such considerations provided the "relevance" for the research. The "neutrality" meant that the research had to be designed and carried out so that anyone, whatever their personal opinion, would have to reach the same conclusions. Briefly, the fact that I found that 90 percent of those who went through the residential "brainwashing" experience decided *not* to join the movement, and that the majority of those who did join went on to leave it within two years, seriously questioned the proposition that the Unification Church possessed anything like efficient mind-control techniques, however much it may have wanted and/or tried to influence potential converts.[13] Other variables, such as the individuals' values, hopes, previous experiences, and expectations of life in non-Unification society also needed to be examined if we wanted an explanation of why people joined the movement. It seemed obvious to me that anyone with access to the statistics would have to agree that the influences exerted by Unificationists were neither irresistible nor irreversible – an opinion I was soon to learn to be somewhat naïve.

But for me there was something more wide-ranging underlying a study of Unification conversions. This involved the free will/determinism debate. Both actors and sociologists are faced with a recurrent exploration of the extent to which, under what circumstances and with what consequences, individuals are affected by and themselves affect the social situation. At one extreme, the social situation could pretty well determine the behavior of individuals; at another extreme, the individuals could themselves pretty well decide what it was that they would do. While I felt I had demonstrated that the social situation provided by the Unification Church did not exert the strong influence that was popularly assumed, this did not mean that it didn't exert any influence; nor did it mean that other social situations might not exert well-nigh irresistible pressure on an individual. Indeed, through a series of in-depth interviews, I was later to study a convicted terrorist – a woman who, after joining a group with the expectation that by doing so she could help to make the world a better place, had become prepared to kill both herself and others. This research led me to the conclusion that it was a series of social variables that had had the effect of controlling her mind to what, it could be argued, was an *almost* irresistible and irreversible degree.[14]

It would, of course, be a mistake to assume that there is a straightforward dichotomy or even a lineal continuum between freedom and determinism. While studying members of closed communities, I have repeatedly been struck by how often they have insisted that they now felt freer than they had before joining what may seem to others to be an authoritarian group severely restricting the freedom of its members. On the other hand, I have observed groups which proclaim that they embrace total freedom and that everyone can do just whatever they choose when, in fact, these "free souls" may be perceived to be quite severely constrained in a number of ways. These apparently paradoxical situations I have described as, respectively, "the freedom of the cage" and "the cage of freedom."[15]

Indeed, one of the more fascinating aspects of sociology is the number of tensions and juxtapositions that it embraces.[16] To begin with, the social constructionist approach involves seeing social reality as an ongoing process that is constantly changing, yet always relying on something that went before and, thereby, involving more or less continuity, though never total stability. Second, social reality is real in the sense that it exists independently of any particular individual's volition; but, unlike most of the physical reality studied by the natural sciences, it (social reality) does not exist except insofar as it is recognized by one or more individuals at either a conscious or subconscious level. Third, every individual perceives any particular social reality in a unique way, depending on where they are standing or "coming from"; but at the same time, perceptions of social reality have to be more or less shared – were this not so, society would be well-nigh impossible.

Thus it is that a social phenomenon, such as a new religious movement, will be viewed in a different light by different people. Members of the movement will share certain perceptions that will differ more or less discernibly and systematically from those of non-members; and within the group, leaders' perceptions will differ from those of rank-and-file members. If the social scientist hopes to present a rounded picture of a social phenomenon, it is necessary to try to understand it from as many different viewpoints as possible. In some cases these different perceptions will conflict with each other quite sharply. However, while one would expect different individuals and different groups with different interests to present different images of the new religions (or "cults" or "sects"), and while it is the task of the sociologist to describe these different images rather than to judge them, it did seem to me that when I came across descriptions that were demonstrably wrong, these ought to be denounced.

Making a difference

As a student, I had accepted as pretty well self-evident, that scientists should be careful not to contaminate their data, although it had to be recognised that just by asking questions or by living in a closed community of which one was not oneself a member, one was almost bound to affect the people one was studying. While there could be situations in which one observed without being observed, it was difficult to believe that this was always, or even usually, the best way to understand a movement that had unusual beliefs and practices. When I first started studying the Unification Church, I would try to place myself in a situation where I could watch and listen without drawing attention to myself – washing-up dishes provided one such opportunity. After some time, however, I would interact more obviously with the members and it was then that I would make mistakes and be corrected, thereby having drawn to my attention things that I might otherwise not have noticed.[17] A parallel could be drawn between someone learning a language from a textbook and then actually using it in the company of native speakers. A third stage in my participation was once I had felt I had mastered sufficient understanding of the movement to be able to ask questions without being fobbed off with evasions or accusations of not being able to understand.

But there was an important lesson I was to learn just when I was starting to congratulate myself that I was really beginning to understand the Unificationists and was finding that things I had first thought to be strange now seemed perfectly normal. My husband and I happened to meet a couple of members while we were on holiday. We chatted to them over coffee, then made our excuses and left. "They weren't that bad, were they?" I said to my husband, who had always expressed a deep suspicion of the movement. "They were all right," he said, "but you – you were really weird!"

I was completely taken by surprise. There is, of course, a sense in which we all behave differently in the company of different people. One does not behave as one does with fellow students in the company of an elderly maiden aunt, but I had not realized the extent to which I had "changed gear." My husband's reaction raised my awareness of how important it is for sociologists to recognize changes in their perception as the worldview of those they are studying grows more familiar. This is partly because the researcher's job, like that of the actor, includes the task of communicating to others for whom such worldviews are unfamiliar and/or incomprehensible. Allied to this, I was to learn that just merely reporting or reproducing the perceptions and/or behavior of Unificationists was not sufficient to enable others to understand them. I was also to learn that when I tried to "make sense" by too accurately reproducing the point of view of those I was studying, I was to find myself being accused of "being one of them."[18] I eventually realized that it is sometimes necessary to "translate" in such a way that one is *not* reproducing the original behavior. An analogy that may be drawn from the theater is that the really brilliant actor portraying a bore will be riveting rather than boring as he portrays what it's like to be a bore far more convincingly than if he himself were giving a boring performance.

It was through trying to explain to non-members why Unificationists might believe and do the things they believed and did that I increasingly found myself "making a difference" in the "cult scene." I was mediating between Unificationists and relatives who had not spoken to each other for years; I appeared on radio and television programmes; I was called as a witness both for and against the Unification Church. At first, I had told myself that I would give the same answer (my truth) whichever side asked the question. Soon, however, I realized that it was different questions that elicited crucially different answers, and that one side was not going to ask the same questions as the other side would ask. But, whoever had called me as a witness, I was likely to be "making a difference." And of course, as I published my findings, I was disseminating an image of the Unification Church (and the many other new religious movements I came to study) which often differed radically from the images that the movements promoted of themselves – or those disseminated by the media or the various "anti-cult groups" that had emerged in opposition to the movements.[19]

However, I reasoned that part of the *raison d'être* of any social scientist is to present his or her findings to a wider public. Indeed, it would be ridiculous *not* to want to present one's findings. One could even argue that the problem was not so much that one's findings were affecting the scene as that one's findings were *not* affecting the scene. And then, in the mid-1980s, I was to take a further step in my "making a difference" by becoming a fully fledged, proactive member of the "cult scene."

I had been worried for some time about what seemed to me unnecessary suffering due to inappropriate actions being taken on the basis of ignorance or misinformation about the so-called cults. At the individual level, there was the trade in deprogramming; at the societal level, there was a "Waco" waiting to happen.[20] The tipping point came when I was attending a meeting of Britain's largest anti-cult group, FAIR,[21] at which some former members were describing their experiences of their respective groups. The audience was becoming irritated because the speakers were denying that they had been brainwashed or even manipulated, claiming instead that they had believed their groups could offer them something, but then they had moved on to other things. The chairman tried to pour oil on troubled waters by asking the former members if there was anything they would like to say that would be helpful for relatives. At this point, a woman stood up and started shouting "we don't want to hear this! We don't want to hear this!" And, indeed, it was clear that the audience did not want to hear anything that might threaten their image of the movements.

Repairing to a nearby pub with the chairman and one of the former members, I declared that "something needed to be done." My companions agreed, but, it seemed, if something were to be done, then it was I who ought to be doing the something. To cut short a long story,[22] I founded Inform (Information Network Focus on Religious Movements), an educational charity with the aim of providing information that was as objective and up-to-date as possible about minority religions. My hope was that we could direct enquirers to some of the work that was being done by social scientists throughout the world. The British government and mainstream churches supported (and continue to support) the venture.

The "cult wars"

I hadn't expected everyone to applaud, but the response was overwhelming. Sections of the media exposed me as a "cult lover" and members of anti-cult groups wrote to their MPs, fed the media stories about me (almost all of which were either silly and/ or untrue), and a petition was presented to 10 Downing Street. Some of this was pretty bruising, but there was a sense in which it was also rather invigorating. At Inform we never know who will be at the other end of the telephone. What might at first seem an innocent enquiry has not infrequently turned out to be either a new religious movement or an anti-cultist trying to trick us into saying something that would discredit Inform. In a way, however, this may be seen as having a positive effect on our work as we have had to be careful that anything we say can be backed up and that neither "side" would be able to accuse us of not giving an objective and balanced account.

The so-called cult wars had been raging since the mid-1970s and, although they involved a variety of protagonists, one set of virulently opposing "sides" consisted of two types of "cult watchers" labeled by their respective opponents as "anti-cultists" (which included the deprogrammers) and "cult apologists" (which included academics). As I have already intimated, one of the reasons that I set up Inform was to combat the anti-cultists and their generalizing descriptions of all the cults as dangerous pseudo-religions involved in financial rackets and political intrigue, indulging in unnatural sexual practices, abusing their women and children, using irresistible and irreversible brainwashing techniques, frequently resorting to a variety of criminal activities, and likely to commit mass suicide. Partly as a reaction to the attacks that I underwent as a result of my work, I was building up a picture of "anti-cultists" that consisted of just as many sweeping generalizations as those of which we were accusing them. A few of the British anti-cultists had entered into dialog with me, but this was always on a one-to-one basis with the individual concerned explaining that they would get into trouble if their colleagues found out that they had any kind of association with me. The British anti-cult groups were, unequivocally, Inform's enemies.

However, ten years after Inform had opened, I came to the conclusion that if I really wanted to understand the cult scene, it was necessary for me to try to understand the anti-cultists, in much the same way as I was trying to understand the movements that they opposed. With some trepidation, I grasped the nettle and wrote to the Executive Director of the American Family Foundation (AFF),[23] requesting permission to attend their 1998 annual conference in Philadelphia. Somewhat to my surprise, I received a courteous response saying that I would be welcome. Still very nervous, I arrived at the conference hotel and almost immediately received a phone call asking me to go up to the Presidential suite for a drink with some of the AFF officers. It seemed that they were as curious about me as I was about them.

By no means all the other participants were as friendly. Several were openly hostile, and included attacks on sociologists in general and me in particular in their talks.[24] However, both the Executive Director and the President and several of the other participants made a point of being kind to me. Recognizing that they were asking "How can she?" just as curiously as I was asking "How can they?," I suggested that we should spend a day before their next annual conference with four of "them" and four of "us" discussing our different perspectives. This was agreed and resulted in my learning a great deal. We certainly didn't reach agreement on all, or possibly even most, of the subjects we raised; but we had an interesting and informative day exploring a number of controversial issues. Just one of the realizations with which I came away was that they were primarily concerned with asking the question "What harm do the cults do?" while we were more interested in the question "What do new religious movements believe and do?" There was certainly some overlap here, but just recognizing how we were coming from somewhat different directions helped both sides to understand, and even respect, some of what it was that at least some members of "the other side" were doing.

Since that time, I have had numerous contacts with "anti-cult groups," not only in America, but also in various European and Asian countries. Perhaps the two most important lessons I have learnt are, first, that, as with new religious movements, one cannot generalize about these "cult-watching groups"; and, next, like new religious movements, they can change quite radically over time. However, the British groups continue to attack me, with the current Chairman of FAIR complaining in the European Parliament and various other places about the British government's using Inform as "its principal source of advice," which, he says, is responsible for "the total lack of official action to restrict or discourage the activity of cults, or to warn students and others of the dangers of becoming involved"[25] – an accusation I tend to find more flattering than plausible.

Whose side are you on?[26]

I am often asked by students how I manage to gain access to new religions, but in fact this is a problem I have encountered remarkably seldom. Interestingly enough, it has often been the most vilified that are the most prepared, if not eager, to tell someone their side of the story. Of course, they may not tell you the truth – they, like everyone else, are certainly unlikely to tell you the whole truth. However, listening to former members and various other informants can help one to build up a fuller picture. This can, however, give rise to some serious methodological misgivings.

In a keynote talk given at an ICSA conference, Steven Mutch[27] cited with approval my statement that "it is important to understand the movements from a variety of perspectives, which, themselves, need to be understood as part of the ongoing process of the situation." However, he then went on to declare that it is "difficult for any individual scholar to attempt successfully to gain access to a controversial NRM and at the same time study the accounts of leavers." This, he argued, is because a researcher who has engaged with either party cannot expect to have any "street credibility" with the other. What is needed is a methodological division of labor, or what Mutch calls a triangulated approach, with different individuals or groups having to choose to specialize in *either* "leaver research" *or* "invited-access research," and then a third party (such as the ICSA) "combining the two approaches."

Mutch has a point – to be labeled as either a cult apologist or a cult critic can make access to "the other side" difficult. But while it can be difficult, it is certainly not impossible. And, whenever it is possible, it is, I believe, desirable.

Quite apart from the fact that one cannot simply add up two extreme images of a social phenomenon to get the "real" picture,[28] to accept Mutch's dichotomous perspective of there being only two sides is to accept "their" perspective. There are now many people whom I first met when they were members of a movement who have long since left, yet have kept in touch with me over the years. Although some leavers are undoubtedly antagonistic towards their erstwhile movement, by no means all leavers are; many now maintain perfectly amicable relations with those who remain in the movement. Furthermore, even when there is antagonism between leavers and current members, it does not follow that researchers are necessarily denied access to one side because they have researched the other. My own work over the past few decades provides plenty of empirical refutations that such must necessarily be the case.

Right from the beginning of my research into the Unification Church I made it clear that I intended to speak to former members and others who were opposed to the movement. This seemed to be accepted without much question. But it has not only been Unificationists who have accepted that my research involves interactions with opposing sides. The Exclusive Brethren, whose reading of the Bible supports their Doctrine of Separation, which involves their cutting themselves off from the rest of society as far as is possible, have invited me into their schools and homes (although I always have to eat in a separate room).[29] Not only are they well aware that I have interviewed several former Brethren who have been "put out" or "withdrawn from" since their departure from the movement, the Brethren have arranged for me to talk to the relatives of some of these former members (with whom they themselves will have no dealings).

The Family International, formerly known as the Children of God, which I have studied in considerable depth (interviewing members at length and staying in several of their Homes around the world), is another movement that has always been well aware of my contacts with former members (including those who are active in "anti-cult" groups). Among the occasions when my contact with "both sides" was abundantly clear, was one when I arranged for a mother, who had left the movement in its early days, to spend a day in my kitchen with her daughter, who was still in the movement and with whom she had had no contact whatsoever for 14 years.

To take just one further illustration out of the numerous examples from which I could draw,[30] I have been a participant observer at Falun Gong gatherings and interviewed several of its practitioners at length, including those who have been granted asylum in the West after having been detained for "re-education" by the People's Republic of China, where the movement is consistently referred to as an "evil cult" (*xiejiao*); and I have stayed on the campus of the Chinese People's Public Security University in Beijing, where, on three separate occasions, I have given ten-day-long courses on social science methodology to police cadets and staff. I have also interviewed former practitioners who are now responsible for "re-educating" practitioners in China, as well as a number of government officials and representatives of the official Chinese Anti-Cult Association. Again, both the practitioners and their opponents knew I had contact with the "other side" yet seemed eager to respond to questions that explicitly drew on allegations I had heard from their opponents.[31]

There are, of course, people on "both sides" who refuse to have anything to do with me or Inform – but many of these people refuse to have contact with *any* outsider. For this reason it is sometimes assumed that covert research is more productive than overt research, and there are some cases in which this can be persuasively argued.[32] However, quite apart from ethical and psychological issues, my experience has led me to believe that in most cases it would be not only unnecessary but also likely to be methodologically counter-productive to go undercover and pretend to join. Once accepted in the researcher role, one is granted permission to question in ways that would be unthinkable for a covert researcher – female members are frequently separated or discouraged from interacting with male members, and rank-and-file members might have little opportunity to question or even observe those in leadership positions.

Another "methodological risk," one that I have already mentioned and have frequently been warned about is inherent in living with a religious community (or a tribe or any group that one wishes to study), is that of "going native." One could, however, argue that by associating with a large variety of people holding opposing perspectives one is less likely to "go native" than if one immerses oneself exclusively within what Mary Douglas would term "a strong group control" situation.[33] Be that as it may, neither I nor any of the Inform staff have ever felt the slightest inclination to join any of the scores of movements we have studied.

Concluding remarks

Both as an actress and as a sociologist of religion I have enjoyed a rich and interesting life. I have met literally thousands of people who see and understand things in ways that frequently conflict quite fundamentally with the ways I see and understand things. With a growing awareness of the wisdom embodied in Kipling's aphorism "What do they know of England, who only England know?",[34] I have traveled throughout the world and encountered numerous different cultures that have confronted my taken-for-granted assumptions of what is the "natural" way of behaving.[35] Of course, not all my experiences have been ones that I am eager to repeat. I wasn't entirely enamored with cleaning Moonie loos – but somebody had to do it and I was there. More seriously, we underwent a very uncomfortable period at Inform when the Crown Prosecution Service demanded we should reveal information that had been given to us in confidence. Determined to resist this, we went to court where, fortunately, the judge decided in our favor. But this was after we had had to pay over £20,000 in lawyers' fees.[36]

But no one has ever suggested that the sociology of religion is an easy option – well, no one who has any idea of what may be involved. Anyone who has an idea of what is involved must surely consider that it can be one of the most challenging of occupations – and one of the most interesting – and one of the most fun.

Notes

1 Constantin Stanislavski, *An Actor Prepares* (London: Geoffrey Bles, 1937).
2 The "gods" is a term referring to the seats furthest from the stage in the highest balcony or circle in a theater.

3 Eileen Barker, "Brahmins Don't Eat Mushrooms: Participant Observation and the New Religions," *LSE Quarterly* June (1987):127–152.
4 I had, however, appeared in plays which relied quite heavily on improvisation, particularly when I was working with the Theatre Workshop at Stratford East.
5 Eileen Barker, "You Don't Get Marxists in Fundamentalists' Boots: A Comparative Exploration of Self as Implicit Religion," in *LSE on Social Science*, ed. Helen Sasson and Derek Diamond (London: LSE Books, 1996).
6 I can become absorbed in the intricacies and twists and turns of philosophy, and since childhood I have enjoyed mathematical and logical puzzles, such as Martin Garner's "Mathematical Games" column in *Scientific American*; one of the more treasured compliments that I have been paid was by a PhD student inscribing his book with the claim that I had taught him how, but not what, to think. But while I certainly consider clear, imaginative and open thinking to be necessary tools in the sociological endeavor, these are only tools and, taken by themselves, cannot help us in our journey of discovery as to what is actually (as opposed to potentially) going on "out there" in the "real world."
7 Peter L. Berger and Thomas Luckmann, *The Social Construction of Reality: Everything that Passes for Knowledge in Society* (London: Allen Lane, 1967). While still a student, I met the psychologist Richard Gregory, which resulted in my becoming, and remaining, interested in, his and various cognitive neurologists' constructionist approach to perception. Richard L. Gregory, *Seeing Through Illusions: Making Sense of the Senses* (Oxford and New York: Oxford University Press, 2009); Eileen Barker, "The Objective Study of the Subjective or the Subjective Study of the Objective? Notes on the Social Scientific Study of Religious Experience and the Social Construction of Reality," in *The Comparative Study of Religious Experience in Taiwan*, ed. Yen-zen Tsai (Taipei: National Chengchi University, Taiwan, 2012).
8 Eileen Barker, "Thus Spake the Scientist: A Comparative Account of the New Priesthood and its Organisational Bases," *The Annual Review of the Social Sciences of Religion* 3 (1979): 79–103.
9 Eileen Barker, *The Making of a Moonie: Brainwashing or Choice?*(Oxford: Blackwell, 1984).
10 Ted Patrick and Tom Dulack, *Let Our Children Go* (New York: Ballantine, 1976); David G. Bromley and James T. Richardson (eds), *The Brainwashing/Deprogramming Controversy: Sociological, Psychological, Legal and Historical Perspectives* (New York: Edwin Mellen Press, 1983); Eileen Barker, *New Religious Movements: A Practical Introduction* (London: HMSO, 1989), Appendix III. It should be noted that by no means all deprogrammers demanded large sums or were responsible for physical violence. Nonetheless, they were involved in illegal kidnappings. It should also be noted that the practice is practically never carried out in the West nowadays, although it continues in Japan and some other countries. Willy Fautré (ed.), *Japan: Abduction and Deprivation of Freedom for the Purpose of Religious De-conversion* (Brussels: Human Rights Without Frontiers International, 2011) [http://www.hrwf.net/Joom/images/reports/2011/1231%20report%20final.pdf] (accessed May 3, 2012).
11 Max Weber, *The Methodology of the Social Sciences* (New York: The Free Press, 1949).
12 Article 18: Everyone has the right to freedom of thought, conscience and religion; this right includes freedom to change his religion or belief, and freedom, either alone or in community with others and in public or private, to manifest his religion or belief in teaching, practice, worship, and observance.
13 I have, furthermore, since discovered that the vast majority of the first cohort of second-generation members have left the movement.
14 Eileen Barker, "In God's Name: Practising Unconditional Love to the Death," in *Dying for Faith: Religiously Motivated Violence in the Contemporary World*, ed. Madawi Al-Rasheed and Marat Shterin (London and New York: I.B. Tauris, 2009), 49–58.
15 Eileen Barker, "The Cage of Freedom and the Freedom of the Cage," in *LSE on Freedom*, ed. Eileen Barker (London: LSE Books, 1995a), 103–118.
16 Eileen Barker, "The Scientific Study of Religion? You Must be Joking!," *Journal for the Scientific Study of Religion* 34(3) (1995b): 287–310; also pp. 7–25 in *Cults and New Religious*

Movements. A Reader, ed. Lorne L. Dawson (London: Blackwell, 2003) [http://zjshkx. com/Upload/Article/2008–1/Barkerpaper1995.pdf] (accessed May 3, 2012).

17 Barker, "Brahmins Don't Eat Mushrooms."

18 I have been accused of being not only a "Moonie," but also a Krishna devotee, a Scientologist, a creationist, and an anti-cultist – all of which imputations would have elicited ridicule from the "genuine articles."

19 Eileen Barker, "Watching for Violence: A Comparative Analysis of the Roles of Five Cult-watching Groups," in *Cults, Religion and Violence*, ed. David G. Bromley and J. Gordon Melton (Cambridge: Cambridge University Press, 2002), 123–148.

20 Stuart Wright (ed.), *Armageddon in Waco: Critical Perspectives on the Branch Davidian Conflict* (Chicago, IL: University of Chicago Press, 1995).

21 Founded in the UK in 1976 as Family Action Information & Rescue, FAIR changed its name in 1994 to Family Action Information & Resource when deprogramming, which several of its members had advocated and taken part in, had become seriously questioned. Then, in 2007, it changed its name again to The Family Survival Trust.

22 Eileen Barker, "INFORM: Bringing the Sociology of Religion to the Public Space," in *Frontier Religions in Public Space*, ed. Pauline Côté (Ottawa: University of Ottawa Press, 2001), 21–34; Eileen Barker, "Misconceptions of the Religious 'Other': The Importance for Human Rights of Objective and Balanced Knowledge," *International Journal for the Study of New Religions* 1(1) (2010): 5–25.

23 The AFF changed its name to the International Cultic Studies Association (ICSA) in 2004.

24 A renowned diva of the anti-cult world deliberately turned her back on me in an otherwise empty elevator when I wished her a good morning, while a well-known deprogrammer actually spat at me!

25 Tom Sackville, "Why Cults are Bad," *The Spectator*, May 29, 2004.

26 This was a question addressed to me by a Scientologist lobbying outside an ICSA conference I attended.

27 Stephen Bruce Mutch, "Cultism, Terrorism, and Homeland Security," *Cultic Studies Review* 5(2) (2006): 169–197. Dr. Mutch, a lawyer of the Supreme Court of New South Wales and an Honorary Associate at Macquarie University, is an active patron of the Australian Cult Information and Family Support Inc., founded in 1996 by "parents and family members of loved ones caught up in abusive groups."

28 This is the "fairness" that the media frequently claim to achieve by inviting two extreme antagonists to present their respective "truths," assuming that the truth lies "somewhere in the middle" when it may do nothing of the kind. It might again be argued that the law also assumes that there are just two opposing sides, but it assumes that the truth lies with only one of these.

29 "Be not diversely yoked with unbelievers; for what participation [is there] between righteousness and lawlessness?" (II Corinthians 6:14); "But now I have written to you, if any one called brother be fornicator, or avaricious, or idolater, or abusive, or a drunkard, or rapacious, not to mix with [him]; with such a one not even to eat" (I Corinthians 5:11, trans. J.N. Darby).

30 Eileen Barker, "Stepping out of the Ivory Tower: A Sociological Engagement in 'The Cult Wars'," *Methodological Innovations Online* 6(1) (2011a):18–39 [http://www.pbs.plym. ac.uk/mi/viewissue.html] (accessed May 3, 2012).

31 Eileen Barker, "A Sociological Approach to Cultic Studies," in *International Forum on Cultic Studies (Shenzhen 9–11 January 2009) The Harms and Social Administration of Destructive Cults,* ed. CASS (Shenzhen: Centre for the Study of Destructive Cults, Chinese Academy of Social Sciences, 2009b), 113–133.

32 Laud Humphreys, *Tearoom Trade: Impersonal Sex in Public Places* (London: Transaction, 1975); Matthew A. Lauder, "Covert Participant Observation of a Deviant Community: Justifying the Use of Deception," *Journal of Contemporary Religion* 18(2) (2003): 185–196.

33 Mary Douglas, *Purity and Danger: An Analysis of Concepts of Pollution and Taboo* (London: Routledge & Kegan Paul, 1966); Mary Douglas, *Natural Symbols: Explorations in Cosmology* (London: Barrie & Rockliff, 1970).

34 Rudyard Kipling, "The English Flag," *The National Observer*, April 4, 1891.

35 Eileen Barker, "But Who's Going to Win? National and Minority Religions in Post-Communist Society," in *New Religious Phenomena in Central and Eastern Europe*, ed. Irena Borowik and Grzegorz Babinski (Kraków: Nomos, 1997), 25–62; Eileen Barker, "Religion in China: Some Introductory Notes for the Intrepid Western Scholar," in *Social Scientific Studies of Religion in China: Methodology, Theories, and Findings,* ed. Fenggang Yang and Graeme Lang (Leiden, and Boston, MA: Brill, 2011b), 109–132.

36 The case involved a guru who was eventually charged with rape, partly because Inform had persuaded some of his many victims who had spoken to us to go to the police, a fact that stood us in good stead when, fortunately for us, the judge also ruled that the Crown Prosecution Service should pay our costs. In the event, the CPS refunded only part of the fees we had had to pay. Then, to our considerable relief, the government made up the difference, agreeing with us that we would be unlikely to obtain important information in the future if our informants thought that we would readily hand over confidences without their permission.

5

CONSTRUCTING RELIGION

Serendipity and skepticism

James A. Beckford

The history of ideas has fascinated me since my days as an undergraduate student of French literature, philosophy, and politics. My undergraduate dissertation, prepared during a year at the University of Lyon in 1963–1964, was about the intersection between the biography, the aesthetics, and the politics of Léon Blum. He was not only the first socialist and Jew to become Prime Minister[1] of France – in the Front Populaire government of 1936–1937 – but also a distinguished literary critic and theorist, among other things. At the same time, Léon Blum was the target of vicious campaigns of ultra-right-wing anti-Semitic abuse and even physical violence. It was his combination of erudition and socialist resistance to bigoted nationalism which proved irresistible to me.

If my early interest in Léon Blum showed the importance of placing intellectual work and political action in the context of biography, I had never given much thought to this aspect of my own life. But two events in recent years started me thinking about possible links between my own intellectual interests and life history. The first was a pair of interviews that Laurent Amiotte-Suchet and Véronique Altglas conducted with me in 2005–2006.[2] They prompted me to ponder for the first time the personal and social contexts in which my research and teaching had taken place.

The second event which prompted some self-reflexive thoughts about the possible links between biography and intellectual work was the experience of reading contributions to the flattering volume that Eileen Barker had edited in my honor.[3] The opportunity to see aspects of my own work, filtered through the eyes of respected colleagues and friends, raised questions about the directions it had taken over a period of 40 years. It also made me wonder to what extent there were any coherent links among my research projects. The missing links and missed opportunities became all too clear to me, but the experience was also good preparation for the current exercise of reflecting on the intersection between my personal life and my professional engagement in sociological research.

Skepticism and serendipity

The two main themes that emerge from the following reflections are skepticism and serendipity. The first owes much to the influence of the writer Michel de Montaigne who managed to survive the 16th-century Wars of Religion in France by preserving his distance from all extremisms. His long essay on vanity made a particularly strong impression on me as a 20-year-old student, but it was his skeptical motto "What do I know?"[4] that has had the most enduring influence on my approach to scholarship. I interpret it as an encouragement to adopt a critical and skeptical attitude towards all claims to truth or knowledge. It is an injunction to take nothing for granted; to be suspicious of fashionable ideas or trends; and to regard one's own arguments as never more than provisional. It owes nothing to nihilism or cynicism, however, and everything to a cautious, self-critical humanism.

The other theme is serendipity. This is the belief that it is possible to make fortunate and useful discoveries at least as much by accident as by design. Admittedly, rigorous methods and diligence are essential requirements for good scholarship, but unexpected opportunities, accidental discoveries, and counter-intuitive findings also occur. It seems to me that serendipity sits well with skepticism insofar as both of them can restrain tendencies towards intellectual arrogance, rigidity, or fundamentalism. In this respect, they are also comfortable bedfellows within a broader humanism which acknowledges the sublime *and* the grotesque aspects of social life – including religion. Indeed, the sociological study of religion calls – often in vain – for an even-handed attitude towards the sublime and the grotesque. This sometimes leads to accusations of relativism from scholars committed to a version of absolute truth, but a skeptical, humanistic sociology is, by nature, undaunted by claims to absolute truth and must be, in any case, willing to entertain criticisms of its own foundations.

From the personal to the social, the sectarian, and the cultic

The process of coming to see religion as a social phenomenon took me a long time. Having been immersed as a child and an adolescent in Calvinistic piety, compulsory attendance at Sunday School and evening worship, Bible classes, scripture examinations, church parades, and a youth organization "for the advancement of Christ's kingdom among boys," I entered early adulthood feeling thoroughly familiar with organized Protestantism and increasingly dubious about its value for me. Studying the writings of Jean Calvin, Blaise Pascal, Denis Diderot, Voltaire, and Jean-Jacques Rousseau only strengthened my ambivalence towards Christianity. But taking a wonderful course in my final year as an undergraduate on "The Critique of Liberalism in France from 1815" finally gave me the opportunity to cultivate an analytical attitude towards religion as a social phenomenon. In particular, I came to see that in the first half of the 19th century both liberal Catholics such as Félicité de Lammenais,

Henri-Dominique Lacordaire, and Charles de Montalembert, and reactionary Catholics such as Louis de Bonald and Joseph de Maistre regarded their religion as integral to the fabric of French society – long before Emile Durkheim made a similar observation. I was also intrigued by the fact that Frédéric Le Play forged a specifically Catholic kind of empirical sociology alongside – and in competition with – the emerging sociologies of Henri de Saint Simon, Auguste Comte, Herbert Spencer, Karl Marx, and others.

My entry into postgraduate study began, then, with a review of the contribution of French "social Catholicism" towards the fragmented and contested emergence of sociology as an academic discipline. It was an opportunity to try to correct some of the Anglocentric histories of sociology and to show that a discipline which was widely regarded as having secularizing tendencies actually had some important roots in progressive and conservative religious ideologies – at least in France.[5] This work, initially undertaken in the Department of French Studies at the University of Reading, reflected my skeptical attitudes towards some taken-for-granted accounts of sociology. It also reflected a narrow conception of religion as beliefs and doctrines.

The direction of my doctoral research changed dramatically in 1966, however, while I was delving into the intellectual history of sociology in France. By chance I stumbled across a supplement of *Comparative Studies in Society and History* on millennialism.[6] It chimed well with a little-known article by Bryan Wilson on sects that I had read a few years earlier as a subscriber to the *Rationalist Annual*[7] – as well as with my readings about communitarian movements in 19th-century France and the USA. Millenarian sects came to hold a fascination for me that gradually eclipsed my interest in social Catholicism as a set of ideas and opened my eyes to the truly social aspects of religion.

My "discovery" of millennialism was the first significant episode of serendipity in my intellectual life but, with hindsight, I can see that it was far from being completely accidental. In fact, there was considerable continuity between my previous interest in French social Catholicism and my new interest in millenarian movements. Both of them centered on expressions of religion which aimed at creating and sustaining totalizing forms of life governed by explicit religious ideas and organizations. They shared a number of other characteristics such as relatively high degrees of formality, clear boundaries between insiders and outsiders, and a controversial image in public life. To put this negatively, my interests were not in informal, banal, everyday, liturgical, or popular forms of religion. Instead, my interests lay in the distinctive and varied rationalities of high-demand, contested, and mobilizing organizations. It is no surprise, then, that I eventually came to teach courses on the mobilization of social movement activists for about 30 years in Durham, Chicago, and Warwick – alongside my research on religion.

Having switched the registration of my PhD from the Department of French to the recently formed Department of Sociology at the University of Reading in 1967, I received strong encouragement from my supervisor, Stanislav Andreski,[8] to locate my research in the context of Max Weber's philosophical and methodological approaches to social science. And, in addition to feeling overawed by the wealth of erudition in Weber's many studies of religions, I threw myself into the intricacies of his discussions of the church-type, the sect-type, and mysticism – as well as into the equally impressive writings of his friend Ernst Troeltsch on the organizational and ethical outworking of the *Social Teachings of the Christian Churches*.[9] I also warmed to the methodological precepts of *verstehende Soziologie* and to Weber's insistence that social order is a constant process of construction, challenge, and legitimization.

But sanctification of my full conversion from a historian of ideas about French social Catholicism to a would-be sociologist of sectarian religion depended on three more episodes of serendipity. First, Bryan Wilson, the pre-eminent expert on the sociology of religious sects, who lived and worked not far from Reading at All Souls College, Oxford, kindly agreed to meet with me to discuss my interest. I cannot overestimate the importance of the guidance he offered, especially as I was alone in focusing on religion in my own department. In particular, he invited me to partici-pate in his weekly seminars on the sociology of religion where many of the leading authorities gave presentations – and where I first made the acquaintance of, among others, John Whitworth, the late Roy Wallis, Steven Lukes, and Douglas Davies.[10] I could not have wished for a better introduction to the key debates in the sociology of religion. Second, Bryan Wilson strongly backed my idea to try to conduct empirical research with Jehovah's Witnesses – a movement that he had tried, but failed, to study for his own doctoral research 15 years earlier.[11] The fact that no other British scholar had managed to complete research on the Witnesses seemed like a bonus for me. In the words of the cliché, I was in the right place at the right time. Third, my initial overtures to the Witnesses at local level in Reading and at national level in Mill Hill, London met with a guarded – but not dismissive – response. They had a long-standing reputation for rejecting applications for permission to conduct research, but my approach happened to coincide with a slight thawing of their relations with people who were "not in the truth." I was also fortunate to gain the personal support of one of their Special Pioneers in Reading – serendipity in spades.

Just as my doctoral research was ending, another instance of serendipity propelled my research in a new direction. I learned from one of my undergraduate students that a Korean religious movement with a millennial ideology, called the Unified Family, had established a center close to the town of Reading. After visiting the center and analyzing as much of the movement's literature as possible, I wrote a conference paper about the movement and soon discovered that it was becoming highly con-troversial. The movement was eventually to become much better known under such names as the Unification Church, the Holy Spirit Association for the Unification of World Christianity, the Unificationist movement or – in popular parlance – the Moonies.[12]

In many respects, the new object of my interest showed a high degree of con-tinuity with the central themes of my research on Jehovah's Witnesses: millennialism, totalizing forms of organization, emphasis on the mobilization of members, and cross-national outreach. But what initially caught my attention about the Unificationist movement was that it allied itself with English nationalist sentiments and that its predominantly young devotees were prepared to distance themselves from their families in order to devote most of their waking life to raising funds and recruiting new members. It was this latter aspect of the movement that gave rise to journalistic *exposés* of the founder, Sun Myung Moon, and to numerous controversies extending right up to the level of parliamentary debates in the UK and congressional hearings in the US. I responded by trying to understand how and why these controversies were developing and what effect they were having on the emergence of a broader category of events that I called "cult controversies." More significantly, I obtained a grant from the Social Science Research Council in 1976–1979 to conduct a "sociological investigation of withdrawal from an authoritarian religious sect."[13] In response, leaders of the Unification Church in the UK tried to obstruct my research and sued me for libel in respect of inaccuracies in an article I had written for *Psychology Today*. With the support of my employers, the University of Durham, and the Association of University Teachers the case was settled out of court several years later. The experience taught me two important lessons: the necessity to double-check information received by me in good faith, and the danger of thinking that academic research might enjoy any "privilege" in law.

Research and teaching on a wide variety of new religious movements (NRMs) or "cults" expanded and accelerated rapidly in many countries in the late 1970s, thereby giving me the opportunity to reflect on underlying issues. As with my research on the Witnesses, my first inclination was to concentrate on questions of ideology, organization, and mobilization, but contextual issues came to preoccupy me. As the controversies unfolded, it became clear to me that questions about media portrayals, legal problems, political framing of "cults," and public opinion demanded much closer attention. Above all, the hostile attitudes of relatives and close friends of some NRM members – as well as of ex-members or apostates – were feeding into the activities of "anti-cult" groups, in some cases leading to attempts to kidnap and "deprogram" members. New information technologies were also helping to accelerate the spread of these controversies across national boundaries. This was my first serious encounter with questions about law and minority religions, and it whetted my appetite for comparative studies of the legal and political contexts of "cult controversies" in countries as diverse as France, the former West Germany, and Japan.[14] It also proved to be useful preparation for my appointment in 1990 as a Governor of Inform – the government-funded organization that Eileen Barker had founded two years earlier for the purpose of collecting, assessing, and disseminating the most reliable information about religious movements.[15]

Religious organizations

Although my PhD thesis of 1972[16] paid a lot of attention to the beliefs and ways of life of individual Jehovah's Witnesses in the UK, it also took into account the changing organizational forms of the Watchtower Society. Questions about authority, power, and compliance in what I called a "totalizing" organization were to the fore of my analysis. Indeed, soon after completing the thesis I published a book-length

Trend Report on "Religious Organization"[17] which attempted to assess the distinctiveness of religious organizations. Some of my other publications on related topics have also sought to extend and to intensify the sociological understanding of the organizational structures and processes that are characteristic of (without necessarily being unique to) religious organizations.[18]

No doubt the writings of Max Weber and Ernst Troeltsch had initially guided me towards questions about the formal organizational characteristics and "vehicles" of religion. But I became increasingly interested in the impact of new technologies of communication on the capacity of religious organizations to spread their messages, to recruit members, and to mobilize followers. In some ways, I was doing supply-side analyses of religious organizations long before this became fashionable among rational choice theorists. Although this had only rarely been regarded as an important dimension of the sociology of religion in the UK, I thought it deserved more careful study. At the same time, I was becoming skeptical about the value of the church-denomination-sect-cult typology which still featured prominently in textbooks on the sociology of religion in the 1970s. My preference was for a less theologically inflected way of characterizing religious organizations in terms of, for example, their degrees of centralization, segmentation, standardization, etc.

In fact, this focus on organization became part of my broader concern to forge better links – theoretically and analytically – between the study of religious and non-religious collectivities. Rather than trying to understand religious activity and structures in terms of specifically religious factors, I have always found it more interesting and productive to examine religious and non-religious phenomena in the same, or similar, terms. For example, processes of recruitment, socialization, mobilization, regulation, marginalization, and rejection are common to all voluntary associations. The challenge is to discover the extent to which particular religious organizations do – or do not – give a distinctive twist to these processes. The other side of the coin, of course, is to consider how far ostensibly non-religious organizations display characteristics that are widely associated with the sacred and religion.[19]

By the time I came to publish an article in 1985 on the "insulation and isolation of the sociology of religion"[20] I was advocating an approach to the sociological understanding of religion that made full use of the theoretical and explanatory resources of sociology in general. The aim was not only to enrich the sociology of religion but also to oblige other sociologists to take notice of what sociologists of religion were doing. I thought it was essential to re-energize the two-way flow of influence between general sociology and the sociology of religion which had been a prominent feature of the sociological classics crafted by such scholars as Emile Durkheim, Max Weber, and Georg Simmel. I remain convinced that this ideal is still valid; and I was happy to acknowledge in 2000 that the degree of insulation and isolation had begun to shrink – especially in relation to understanding the gendering of religion.[21] My own attempts to close the gap between the sociology of religion and the concerns of other mainstream sociologists have included discussions of social problems,[22] social movements,[23] self-help groups,[24] and social policies[25] – all with regard to their religious dimensions.

Since the early 1990s, my aim of forging closer links between mainstream social science and the study of religion has taken two further routes. One has been the study of the place accorded to religion in prisons, notably in Britain and France.[26] The other is an investigation of the response of public institutions to the growth of religious diversity.[27] In particular, I am actively engaged in the seven-year Major Collaborative Research Initiative on "Religion and diversity" which is directed by Lori Beaman at the University of Ottawa.[28] Questions about rights, equality, and justice – especially with regard to gender and ethnicity – lie at the root of these projects.

Theorizing and religion

When I moved from Loyola University, Chicago to the University of Warwick in 1989 I stopped teaching courses on the sociology of religion, although the focus of most of my research remained on religious topics. One of the reasons for abandoning this side of my teaching portfolio was that my new department wanted me to teach other things. But this change of direction also reflected my own concern to maintain a good balance between my interest in religion and other, equally important aspects of social life. Working with Charles Turner, a younger colleague with an excellent understanding of sociology in Germany and Central Europe, I developed a new undergraduate course at Warwick on Theoretical Ideas in Sociology that gave me the opportunity to expand my theoretical horizons and – eventually – to think about religion in the context of more general sociological theories.

My 1989 book *Religion in Advanced Industrial Society*[29] had been commissioned by Tom Bottomore and Mike Mulkay for their series on "Controversies in Sociology." The idea was that the book would help to persuade sociologists who were not specialists in religion that religion remained interesting – and might even be on the way towards becoming more controversial in advanced industrial societies. Thus, in addition to assessing the theoretical contributions of classical and modern thinkers, I tried to tease out the potential relevance to the sociology of religion of works by Antonio Gramsci, Louis Althusser, Michel Foucault, Jürgen Habermas, and Alain Touraine, among others. My aim was also to suggest that the "deregulation" of religion might lead to new controversies. The central claim was that "Religion has come adrift from its former points of anchorage but is no less potentially powerful as a result. It remains a potent cultural resource or form which may act as the vehicle of change, challenge, or conservation."[30] This was a clear expression of my skepticism about simplistic theories of secularization; and I subsequently took the argument further by reasoning that simplistic claims about a "resurgence" of religion in advanced industrial societies are equally suspect.[31]

I have never thought that it would be interesting or worthwhile to devise a theory of religion. This is because religion is not, in my view, a fixed or unitary thing that could be explained by a single set of propositions. Rather, I believe that human agents – and, by implication, social organizations – attribute a wide variety of meanings to religion in different social and cultural settings. From my point of view, then, the most interesting sociological questions are about how religion is constructed and enacted in particular contexts – without making any inferences about its "essential" or would-be universal properties. This is a theoretical approach which draws heavily on the traditions of interpretive and interactional perspectives on social life and which can be usefully extended to discourse analysis and ethnomethodology.[32]

I find these theoretical ideas to be useful in the sense that they can help to generate persuasive accounts of social processes, settings, structures, roles, and so on. But they cannot possibly exhaust all theoretical possibilities; nor are they definitive statements about the phenomena that they help to explain. I make use of them as frameworks of ideas with which it is good to think. This is an instrumental use of middle-range theoretical ideas rather than high-level theorizing for its own sake. Indeed, the main aim of my *Social Theory and Religion* was to assess the usefulness and robustness of social constructionist ideas in relation to specific topics such as secularization, pluralism and religious diversity, globalization, religious mobilization, individualization, and privatization.[33] At the same time, my empirical investigations of prison chaplaincies in England and Wales and France also focused on what is at stake in the institutional processes of defining and categorizing religions and religious practices for administrative and disciplinary purposes.[34]

Fostering the instrumental and pragmatic uses of theoretical ideas about religion was also one of the aims of the volume I edited in 2006 with John Walliss on *Theorizing Religion*.[35] In fact, my own contribution to the volume was an assessment of the practical value of the "minimalist" approach to understanding religion advocated by the French social anthropologist Albert Piette[36] – another instance of the "French connection" that percolates through my intellectual biography. What attracted me to Piette's work was the promise it offered of disclosing the mundane, banal, routine, and – on occasion – boring aspects of many religious occasions and activities. I also took seriously Piette's accusation that sociologists of religion tend to over-theorize their work in the sense of imposing excessively high-level generalizations on the flow of social life at the expense of insights into its richness and variety. Again, it seemed to me that Piette's perspective was helpful insofar as it deflated claims that religion was somehow in a category of its own and not, therefore, accessible by social scientific procedures. As there is no disjunction between his studies of religion and his studies of photography, festivals, and what he calls "secular religions," I argued that his work goes a long way towards closing the gap between the sociology of religion and sociological understanding of other social and cultural phenomena.

My welcome for Albert Piette's strictures against the alleged tendency for sociologists of religion to over-theorize their work sits well with my own skepticism about three theoretical schemes in particular. First, the fashion for trying to force religious changes into the single mold of "postmodernity," beginning in the 1980s, struck me as unwise and unhelpful.[37] I thought that the term "postmodernity" was too vague, too abstract, and too detached from material and organizational considerations to be useful in sociological explanation. Moreover, its application to religion tended to be selective and resistant to empirical testing.

Second, while I have often found it helpful to analyze religious organizations in terms of their deliberate – and arguably rational – strategies for improving their material resources and their share of the religious "market," attempts to reduce all aspects of religion to "rational choice" – or any other single factor – strike me as unprofitable.[38] Following Max Weber's line of reasoning, I argue that if a social theory purports to explain everything, it cannot account for social differences. Another of my criticisms of what now passes as the "subjective rationality" approach to religion is that it is based on questionably narrow assumptions about individual psychology. In addition, as an advocate of a social constructionist approach, I am strongly critical of the rational choice theorists' tendency to ignore all questions about the construction, contestation and enactment of definitions of religion in public life.

Third, the term "post-secular," which is currently in vogue among growing numbers of scholars of religion, seems to be flourishing mainly on the basis of being associated with the name of Jürgen Habermas. Nevertheless, the term suffers from some of the same defects as "postmodernity." In addition, it is associated with dubious claims about the "resurgence" of religion in the public sphere of Western societies.[39] In short, the idea of the post-secular seems to me to be unnecessary, confusing, and unproductive.

Professional contexts

So far, I have emphasized the intertwining of episodes of serendipity and a constant thread of skepticism in my intellectual biography, but it would be entirely wrong to neglect their social contexts. Above all, I need to take account of the many ways in which I have benefited from participation in scholarly associations both at home and abroad. Conferences, seminars, and workshops in many parts of the world have been essential settings for learning about other scholars' research and for obtaining critical feedback on my own ideas. Participating in joint research projects; organizing conference sessions; contributing to edited volumes and encyclopedias; editing volumes and a journal; serving on editorial boards and scientific committees; assessing applications for research funding; advising public policy-makers; being elected to help run scholarly societies – all these activities can help to enrich the experience of participating in a collective enterprise of studying the place of religion in social continuity and change.

Having strong links with individuals and groups of scholars in other countries has been a particularly formative influence on my work. The connections with French colleagues – including two periods of teaching at prestigious institutions in Paris – have been especially influential, but long-term engagement with colleagues in the USA,[40] Canada, the Nordic region, and Japan has also been stimulating and rewarding. These connections have been all the more valuable to me since – apart from the two years with Ross Scherer and Roger Finke at Loyola University, Chicago – I have never worked in academic departments alongside other sociologists of religion.

Nevertheless, my professional life as a sociologist is not entirely without regrets. For example, the untimely death of certain colleagues – notably Phillip Abrams in 1981 and Roy Wallis in 1989 – deprived the academy of the outstanding contributions that they would undoubtedly have continued to make to scholarship. A more selfish regret is that the formal offer of a grant for me to conduct research with Georg Feuerstein on yoga was withdrawn when Mrs. Thatcher slashed the budget of the Social Sciences Research Council in the early 1980s; and a subsequent application for funds to study the spiritual aspects of self-help groups was a failure. At a more general level, I also regret that issues of gender and ethnicity have not had a higher profile in my work.

These regrets about professional life are balanced, however, by the sense of satisfaction that comes from knowing that former PhD students have managed to secure good jobs or promotions and that they are publishing the findings of their independent research. It is also pleasing to note the continuing expansion and success of scholarly associations and journals for the sociology of religion. In addition, the investment of substantial public funds in the UK, Canada, Australia, the European Union, the Norface consortium of research councils, and the Council of Europe in programs of research on the social aspects of religion in the first decade of the 21st century augurs well for the future.

Conclusion

My interest in religion has ranged over social Catholicism, millenarianism, "cult controversies," religious organizations, theorizing religion, regulation of religion, chaplaincies, and religious diversity. Serendipity and the "French connection" have played an important role at times, but skepticism is the organizing principle. It kindles my curiosity about the ways in which religions – like other social and cultural phenomena – are constructed, framed, and enacted. This helps to "mainstream" sociological studies of religion and to bring them into a productive relation with other fields of sociology. Admittedly, my emphasis on the social contexts of what counts as religion in public life may be oblique to other sociologists' interests in religious belief, experience, activities, identity, and so on but I believe that it provides a good basis for raising important questions about cross-national studies, public policy, equalities, and justice.

Notes

1 His official title was President of the Council of Ministers.
2 L. Amiotte-Suchet and V. Altglas, "Sectes, controverses et pluralisme: une sociologie sceptique des religions. Entretien avec le sociologue des religions James A. Beckford," *Ethnographiques* 15 (February 2008) [http://www.ethnographiques.org/2008/Amiotte-Suchet,Altglas.html] (accessed July 15, 2008).
3 Eileen V. Barker (ed.), *The Centrality of Religion in Social Life* (Aldershot: Ashgate, 2008).
4 This motto, *Que-scay-je?* (or *Que sais-je?*, in its modern French form) is perhaps best known nowadays as the title of a series of about 4000 popular paperback books published

by the Presses Universitaires de France which introduce readers to an astonishingly wide array of topics including the sociology of religion and cults.

5 The Protestant influence on early sociology in the USA has been well documented by William H. Swatos, *Faith of the Fathers: Science, Religion and Reform in the Development of Early American Sociology* (Bristol, IN: Windham Hall Press, 1984), and Arthur J.Vidich and Stanford M. Lyman, *American Sociology. Worldly Rejections of Religion and Their Directions* (New Haven, CT: Yale University Press, 1985).

6 *Comparative Studies in Society and History*, Supplement 2, "Millennial dreams in action," 1962.

7 Bryan R. Wilson, "On the Fringe of Christendom," *Rationalist Annual* (1963): 40–50.

8 He is best known for pioneering works on military sociology, Herbert Spencer, parasitism and subversion in newly industrializing countries, comparative sociology, Max Weber, and – above all – a magisterial demolition of the pretensions of positivistic sociology in *Social Sciences as Sorcery* (London: André Deutsch, 1972).

9 Ernst Troeltsch, *The Social Teachings of the Christian Churches*, trans. Olive Wyon (London: George Allen & Unwin, 1931). These two volumes, purchased second-hand in their original two-volume hardback form for £5, still occupy a place of pride on my bookshelves.

10 For an indication of the richness of Bryan Wilson's founding "stable" of research students at Oxford, see the contributions to Bryan R. Wilson (ed.), *Patterns of Sectarianism* (London: Heinemann, 1964) and the testimonies to his erudition and kindness in Eileen Barker, Karel Dobbelaere and James A. Beckford (eds), *Secularization, Rationalism and Sectarianism. Essays in Honour of Bryan R. Wilson* (Oxford: Clarendon Press, 1993).

11 Bryan R. Wilson, "Social Aspects of Religious Sects: A Study of Some Contemporary Groups with Special Reference to a Midland City," unpublished PhD thesis, University of London, 1955. This thesis was revised for publication as Bryan R. Wilson, *Sects and Society* (London: Heinemann, 1961).

12 James A. Beckford, "A Korean Evangelistic Movement in the West," in *The Contemporary Metamorphosis of Religion?* (The Hague: Conférence internationale de la Sociologie des Religions, 1973): 319–335.

13 The results appeared in James A. Beckford, *Cult Controversies. The Societal Response to New Religious Movements*, (London: Tavistock, 1985).

14 James A. Beckford, "The Cult Problem in Five Countries: The Social Construction of Religious Controversy," in *Of Gods and Men: New Religious Movements in the West*, ed. Eileen V. Barker (Macon, GA: Mercer University Press, 1983): 195–214.

15 See www.inform.ac.

16 James A. Beckford, "A Sociological Study of Jehovah's Witnesses in Britain," unpublished PhD thesis, University of Reading, 2 vols, 1972. It was revised for publication as James A. Beckford, *The Trumpet of Prophecy. A Sociological Analysis of Jehovah's Witnesses* (Oxford: Blackwell, 1975).

17 James A. Beckford, "Religious Organization," *Current Sociology* 21 (1973): 1–117.

18 James A. Beckford, "Religious Organization: A Survey of Some Recent Publications," *Les Archives de Sciences Sociales des Religions* 57 (1984): 83–102; James A. Beckford, "Religious Organization," in *The Sacred in a Secular Age,* ed. Phillip E. Hammond (Berkeley, CA: University of California Press, 1985): 125–138; and James A. Beckford and Sophie Gilliat, *Religion in Prison. Equal Rites in a Multi-Faith Society* (Cambridge: Cambridge University Press, 1998).

19 The *locus classicus* of cross-pollination between the foci on sacred and secular aspects of organization is N.J. Demerath III, Peter Dobkin Hall, Terry Schmitt and Rhys R. Williams (eds), *Sacred Companies. Organizational Aspects of Religion and Religious Aspects of Organizations* (New York: Oxford University Press, 1998).

20 James A. Beckford, "The Insulation and Isolation of the Sociology of Religion," *Sociological Analysis* 46 (1985): 347–354.

21 James A. Beckford, "'Start Together and Finish Together': Shifts in the Premises and Paradigms Underlying the Scientific Study of Religion," *Journal for the Scientific Study of Religion* 39 (2000): 481–495.

22 James A. Beckford, "The Sociology of Religion and Social Problems," *Sociological Analysis* 51 (1990): 1–14.

23 James A. Beckford, "Religious Movements and Globalization," in *Global Social Movements* ed. Robin Cohen and Shirin Rai (London: Athlone Press, 2000): 165–183.

24 James A. Beckford, "Great Britain: Voluntarism and Sectional Interests," in *Between States and Markets. The Voluntary Sector in Comparative Perspective*, ed. Robert Wuthnow (Princeton, NJ: Princeton University Press, 1991): 30–63; James A. Beckford "Religion, Self-help and Privatization," in *Die Objectivität der Ordnungen und ihre kommunikative Konstruktion*, ed. Walter M. Sprondel (Frankfurt am Main: Suhrkamp, 1994): 318–341.

25 James A. Beckford, Richard Gale, David Owen, Ceri Peach and Paul Weller, "Review of the Evidence Base on Faith Communities" (London: Office of the Deputy Prime Minister, 2006).

26 James A. Beckford and Sophie Gilliat, *Religion in Prison. Equal Rites in a Multi-Faith Society* (Cambridge: Cambridge University Press, 1998); James A. Beckford, Danièle Joly and Farhad Khosrokhavar, *Muslims in Prison. Challenge and Change in Britain and France* (Basingstoke: Palgrave, 2005).

27 Wendy Ball and James A. Beckford, "Religion, Education and City Politics: A Case Study of Community Mobilisation," in *Transforming Cities. Contested Governance and New Spatial Divisions*, ed. Nick Jewson and Susanne MacGregor (London: Routledge, 1997): 193–204.

28 See www.religionanddiversity.ca.

29 James A. Beckford, *Religion and Advanced Industrial Society* (London: Unwin-Hyman, 1989).

30 Beckford, *Religion and Advanced Industrial Society,* 170.

31 James A. Beckford, "The Return of Public Religion? A Critical Assessment of a Popular Claim," *Nordic Journal of Religion and Society* 23(2) (2010): 121–136.

32 For example, James A. Beckford, "Accounting for Conversion," *British Journal of Sociology* 29(2) (1978): 249–262; James A. Beckford, "Talking of Apostasy, or Telling Tales and 'Telling' Tales," in *Accounts and Action*, ed. Nigel Gilbert and Peter Abell (Aldershot: Gower, 1983): 77–97.

33 James A. Beckford, *Social Theory and Religion* (Cambridge: Cambridge University Press, 2003).

34 James A. Beckford and Sophie Gilliat, *Religion in Prison;* James A. Beckford, Danièle Joly and Farhad Khosrokhavar, *Muslims in Prison.*

35 James A. Beckford and John Wallis (eds), *Theorizing Religion: Classical and Contemporary Debates* (Aldershot: Ashgate, 2006).

36 James A. Beckford, "A Minimalist Sociology of Religion," in Beckford and Wallis (eds), *Theorizing Religion*, 183–197.

37 James A. Beckford, "Religion, Modernity and Postmodernity," in *Religion: Contemporary Issues*, ed. Bryan R. Wilson (London: Bellew, 1992): 11–23; James A. Beckford, "Post-modernity, High Modernity and New Modernity: Three Concepts in Search of Religion," in *Postmodernity, Sociology and Religion*, ed. Kieran Flanagan and Peter Jupp (London: Macmillan, 1996), 30–47.

38 Beckford, *Social Theory*, 167–171.

39 James A. Beckford, " The Uses of Religion in Public Institutions: The Case of Prisons," in *Exploring the Postsecular. The Religious, the Political and the Urban*, ed. Arie Molendijk, Justin Beaumont and Christoph Jedan (Leiden: Brill, 2010), 381–401.

40 For example, Robert Bellah kindly hosted me as a Fulbright Scholar at the University of California, Berkeley in 1982–1983.

6

STRADDLING BOUNDARIES

Disciplines, theories, methods, and continents

Peter Beyer

One of the most durable and consistent self-evidences of our time and society is that each of us is or should be an individual, a person with agency who forges for her- or himself a meaningful life, albeit a life embedded in society and situated in a web of relations. This narrative or myth makes it appear that each of us is unique, has a story that is intrinsically worth telling; but that we are also all products of our time and place, creatures of our physical surroundings and bodies, reflections of our upbringing, social networks, and social contexts. The personal story I tell in the following pages is therefore a situated story, one in which autobiography is not just about a particular individual, but about the society and times in which that life has been taking place and of which it is an expression. Since it cannot be about all aspects of either the personal or the contextual, it concentrates only on certain aspects, in this case ones that have to do with selected boundaries.

The boundaries in question have mostly to do with becoming and being an academic, a peculiar role and pursuit in contemporary society that is centered around the doing, production, and dissemination of what we call science, in the broader sense of that term. Being an academic is about knowledge production of a particular kind and according to complex sets of rules and categories that include the division into disciplines, subdisciplines, and fields of specialization. Individual academics do this differently, even if in normative ways; and that individuality, expressed through the individual career or academic life-course (*curriculum vitae*), can be instructive of some of the peculiarities and contingencies of the scientific enterprise itself. It is with this in mind that I tell my personal story.

Academic training and the development of lifelong preoccupations

I begin with a few personal characteristics that make certain twists and turns less surprising. I was born into a German family in the immediate post-World War II era.

That family joined thousands of others and migrated during the mid-1950s to North America. As a direct consequence of a minor difference in the immigration policies of the United States and Canada, the Beyer family ended up in southwestern Ontario in Canada. This has somewhat accidentally made me a Canadian 1.5 generation immigrant – I was 5 years old on arrival – who grew up during the 1950s and 1960s in a German-speaking household as an Anglophone in the demographically, economically, linguistically, and politically dominant part of Canada. I grew up already crossing a number of socially important boundaries and located inside several others.

When, as a "baby-boomer" who came of age in the era of the 1960s counter-culture, I decided in the mid-1970s to undertake graduate studies in religion – spurred as much by R.D. Laing, Alan Watts, and Friedrich Nietzsche as Dietrich Bonhoeffer and Arthur Gibson[1] – I had to do so in a particular academic unit at a particular university. Religious studies as a discipline was then only just coming into its own, institutionally asserting itself as a distinct discipline in North America only as of the 1960s, and so the practical possibilities were still quite limited. I decided to study at the theological faculty of the University of St. Michael's College in Toronto, because it was close and affordable, but mainly because it offered graduate programs in "special religious studies," something that seemed well suited to someone vaguely fascinated by matters deemed religious but also personally, like Max Weber, religiously "tone-deaf." My degrees were therefore formally in theology, but I did as little theology as possible to get them, embarking rather on the sociological and historical study of religion, even though I had received no sociological or historical training as an undergraduate. This combination proved to be a rather risky decision from the point of view of career development: the academic world was and is still structured along disciplinary lines, in spite of constant valorization of inter-disciplinarity. My degrees were more or less in religious studies, and so it is not surprising that I ended up with positions in religious studies departments specifically as a specialist in the sociology of religion. Yet even this was comparatively rare as, for historical reasons, the area of the study of religion – still with clearly theological undertones – was right up until at least the 1970s suspicious of sociology as "reductionist," and sociology departments tended not to hire people with religion as their prime specialization. What Jim Beckford has called the insulation and isolation of the sociology of religion still obtained in the early 1980s,[2] even though the secularization thesis that operated in the background of both these disciplinary orientations was about to lose its paradigmatic status in rather rapid fashion. With hindsight, we can see that both sociology and religious studies were about to undergo paradigmatic sea changes, but that was far from obvious at the time.

It was in 1975 during my MA studies that my supervisor, Herbert Richardson, knowing that I could read German and that I was drawn to abstract theory, suggested that I might find interesting the work of a little-known sociologist, Niklas Luhmann. Thus began the turn to sociology and a lifelong preoccupation, but also the straddling of another important boundary: between "macro" and "micro" and, geographically, between Europe and North America. My personal status as a 1.5 generation immigrant thus translated itself to the professional level. North American sociology, then as now, was not overly receptive to macro theory, especially in the context of disillusionment with the grand theory of Talcott Parsons, whose student Luhmann had at one time been. Their work showed a decided family resemblance. Luhmann is still not overly popular in North America, and the majority of his major works have, as of 2012, not been translated into English. Both my MA and PhD theses were attempts to appropriate various aspects of Luhmann's theory, in the latter case applying it to Canadian and French Canadian religious history and thus beginning another sub-specialization that straddled yet another boundary, namely that between English and French Canada. By the time I had finished my graduate degrees, I was fully aware of not only my relative "hybridity," but also that it was not the easiest location from which to launch an academic career. My decision to engage in postdoctoral studies at the French-speaking Université du Québec à Montréal between 1981 and 1983 was consciously an attempt to address my situation, not by reversing the straddling of boundaries, but by seeking to develop that aspect further through becoming functionally trilingual and developing a broader Canadian religion expertise that, like the Luhmannian orientation, has followed me through the rest of my career. Early choices mark an academic career indelibly, if by no means definitively.

The four years between the end of my postdoctoral studies and my first full-time academic position in 1987 were in some ways unproductive and even desperate. Good positions were not in plentiful supply, even in North America; and by 1985 I had fully realized that my boundary straddling and my combination of somewhat unusual specializations were far from advantageous. Yet those years were in key ways as determinative and as revealing of the nature of the academic profession as any others. From a professional perspective they demonstrated the important role of networking – not what one knows, but rather who one knows. The historical context in which they occurred was perhaps even more significant. The myth of the "ivory tower" may be salient for some academic fields, but not the social sciences. World events matter and change the course of disciplines.

Mentors, networks, and living in interesting times

Mentors are crucial, especially early in a career. There are usually many of them, playing minor to major roles, not necessarily in giving advice and influencing the tenor and direction of one's work, but just as much in providing opportunities and sponsoring or promoting a person. In my case, three men played major roles in this regard. One was Herbert Richardson, my mercurial and maverick graduate supervisor, who provided the occasion of my first academic conference paper in 1982, but whose major facilitation after graduation consisted in hiring me to work in his academic publishing firm between 1984 and 1987. This not only gave me a job when sessional appointments were the extent of my academic employment; it also allowed me to participate in academic conferences in both religious studies and the sociology of religion; which in turn gave me the opportunity to develop my work and network more broadly. In that context, and with hindsight, a seminal experience occurred in 1985 at the annual meetings of the Association for the Sociology of Religion held in

Washington, DC, which I attended as representative of the press. On that occasion, I heard a paper by Roland Robertson (in collaboration with Joann Chirico, I believe) on globalization and religious resurgence.[3] It took the seed a while to germinate, but within the next two to three years it convinced me to turn my Luhmannian theoretical work to the analysis of the religio-political movements that had mushroomed around the world since 1979, and to do so explicitly within a globalization framework.[4] In the process, Roland Robertson became another key mentor, along with John H. Simpson, a colleague at the University of Toronto where I had by that time received my first full-time academic appointment. Simpson's work on the new Christian politics in the United States[5] was another of those confluent influences at that time.

These influences were, of course, not just personal. They reflected a particular historical and disciplinary context which we now see had an even greater import than most of us realized at the time. It is always difficult to see the forest when one is in among the trees.

During the 1970s and the earlier 1980s, new religious movements like ISKCON, Scientology, and the Unification Church seemed to dominate the landscape in the sociology of religion and acquired a decided presence in religious studies as well. It was not just their newness that was at issue, but also that they seemed to run counter to the prevalent expectation inherited from the 1960s: that secularization reigned and that religion was declining or privatizing. A great many careers in both disciplines were influenced and even made in the observation of these movements, above all in trying to figure out why they were happening at all (hence, the obsession with conversion and charisma as key issues).[6] At the time, it did not seem that all this attention would seriously undermine secularization assumptions; the movements were after all small, most were globally speaking rather insignificant, and almost all of them stayed that way.[7] With hindsight, however, we can see that this is in fact what happened, that the heyday of the secularization-as-religious-decline-and-privatization thesis did not last past the early 1980s. In this context, Rodney Stark and William S. Bainbridge's 1985 volume, *The Future of Religion*,[8] is indicative. Its main theoretical argument, namely that dominant forms of religion may decline but resurgent forms always arise to take their place, is based in the analysis of new religious movements. It is, however, arguable that the subsequent collapse in the sociology of religion of that form of the secularization thesis, in which Stark and others played a significant role, had at least as much to do with the rise of religio-political movements, above all the Christian Right in the United States. This development, more than parallel events in places from Iran to Nicaragua, put the spotlight on the strength of institutional religion in the United States, and therefore anti-secularization perspectives which clearly took the American experience as paradigmatic made sense to many. The broader phenomenon of global religio-political movements – "fundamentalisms" – did not receive clear and consistent attention in sociology of religion and in religious studies until the later 1980s.[9]

The global nature of the religio-political movements was nonetheless critical. Under the until then dominant way of looking at the place of religion in modern societies, the United States was generally the exception that proved the rule of a prevailing trend towards increasing secularization, understood as religious decline. As long as the frame of analysis included mostly North America, Europe, the Soviet Bloc, and connected places like Australia, that status of exceptionalism made sense and would still make quite a lot of sense today. The 1980s and especially the 1990s saw a shift away from that limitation such that the same scientific observers more and more took the entire world as their default unit of analysis or at least field of vision. This occurred for complex reasons, including, for example, the constantly accelerating means of global communication, ever more evident and increasing global economic integration, and the intensified global migration that brought the "rest of the world" increasingly into Western "backyards." For the scientific observation of religion this shift to a global view, combined with the evident strength of religion in so many other parts of that world – including in the form of the so-called "fundamentalisms" – meant that now, increasingly, it was regions like Europe that began to look like the exception, no longer the United States.[10]

Adopting globalization

The turn in my own work towards the examination of religio-political movements in a globalization framework was, thus, symptomatic of these broader contextual changes. In the late 1980s, however, as just noted, the disciplines in which I was embedded were only beginning to pay full attention to the global religio-political movements, and the idea of globalization had not yet become the popular buzz-word that it became in the wake of the fall of the Soviet Union in the 1990s; it was still largely confined to specialized usage in the world of business and economics, in sociology, and in political science.[11] Adopting a globalization framework at that time was therefore a rather "early" move on my part, but this was not a case of farsightedness. Aside from the personal influence of mentors like Roland Robertson – who was one of those who had been working on globalization since the 1960s[12] – a perhaps even more critical factor was again the "internal logic" of the specializations I had been developing since my graduate studies: Niklas Luhmann had published an article on "world society" already in 1971,[13] indicating that his theory led logically to taking the whole world as a prime unit of societal analysis. Accordingly, as I turned my attention to the religio-political movements for largely contextual and "career-promoting" reasons, my ongoing aim to use and develop the Luhmannian theoretical frame for the understanding of religion, dating from my MA thesis already,[14] almost suggested a resort to the "world society" frame that Luhmann had intimated. Indeed, the first conference paper I ever delivered (in 1982)[15] was already an embryonic attempt to make the connection, although not one I earnestly pursued until a few years later.

My focus on religion and globalization thus began in the mid-1980s. Since it takes time to do research and get writing done, the earliest of my publications on the theme appear only in 1989 and 1990.[16] The 1994 book, *Religion and Globalization*,[17] took a little longer. It is worth underlining again, however, that all of these earlier works would have been difficult to complete if this period had not coincided with full-time academic employment, even if that employment at the University of Toronto was still contractual and therefore somewhat insecure. Moreover, while in some positions teaching undergraduate courses detracts from research and publication, in my case the opposite obtained: my heads of department – Jim Callahan and Jane MacAuliffe especially – rather than relegating me to core and introductory courses, allowed me to teach courses in the context of which I could pursue my research, courses notably on religion and politics, world religions, religion in Canada, and of course the sociology of religion.

Ottawa and career "take-off"

This symbiosis between the ability to pursue research and having a suitable "job" was most clearly illustrated in the period after I received my first tenure-track position, at the University of Ottawa, in 1995. Access to institutional support, including research funds, but above all the security that comes with knowing that this position was permanent as long as I continued to demonstrate my abilities as an effective teacher and researcher,[18] allowed me to transform academic interests into longer term research programs. Not surprisingly, the programs I thus devised continued the lines I had begun much earlier, including further development of the theoretical work on religion and globalization and the great expansion of empirical work on religion in Canada. The latter direction had only received sporadic attention since my postdoctoral fellowship days at the Université du Québec à Montréal in the early 1980s.[19] Notably, in this regard, the University of Ottawa position was English-French bilingual, and therefore structurally, as it were, linked with those earlier attempts to become a "real Canadian" who spoke and worked in both official languages.

The change and solidification in institutional context was certainly essential for my career development, but the mid-1990s proved to be pivotal in other ways as well. Perhaps of the first importance, the 1994 book, *Religion and Globalization*, clearly had a significant and long-lasting effect. Not only was it instrumental for my being taken on at the University of Ottawa, in the wake of its publication specific invitations to participate in conferences, give plenary or keynote addresses, and the like started to arrive with some regularity. Notably, the vast majority of these invitations came from outside North America (at an approximate ratio of 3:1), mostly from Europe (in majority from the Nordic and German-speaking countries), indicating that the straddling of continents that began with migration from Germany to Canada in 1955 was very much continuing in new forms. There is probably no question that, directly or indirectly, this outcome was in part due to my ongoing emphasis on theory, macro theory, and the theory of Niklas Luhmann in particular. In spite of the even greater integration of the academic world through globalized communication technologies and the process of globalization more generally, the social sciences at the beginning of the 21st century still display a kind of regionalism, albeit not nearly as clearly as they did at the beginning of the 20th century.[20]

The critical role of academic societies

A further development concerns scholarly associations. Earlier I mentioned how involvement in their meetings during the mid-1980s was instrumental in my turn to globalization as a central research and theoretical focus. Such involvement took a couple of new turns that again expressed the boundary-straddling aspect, both disciplinary and regional. When my by that time already long-time mentor, John Simpson, took his turn as President of the Association for the Sociology of Religion (ASR) in 1995, he asked me to act as program chair for that year's meeting. That experience and the visibility that comes with it led in short order to my being elected to the councils or boards of all three of the American-based societies focusing on the social-scientific study of religion, namely the ASR, the Society for the Scientific Study of Religion, and the Religious Research Association. Just as significantly, in 1995 I almost "stumbled upon" the meetings of the French/English bilingual International Society for the Sociology of Religion (ISSR/SISR), held that year only down the road, in Quebec City. A predominantly European society, it was holding its annual meetings only for the second time since its foundation in 1947 outside Europe,[21] serendipitously providing me with the opportunity to forge better professional links with that (sub)continent. I have not missed one of the ISSR biennial meetings since then and, as of 2001, have also been increasingly involved in its executive structure. Around that time, something similar happened with the Canadian societies with religion as their focus, namely the Canadian Corporation for the Study of Religion and the Canadian Society for the Study of Religion.

The consistent and higher level of involvement in all of these societies certainly had an effect on the directions that my own work took, not to mention the shape and composition of my academic networks. What is, however, equally significant is that, with the very partial exception of the Canadian ones, the societies in which I chose to immerse myself all had a cross-disciplinary character between religious studies and sociology. Although I have occasionally attended, I have never felt particularly at home in the "core disciplinary" societies, such as the American Academy of Religion or the American Sociological Association, if anything sensing a greater attraction towards the international versions such as the International Association for the History of Religions. The sociology of religion is for me a pleasant "in-between" place that corresponds to who I have become as an academic scholar; much as one might think of Canada as a pleasant (and polite) place "in between" the United States and Europe – and Ottawa and the University of Ottawa as "in between" French and English Canada.

The pragmatics of research agendas

Once solidly ensconced within the walls of a university, academic and research life is certainly more secure, and one can undertake more extended programs of research. That was certainly the case for me after 1995. Still, the context of universities changes as consistently as so-called disciplinary "paradigms," the burning questions of the day, or the world-historical environment. In the Canadian context of the 1990s and early 2000s, aside from the constant growth of postsecondary institutions, a highly consequential change occurred in the self-understanding of universities, at least at the administrative or governance levels. Universities came to see themselves significantly more as institutions operating in a kind of corporate competitive environment akin to private enterprises. Greater and greater emphasis was thus put on factors such as public relations, corporate image, fundraising, public advertising and recruitment, and a reputation as "research-intensive" institutions which translated into efforts to increase the "impact" and "external funding" of the research of their professors. For myself, that atmosphere translated directly into a decision to adjust the direction and type of research that I did, especially as of the turn of the millennium.

Throughout my career, I had focused my research in two areas: religion and globalization and religion in Canada. Since it is extremely difficult – although obviously not impossible – to develop entirely new research directions in mid-career, the question of how to respond to the (new) institutional pressure translated itself into how I could design a research program that flowed from my specializations and was likely to attract external funding. The answer lay in an aspect of the global and Canadian contextual changes in which I was personally, culturally, and professionally embedded: the phenomenon of post-World War II transnational migration. I am, after all, a postwar baby-boomer immigrant myself. In 1998 I had published an article, a revision of a plenary address delivered to the ISSR meetings in Toulouse in 1997. This article argued for the decentering of religious authority and authenticity in the world's religions in part as a consequence of the accelerated and more globalized transnational migration of the postwar period. In the early to mid-1990s, American sociology of religion had begun to pay focused attention to the religion of post-1960s immigrants in that country, a seminal volume in that case being Steve Warner and Judith Wittner's *Gatherings in Diaspora*, published also in 1998. I was very interested in this work from even before it began to appear,[22] mainly because it so clearly concretized the theoretical question of the relation of religion and globalization. It was therefore but a short leap to conceive a "fundable" research program that combined the religion and globalization direction with the religion in Canada direction through a focus on the religious expression of Canada's immigrant population, especially that which had arrived after 1970 from virtually all regions of the world instead of mostly from Europe as before.

The situation also opened up an opportunity to expand methodologically, to straddle some more methodological boundaries and thereby, frankly, to do something new and interesting. I had started my career using mostly historical method and then concentrated almost entirely on the development of theory. The "fundable" requirement and the contemporary focus of the new research suggested a different approach. I had done very minor and simple quantitative and qualitative work during the 1990s,[23] and so it made sense to expand in those directions. I decided to do a first project using the statistics from the post-1970 decennial Canada censuses, which asked a religious identity question. I could, using that data, "map" changing Canadian religious diversity, its sources and patterns, as a first step in a longer research program. Expansion into new methodological territory, however, suggested that I adopt a team approach, asking others more versed in statistical method to collaborate with me, even though what I had I mind was not complex quantitative analysis. My old mentor, John Simpson, a good "quantoid," seemed the logical person to ask, and he agreed. The experience introduced me to and convinced me of the value of collaborative research, and all my projects have been team projects ever since.

The quantitative project using Canadian census data dovetailed later in the decade (from 2004 on) into two qualitative ones that focused on, not so much the religion of Canada's immigrants, as the Canada-born and Canada-raised offspring of those immigrants. The theoretical reason for this selection was that these populations could be expected to represent transnational religion that was significantly less "diasporic" and differently "glocalized" than that of their parents, whose points of authoritative reference would be comparatively more in the "heartlands" of their regions of origin. Put differently, the second generation would be a good and perhaps better group with which to test and develop the theory that by this time I had published in much more developed form in the 2006 volume, *Religions in Global Society*.[24] These projects had the additional advantage of being eminently "fundable," as the interest in "religious diversity" increased in Canada as elsewhere, in part because both "religion" and "diversity" in public discourse were deemed more and more to be somewhere between a challenge and a problem. Moreover, taking on qualitative research meant crossing another methodological boundary and therefore required new collaborators who would ease the transition. Rather than substitute, I asked new collaborators, in this case principally Nancy Nason-Clark, Lori Beaman, and as of 2008, Solange Lefebvre. That involvement, in turn, bore additional fruit as I came to collaborate with these colleagues and others on other major joint projects.[25]

A new generation and new directions

In many ways collaborators take the place of what mentors did earlier in my career. As in almost any other career, or as perhaps in most human life more generally, these roles are critical for shaping and rendering effective what it is that we do. In the theoretical terms that I have become accustomed to using, these critical others make it possible to make the transition from solipsistic thought to effective social communication. In the academic world, however, there is another class of roles that is equally as germane, namely those who we in turn mentor and from whom we benefit as much as they – hopefully – benefit from us. These are, of course, students, graduate students most particularly. In my case, the ongoing research projects have offered the critical opportunity to assist a further group of up-and-coming academics to become the new researchers and then also the new collaborators. This list grows over time. For me, among the most influential have been Michael Wilkinson, Wendy Martin, Rubina Ramji, Shandip Saha, and Arlene Macdonald. They – and quite a few others I am not mentioning but who are no less significant in this regard – demonstrate the way in which the entire academic profession, like so many others, is always an open network operation for which, as already noted, the old metaphor of the "ivory tower" is utterly and wholly inadequate.

To conclude, I continue with another of the abiding threads that has sought to bind this little narrative together: the course of an academic research career is to some extent set from very early on; not in its details, of course, but in its general orientations. In my case, the underlying impulse that led a fundamentally non-religious person to try to make a career of studying religion, to cross that boundary, was an abiding fascination, even obsession, with observing abstract patterns. As many of my students will attest – some, no doubt, while rolling their eyes – I seem to be incapable of talking about almost anything without starting from abstract observations. Little wonder, then, that so much of my work has been theoretical, sometimes even obscurely so, and that even with the solid turn to empirical research over the past decade or so, the theoretical impulse has persisted. In 2006, with the publication of *Religions in Global Society*, I thought that I had come to a suitable conclusion in the effort to adapt Luhmannian theory to the task of understanding the relation of religion and globalization. Not a last word or a final word, to be sure, but enough (already). I underestimated the strength of an abiding orientation.

Contextual factors again played a role, and in this case it was the context of disciplinary developments. Since the late 1990s, I had become increasingly preoccupied with the question of why "paradigms" – another way of describing the most popular theories, questions, and approaches that people within disciplines take – change; and I have never been convinced by arguments about "cumulative problems" with old paradigms leading to some kind of tipping point. "Endogenous" factors did not seem to be enough, or at least endogenous explanations appeared to be far too tautological. I was and am much more attracted to the idea that these shifts probably happen mostly for "accidental" reasons having to do with changes in the world-historical contexts that we all inhabit. This understanding I outlined above. The disciplinary movements in question were several: the decline in the popularity of secularization assumptions, the increasing and supposedly purely empirical observation that somehow religion was becoming *more* important around the world, the critical currents in both religious studies and sociology of religion which declared that we had been observing religion wrongly – quite aside from its "decline" or "resurgence" – the solid return of the notion that the kind and form of prevailing religion was changing, such as in the idea that "religion" was giving way to "spirituality," and a rising concern with the specific idea of religious diversity.[26]

In this context, I came to ask myself how all these developments could make sense together given the world-historical context in which we lived. Could I arrive at a theoretical model for understanding this combination? And could I do so by developing my career-long theoretical (and empirical) research further? Almost as a kind of playful exercise, beginning in 2003, I asked myself the question: If secularization is no longer the leitmotiv of the contemporary study of religion, what might be taking its place? This half-serious exercise subsequently took on a life of its own, to the point where, as of this writing, I find myself on a new theoretical quest that asks what to call this new observational situation in which we seem to have arrived, both within and outside the academic world. At the risk of adding yet another "post-" word, I have come to play with the idea that the combination of developments in the disciplines is perhaps reflective, not of postmodernism or of postsecularism, but rather – or in addition – of post-Westphalianism, a term borrowed from political scientists, but applied to religion and given a decidedly Luhmannian twist.[27]

I do not know what will become of this new direction, if anything. My purpose in including it by way of a conclusion is to show again that combination which seems to characterize most academic careers: on the one hand, the directions established at the beginning of a career have a way of marking it indelibly all along its course. On the other hand, accidentally and on purpose, those directions lead us into projects, questions, and developments that we could not have foreseen. This relative unpredictability, this penchant to straddle new boundaries, here between the familiar and the unforeseen, is likely one of the main attributes that makes this profession and this career ultimately rewarding and more than occasionally fun.

Notes

1 Arthur Gibson was a Basilian Father who taught at St. Michael's College in the University of Toronto while I was an undergraduate there. He was author of such works as Arthur Gibson, *The Faith of the Atheist* (New York: Harper & Row, 1972); *The Silence of God: Creative Responses to the Films of Ingmar Bergman* (New York: Harper & Row, 1969).

2 See Eric J. Sharpe, *Comparative Religion: A History* (London: Duckworth, 1975); James A Beckford, *Religion and Advanced Industrial Society* (London: Unwin Hyman, 1989).

3 In that same year Roland Robertson and JoAnn Chirico's "Humanity, Globalization, Worldwide Religious Resurgence: A Theoretical Exploration," *Sociological Analysis* 46(3) (1985): 219–242 appeared, itself a seminal article in the history of the sociology of religion and globalization and containing some of the arguments presented in the paper.

4 The first published result of this turn was Peter Beyer, "Globalism and Inclusion: Theoretical Remarks on the Non-Solidary Society," in *Religious Politics in Global and Comparative Perspective*, ed. William H. Swatos (Westport, CT: Greenwood, 1989). Like *all* of my publications between 1984 and 1991, this one owed something to "whom" I knew during that time as a result of the networking and mentoring I am discussing, not just "what" I knew.

5 See especially J.H. Simpson, "Moral Issues and Status Politics," in *The New Christian Right*, ed. R.C. Liebman and R. Wuthnow (New York: Aldine, 1983).

6 The list of scholars and publications could be exceedingly long, but see, as representative examples from the 1970s and early 1980s, Irving Zaretsky and Mark P. Leone (eds), *Religious Movements in Contemporary America* (Princeton, NJ: Princeton University Press, 1974); Jacob Needleman and George Baker (eds), *Understanding the New Religions* (New York: Seabury Press, 1978); Charles Y. Glock and Robert N. Bellah (eds), *The New Religious Consciousness* (Berkeley, CA: University of California Press,1976); Eileen Barker (ed.), *New Religious Movements: A Perspective for Understanding Society* (New York: Edwin Mellen Press,1982); – (ed.), *Of Gods and Men: New Religious Movements in the West* (Macon, GA: Mercer University Press, 1983). Indicative of the importance of this phenomenon, these volumes contain contributions from a great many of the leading scholars in the sociology of religion during the final decades of the 20th century.

7 See the debates in Bryan Wilson, "The Return of the Sacred," *Journal for the Scientific Study of Religion* 18(1979): 268–280; Philip E. Hammond (ed.), *The Sacred in a Secular Age: Toward Revision in the Scientific Study of Religion* (Berkeley, CA: University of California Press, 1985).

8 Rodney Stark and William S. Bainbridge, *The Future of Religion: Secularization, Revival, and Cult Formation* (Berkeley, CA: University of California Press, 1985).

9 The earliest work on the American Christian Right did come from American sociologists of religion, among others, but work on "global fundamentalisms" was clearly the early province of scholars specializing in the areas in which they occurred. For the New Christian Right, see Robert C. Liebman and Robert Wuthnow (eds), *The New Christian Right: Mobilization and Legitimation* (New York: Aldine, 1983); David G. Bromley and Anson Shupe (eds), *New Christian Politics* (Macon, GA: Mercer University Press, 1984); for the "fundamentalisms" outside the United States, see, for example, Charles S. Liebman and Eliezer Don-Yehiya, *Religion and Politics in Israel* (Bloomington, IN: Indiana State University, 1984); Nikki R. Keddie, *Roots of Revolution: An Interpretive History of Modern Iran* (New Haven, CT: Yale University Press, 1981). In the late 1980s and early 1990s the "bulk" of the literature on "fundamentalisms" appears: see, as examples, Bruce B. Lawrence, *Defenders of God: The Fundamentalist Revolt against the Modern Age* (San Francisco, CA: Harper & Row, 1989); Martin E. Marty and R. Scott Appleby (eds), *The Fundamentalism Project*, 5 vols (Chicago, IL: University of Chicago Press, 1991–1995); Martin Riesebrodt, *Pious Passion: The Emergence of Modern Fundamentalism in the United States and Iran*, trans. Don Reneau (Berkeley: University of California Press, 1993). See also the Religion and the Political Order Series under the direction of Jeffrey Hadden and Anson Shupe: Jeffrey K. Hadden and Anson Shupe (eds), *Prophetic Religion and Politics*, Religion and the Political Order Series, Vol.1 (New York: Paragon House, 1986).

10 See, in this regard, Grace Davie, *Europe: The Exceptional Case: Parameters of Faith in the Modern World*, Sarum Theological Lectures (London: Darton, Longman & Todd, 2003); see also Peter Berger's justification for insisting that the world was desecularizing in the opening article of Peter L. Berger (ed.), *The Desecularization of the World: Resurgent Religion and World Politics* (Grand Rapids, MI: Eerdmans, 1999).

11 The earliest instance of the use of the word, globalization, in a scientific publication title that I have been able to find is an article about global communism by George Modelski in 1968. George Modelski, "Communism and the Globalization of Politics," *International Studies Quarterly* 12(1968): 380–393. The business and economics use of the term appears to date from the early 1980s. See e.g., Theodore Levitt, "The Globalization of Markets," *Harvard Business Review* 61(3) (1983): 92–102. In sociology the term surfaces from about the same period: Robertson and Chirico, "Humanity, Globalization, Worldwide Religious Resurgence: A Theoretical Exploration." Related concepts like "internationalization" were, of course, of much older usage.

12 See J.P. Nettl and Roland Robertson, *International Systems and the Modernization of Societies: The Formation of National Goals and Attitudes* (New York: Basic Books, 1968).

13 Niklas Luhmann, "Die Weltgesellschaft," *Archiv für Rechts-und Sozialphilosophie* 57(1971).

14 Peter Beyer, "The Religious Theory of Niklas Luhmann" (1977).

15 Peter Beyer, "Global Society and Particular Cultures: A Formulation of the Problem," in *New Era Winter Advanced Seminar* (Montego Bay, Jamaica, 1982).

16 Peter Beyer, "Globalism and Inclusion: Theoretical Remarks on the Non-Solidary Society."; "Privatization and the Public Influence of Religion in Global Society," *Theory, Culture & Society* 7(2–3) (1990): 373–395.

17 Peter Beyer, *Religion and Globalization* (London: Sage, 1994).

18 The granting of tenure in Canadian universities is typically much more – although not entirely – predictable than it is, for instance, in many American universities, given that it is for the most part based on relatively clearly worded clauses in negotiated collective agreements. Such clauses severely limit such factors as "financial considerations" and arbitrarily shifting standards ("moving goal posts") from becoming germane to the process.

19 See Peter Beyer, "The Mission of Quebec Ultramontanism: A Luhmannian Perspective," *Sociological Analysis* 46(1985): 37–48; –, "The Evolution of Roman Catholicism in Quebec: A Luhmannian Neo-Functionalist Interpretation," in *Sociological Studies in Roman Catholicism*, ed. Roger O'Toole (Lewiston, NY: Edwin Mellen, 1989), 1–26; –,

"Religion and the Transition to a 'New World Order'? Some Preliminary Evidence from Canada," in *Religion and the Transformations of Capitalism: Comparative Approaches*, ed. Richard H. Roberts (London: Routledge, 1995), 121–132.

20 See Rudolf Stichweh, "Science in the System of World Society," *Social Science Information* 35(1996): 327–340.

21 The previous time was also in French-speaking Canada, in Montreal in 1967, somewhat before "my time."

22 See Stephen Warner and Judith G. Wittner (eds), *Gatherings in Diaspora: Religious Communities and the New Immigration* (Philadelphia, PA: Temple University Press, 1998). Another example of the critical role professional association meetings played, since I had heard many of the conference papers leading up to these publications in the years before, and even quite incidentally witnessed part of the planning of this particular volume at a very informal meeting between Steve Warner and a couple of his eventual collaborators at a SSSR conference in the early 1990s.

23 Peter Beyer, "Religion and the Transition to a 'New World Order'? Some Preliminary Evidence from Canada."; "Religious Vitality in Canada: The Complementarity of Religious Market and Secularization Perspectives," *Journal for the Scientific Study of Religion* 36(1997).

24 Peter Beyer, *Religions in Global Society* (London: Routledge, 2006).

25 The principal one of these is a major, seven-year project, entitled the "Religion and Diversity Project," in which a couple of dozen of us from around Canada and from several other countries are collaborating under the direction of Lori Beaman. See www. religionanddiversity.ca.

26 Among the many references one could site for these developments, see Peter Berger (ed.), *The Desecularization of the World: Resurgent Religion and World Politics*; Paul Bramadat and Matthias Koenig (eds), *International Migration and the Governance of Religious Diversity* (Montreal and Kingston: McGill-Queen's University Press, 2009); Jeremy Carrette and Richard King, *Selling Spirituality: The Silent Takeover of Religion* (New York: Routledge, 2005); David Chidester, *Savage Systems: Colonialism and Comparative Religion in Southern Africa* (Charlottesville, VA: University Press of Virginia, 1996); Jürgen Habermas, *An Awareness of What Is Missing: Faith and Reason in a Post-Secular Age* (Cambridge: Polity Press, 2010); Paul Heelas et al., *The Spiritual Revolution: Why Religion Is Giving Way to Spirituality* (Oxford: Blackwell, 2005); Danièle Hervieu-Léger, *Le Pèlerin Et Le Converti: La Religion En Mouvement* (Paris: Flammarion, 1999); Ronald Inglehart, *Modernization and Postmodernization: Cultural, Economic, and Political Change in 43 Societies* (Princeton, NJ: Princeton University Press, 1997); Richard King, "Orientalism and the Modern Myth of 'Hinduism'," *Numen* 46(1999): 146–185; Russell T. McCutcheon, *Manufacturing Religion: The Discourse on Sui Generis Religion and the Politics of Nostalgia* (Oxford: Oxford Univeristy Press, 1997); Meredith McGuire, *Lived Religion: Faith and Practice in Everyday Life* (New York: Oxford University Press, 2008); Susumu Shimazono, *From Salvation to Spirituality: Popular Religious Movements in Japan* (Honolulu: Trans Pacific Press, 2004); Jonathan Z. Smith, "'Religion' and 'Religious Studies': No Difference at All," *Soundings* 71(1988): 231–244; Wilfred Cantwell Smith, *The Meaning and End of Religion*, ed. and Foreword John Hick (Minneapolis, MN: Fortress Press, 1991); Rodney Stark and Roger Finke, *Acts of Faith: Explaining the Human Side of Religion* (Berkeley, CA: University of California Press, 2000); Charles Taylor, *A Secular Age* (Cambridge, MA: Belknap Harvard, 2007).

27 From among the political science literature, see Else Kveinen, "Citizenship in a Post-Westphalian Community: Beyond External Exclusion?," *Citizenship Studies* 6(1) (2002): 21–35; Andrew Linklater, "Citizenship and Sovereignty in the Post-Westphalian State," *European Journal in International Relations* 2(1) (1996: 77–103):. My earliest published attempt focuses on the idea of pluralization. See Peter Beyer, "Globalization and Glocalization," in *The Sage Handbook of the Sociology of Religion*, ed. James A. Beckford and N.J. Demerath III (London: Sage, 2007), 98–117. Early versions of the post-Westphalian

thesis are in – "Religious Pluralization and Intimations of a Post-Westphalian Condition in a Global Society," in *Annual Review of the Sociology of Religion, Volume 2: Religion and Politics*, ed. P. Michel and E. Pace (Leiden: Brill Academic Publishers, 2011), 3–29; – "Socially Engaged Religion in a Post-Westphalian Global Context: Remodeling the Secular/Religious Distinction," *Sociology of Religion* 73(2) (2012): 109–129.

7

WORK AND ADVENTURE

From poetry to the sociology of religion

Irena Borowik

During my school days, and at university too, it was not just the fact that I'd later deal with religion that didn't cross my mind – it seemed extremely improbable too that I would be interested in academia at all. My whole creative energy went into poetry, both in a writing sense and in participating in the more or less organized artistic life of the Bohemian set of the city of Białystok in Poland. This entailed participation in literary contests, poetry festivals, evenings involving readings of poems, and also meetings of a social-literary group of a few people discussing our latest works and organizing workshops.

In some ways I am a symbolic example of the part of the world in which I grew up; that is, north-eastern Poland, the Polish-Belarusian and Polish-Ukrainian borderland. I wrote poems in three languages: Belarusian, Ukrainian dialect, and Polish. My first publication appeared in the youth press in Polish, my first little volume of verses came out in Belarusian in 1978 (in my second year at university), my first longer poem was in the dialect, and three poetry books in Polish (two collections and the longer poem *Weekday*). Was this of any significance for my later academic interests, and if so, what kind? Of course it was. Who we are and where we are is what we become.

My birthplace and my ancestors, the East Slavic ethnic group

The small village of Morze, where I was born in the autumn of 1956, could just as easily have been on the other side of the border. In that case I would have been a citizen of the USSR in the Belorussian or Ukrainian Republic. I would not only have had different memories from childhood but many things in my life would have turned out differently. In spite of its political restrictions of various kinds, Poland enjoyed freedom to a far greater degree than did the other countries of the Eastern Bloc.

All of the villagers were members of what is referred to as the East Slavic ethnic group (what this means is a separate matter – an extensive debate has gone on about this subject, and continues to do so – more of which later), located in the aforementioned Polish-Belarusian-Ukrainian borderland. The traditional community of such villages, like that in which I grew up, is often described in nostalgic terms by sociologists and anthropologists. I did not share this romantic sense. From my point of view this was a community in which the individual is strongly, even ruthlessly controlled by the group, to which it must be subordinated; this is the dominance of collective life over individualized needs, uniformism, hypocrisy, and many other defects. The struggle for my own freedom was one of the most characteristic rifts of my youth.

Childhood in this traditional village also meant rituals in the Orthodox Church, full of magic and incomprehension, and joyful holidays, particularly the period leading up to Christmas and Christmas itself. Even today, every year I go to celebrate Orthodox Christmas together with my family and the villagers, including the remnants of my peer group. We sing carols long into the night and walk leisurely from home to home, singing about Christ's birth, listening to the snow crunching underfoot, from time to time allowing ourselves to be tempted by the offer of something stronger for fortification from the home owners, as it can get bitingly cold in this part of Poland.

One of the most important values drummed into a child from the first years of consciousness was work. My first experience of work was not pleasant. I might have been 5 years old, and my father was cutting straw for chaff using a chaff-cutter attached to a mill, whose mechanical movement was provided by our big horse known as Chestnut, the same one which I was later to ride bareback. Poor Chestnut walked around in circles on the mill, and I followed him – to prod him on if he stopped. This took half a day, and in the course of this I made up the first poem in my life, which I sang to myself and Chestnut. The heroine of the poem was a princess, living in a tomb in a nearby cemetery. The princess slept by day, and by night she would awake and see her prince. She went from grave to grave, and at each one she sang longingly, called out, carried on, and called out again. And so the night went by, she fell asleep again and the next nights passed the same, just like my hours on the treadmill. This is when I became a poet.

My ancestors, progenitors of the East Slavic ethnic group – as the subject literature tells us – arrived in present-day north-eastern Poland in the 13th and 14th centuries, from the region of Volhynia, in today's Ukraine. They settled in the then virgin and huge Białowieża Forest, taking from it patches of land to cultivate, making honey and hunting animals. They used an archaic dialect, which still today allows me, with a fairly good knowledge of four literary Slavic languages, to understand all the others. We also know for certain that they constructed wooden churches in the region, crowned by characteristic Orthodox copulas and crosses. As a result of the Mazovian tribes arriving from the other side – that is, from the west – and populating the nearby areas, this land became pluralistic in ethnic, religious, and linguistic terms even then, in the 13th and 14th centuries.

Describing the character of this minority was never straightforward. I attempted to show the values of this disappearing world – in a literal sense today – in a poem written in the language of Morze entitled *Vineć*.[1] The protagonists of this poem are the villagers so close to me, speaking in the name of its culture. These are the monumental lessons of old grandfather Nikifor.

A ty Irka pomentaj
Ne kłaniajsia za czasto
Hołowoju dorohi ne zamitaj
Na toje nohi kob znali dorohi
Na toje ruki kob zaznali muki
A na toje hołowa
Kob wysoko buła!

> ("And you Irka remember, do not bow too often! Do not sweep the road with your head! The legs are there to know the roads, the hands are there to know suffering, and the head is there to carry it all.")

I suspect that the fact that I carry within myself this borderland in which I grew up is directly connected to my academic interest in examining various Christian traditions from a comparative standpoint, starting from the research for my doctorate and continuing until today. It also connected with the fact that of late I have been interested in Islam. Looking back on the years, I see this motif clearly. It is in some sense also a search for the truth about myself, raised on the cusp of the culture of Byzantium and Rome.

Friends, masters, and first serious research

I don't know about other people, but I do not believe in chance happenings. What seems to be chance never is, but is brought to a certain moment by a string of events, causes, and consequences. The high school which I attended was the Medical Lyceum in Bielsk Podlaski, a small town located 18 km from my family village and inhabited half by Catholics and half by Orthodox Christians. This was a five-year school culminating in the *matura* school-leaving examination and a diploma exam in nursing. My experiences associated with these studies were certainly formative, especially the hospital work experience, which, starting from the second year, i.e. from the age of 16, became increasingly important. This hospital was a remarkable place. I remember the first time I observed a birth, the beginning of a life. Everything happened at the same time: the loud, painful shrieks of the woman in labor, the little head of the baby emerging, covered in blood, and after a moment the mother looking at her child, radiant with delight, elation, and love. I remember too other looks, through suffering and misty eyes, leading to an encounter with death and the dropping hand of a dying man, who had just a moment, a fraction of a second before, held mine so hard that it hurt. I remember his chest, which I looked at, unable to believe that it no longer bore his breath. It's impossible, I thought at the time. That's how people are born, that's how they die, and life goes on? Is this how it's supposed to be?

I repeat: I do not believe in chance occurrences, but I believe in something quite the opposite, that events and their consequences are bound in time with a kind of logic which eliminates chance at the outset. This is shown wonderfully in literature by Mikhail Bulgakov, whose book *The Master and Margarita* is among my most treasured: What would have happened if that oil, which caused a certain chain of events, had not been spilt? In the third year of school we had work experience in a unit of the health clinic that dealt with social support. As part of this work experience we looked after those who needed this kind of help: multiple-child families living in uncared-for and dirty accommodation, sick people who needed care, physically infirm and disabled people, and so on. I had entrusted to me a family with many children, and my friend Marysia had an elderly, hard-of-hearing woman living alone. Theoretically by chance, and in fact by design, Marysia asked me to fill in for her one day and I went there in her place, to the second-floor flat in the center of Bielsk Podlaski to ask in what ways I could help. I was met by the beautiful face of a 74-year-old woman, slim, oval-shaped, her wise hazel eyes looking at me, at her crown grey, lightly wavy hair. She invited me in, and once in the hallway, full of amazement, simply dazzled, my jaw dropped at the bookshelves occupying every wall. On this day one of the most important friendships of my life began.

We sociologists talk of "significant others." Leaving aside the family, it was Janina who opened the sphere of those important relationships which formed me as a person, but also my interests and aspirations. A few words are needed on who she was and what she was like in order to demonstrate the importance of this meeting to me. She belonged to the ranks of those known in Poland as the "pre-war intelligentsia,"[2] which meant that she had received a decent high school education, culminating in a "pre-war" *matura*. Janina's husband, who was no longer alive when I met her, had founded and for many years been the headmaster of the Agricultural Technical School in Bielsk Podlaski, which in 1973 was thriving. Most of the books that filled the shelves at Janina's home were from the broad field of the humanities, and those that she was most interested in were on religious affairs. What was remarkable about her inner world was that she was able to combine the ardor of mystical religiosity[3] with an analytical and creative mind. I believe it was then that this picture of religion which is consistent but open and subordinate to life (she was a member of a secular order in the Roman Catholic Church) took root within me. At the time it reminded me of religion in a Dostoevsky novel. This meant living on high emotions, and for Janina these emotions were borne by religion. Good and evil, Satan wearing a hat on Mickiewicz Street in Bielsk Podlaski, God the Son moving in the heart. It was as if *The Brothers Karamazov* was brought to life in a tangible sense.

We wrote to each other and I visited her regularly, even after I started my university studies. At the time I was indifferent to religion, leading the life of a prodigal daughter of Białystok artistic bohemians. Nevertheless – and I still cannot say why – I always swept my hair away from my forehead with joy and trust so that Janina could, as was her habit, say goodbye by marking the sign of the cross on it with the forefinger of her right hand.

It was my husband, Włodzimierz Pawluczuk, who opened the doors to academia to me. A sociologist, anthropologist, and religious studies scholar, he was a professor at the time when I was writing my Master's dissertation. It was he who showed me how attractive discursive thinking could be and how emotional academic enquiry was. He was my mentor, and he read my first articles and the clumsy chapters of my doctoral thesis. His criticism was much more balanced than anything I have been able to give to my students and his praise lifted me higher. It was, however, not easy when everything was tied together: our personal and professional roles overlapped and our dependence grew stronger. Even 30 years after our first joint trips, after the storms that we did not survive as a couple, I see clearly how important his role was, how close his thinking was to mine, and how intellectually attractive and creative his concepts were. I can only say that I have been lucky.

My husband's interest in phenomenology also pushed me in that direction. I remember extremely distinctly how, awaiting the birth of our son, I read *Ideas II* by Edmund Husserl. That was April 29, 1983. It's good that my son Mateusz decided to arrive the next day because the day after that – May 1 – was not a good day to be born in the Poland of that time. Doctors, nurses, just like everybody else, pushed by the communist ruling party, had to go and celebrate Labor Day, go on parades, wave flags, give speeches, stand in grandstands, dance at the gala in the evening. Not many people were left in the hospital to take care of expectant mothers.

The ideas of Edmund Husserl, Martin Heidegger, Jean-Paul Sartre, Alfred Schütz, Erving Goffman, and Florian Zaniecki provided the foundation for the theoretical framework of my doctoral thesis. Observing daily life in the Orthodox villages which I knew so well, I became convinced that religion is festive in character, and daily life is determined by hard work in the fields. I was curious about the question whether – and if so to what degree – religions were different from each other in this respect, and chose this as my thesis topic. My research was carried out in villages in north-eastern Poland, among Orthodox Christians, Catholics, Muslims,[4] and Pentecostals. The material for my analysis comprised notes from participant observation, recordings of prayer meetings, sermons, and also – and this was crucial – conversations taking place in people's homes, in the conditions of daily life. After five years, in 1988, I defended my doctoral thesis at the Jagiellonian University in Krakow; it was later published in modified form as a book.[5]

In hindsight, several issues from this research seem important to me. First, it turned out that the relationship between religion and everyday life for the Pentecostals was decidedly different from the other groups. For the Pentecostals, religion was a sacred canopy, the transcendence shrouding everyday life, at the level of both actions and their justifications. This was expressed in all conceivable situations: in their way of work, at rest, in the daily rhythm of life, in their concerns and the answers to those concerns. For example, I was driving with a man named Piotr to the fields to gather the crops, in a cart pulled by a horse, when on the other side of the road a man tottered along towards us, pushing a bike. Piotr looked at the man and said, "They ask where hell is and what it's like! Hell is here, this is hell bubbling over with sulphur!" That same harvest time, a Sunday, the skies clouded over. Every few moments a cart came careering noisily through the village, the horses racing: "Oh!" commented Piotr, "they're racing, racing, the devil's chasing them!" Similarly, Lidia and Paweł used to sing hymns all the time while drying hay, and kept on singing when they were insulating their modest wooden home with hay for the winter.

These examples show how religion is present in the everyday life of the Pentecostals in the village. Religion gives everyday life meaning, dictates the daily rhythm, and guides people's decisions. The daily life of Catholics, Orthodox Christians and Muslims, on the other hand, was dominated by worry, in which Heidegger's Self was entirely immersed. The villagers' daily problems included unmilked cows, late buses, someone's gossip, someone arguing with someone, someone visiting someone, problems with health, dances happening on Saturdays, punch-ups which had happened on Saturdays, how to pickle cucumbers, and so on –without any references to religion.

Another important track in this research was to examine Max Weber's thesis about the economic consequences of inner-worldly asceticism. The Pentecostals I studied exhibited many features of this type of ethic, although in their case devotion to work and prayer, rejection of alcohol (which was omnipresent in the life of the village), and rejection of other diversions, such as watching television, listening to the radio, going to dances or to village meetings, smoking cigarettes – all these "empty things not connected with God" – did not in fact lead them to prosperity. On the contrary: since they functioned in an environment dominated by Orthodoxy and – let's say – an irreligious, secular pragmatic ethic, this led them to a kind of isolationism and economic backwardness. The asceticism – although in fact inner-worldly and striving to transform the world into a better one – forced them to be isolated from the "rotten" ones. As a consequence, when the other farmers in the village hired a combine harvester they would not even consider this, since harvester drivers would have to be offered meals, and vodka after work, and that was a sin. While others carried milk to the dairy and received money in return,[6] the Pentecostals eschewed this practice, because they were convinced that the milkmaid was cheating people and they did not want to be party to this dishonest, immoral procedure. These and other factors meant that in this case inner-worldly asceticism led to isolation and resulted in economic regression, far from the "spirit of capitalism." Much closer to this "capitalist spirit" were the immoral, drunk, cigarette-smoking, lying, state-property-thieving members of the kolkhozes, established in Poland according to the Soviet model.[7] In general, minority groups very rarely have opportunities to promote their values and lifestyle, unless they are expansive and gradually transform from minority groups into widely influential universalistic religions, as at some point occurred with world religions.

According to my conclusions at the time, there were no significant differences among the models of everyday life for followers of Islam, Catholicism, and Orthodox Christianity. All of these groups shared similar problems (and solutions), similar patterns of work and rest, similar rules of relations with others, and a similar attitude towards time, often seeing oneself through the prism of completed tasks. I no longer believe that my conclusions can be universalized. On the contrary, I am convinced that various religions and denominations have different ways of conceptualizing everyday life and religion's role in it. But these are less important than dominant and widely distributed cultural models. In the case of my research it was secular culture that dominated in rural areas and the Pentecostals constructed their daily life and religion in opposition to this secular culture.

While working on my doctorate I met people from outside of Poland who would become very important in my later life. In 1986 Professor Eileen Barker of the London School of Economics visited the Institute of Religious Studies of Jagiellonian University, where I was a third-year doctoral student at the time. Her charismatic personality, outstanding lecture, and above all the methodological aspects of her research immediately made me aware that what she did could be a model for me to follow. Her approach to the people she was studying and respect for their different ways of thinking and believing made an everlasting impression on me.

Two years later, I participated in a conference in Krakow attended by Professor Jeffrey Hadden, whose wife Elaine was very moved by their visit because she had Polish ancestors. This meeting had many important consequences. In 1991, after I participated in the annual conference of the Society for the Scientific Study of Religion in Washington, DC, Jeffrey Hadden generously invited me to his home and organized my visits to several cities in the USA. He and the friends who supported him in my travels opened before me, literally and figuratively, the library of the global sociology of religion. I was delighted, amazed, simply dumbfounded. I returned to Krakow with 60 kg of books in my hand luggage! Afterwards a few more deliveries came from Jeffrey, which reinforced the library of the Institute of Religious Studies of Jagiellonian University where I was working. These readings changed my – and many others' – understanding of religion and the world in which it manifested itself.

At a conference in Hungary – it must have been in 1985 or 1986 – I had the pleasure of listening to a paper given by Miklós Tomka.[8] With characteristic fervor he presented the results of some major, representative studies. This was a time when Marxism was the hegemonic perspective in the scientific studies of religion. My religious studies colleagues from the Soviet Union, especially Moscow, cited Lenin, Marx, Engels, and their own contemporary ideologues who thought "correctly" about religion. I don't believe that they were pretending when they said they hadn't even heard of Durkheim or Weber, let alone later theorists. I believe that they were ignoramuses. And they were the ones sitting in the front rows. Miklós's paper was chock-full of the latest theoretical premises of the time, he took issue with global sociology, was statistically sophisticated, and exuded independence and inner freedom. It is these things that I will remember him for.

I mention here only those people who made a mark in my life and academic development at the time when I was a young girl, a doctoral student, and immediately after completing my doctorate. Unfortunately, lack of space means that I cannot list all my academic friendships here, although I consider them to be very important.

I will just mention three areas: Two academic associations – ISORECEA[9] and the International Society for the Sociology of Religion – are crucial here, along with my place of work, Jagiellonian University. Teaching is an opportunity to discuss things with students, but also requires a strong grounding in classical sociology and constant updating on the latest trends.

I am obviously not the only one whose teaching is closely linked to my research interests. Alongside semester lectures each year in the sociology of religion which are a constant element in my teaching, I have run courses, and continue to do so, which reflect my long- and short-term research interests. The geographical, cultural, and political context of one's work of course influences one's interests. Being a sociologist in Poland, an almost mono-confessional country, it would have been hard not to be interested in the role of religion in society. Over the years I have conducted research in this area on many occasions.

Religion, religiosity, and sociological theories of religion

The starting point for my interests in the empirical study of religiosity was the observation of Polish society and its specific nature in this respect. Starting in 1991, on several occasions I researched the subject of religiosity in nationwide representative samples, something that was made possible by research grants. I undertook various attempts at a synthesis, looking for regularities in the religiosity of Polish society[10] and attempting to answer the question of why this religiosity is so stable, and what indicators of changes there are.[11] It is intriguing from a cognitive point of view that in Polish society a strong attachment to the Roman Catholic Church and its rites of passage coexists with an indifference to religious moral teachings, selective acceptance of certain dogmas, and a lack of acceptance of others – all characteristic of the societies of Western Europe. Two parallel processes are going on in Poland: the institutionalization and privatization of religion. However – unlike in Western Europe – they do not cancel each other out. In Poland the privatization of religion does not break or even weaken institutional religion, and does not disturb the process of institutionalization, i.e., the generational transmission of religion.[12]

In carrying out this research I developed my understanding of religion. On the one hand, the domination of the Catholic Church was and continues to be an important framework for my research – not forgetting sensitivity towards the position of all religious minorities. On the other hand, I have been guided by the idea of overcoming the restrictions resulting from adopting either a functional or a substantive perspective in defining religion. My position in this respect is close to that represented by, for example, Roland Robertson, Robert Bellah, Karel Dobbelaere, and James Beckford, who have all expressed that neither a functional nor a substantive view alone is sufficient for grasping religious phenomena.

Therefore – if I may at this point – by religion I understand a certain type of objectivization of social response to the so-called ultimate questions, this objectivization taking the form of a given theory (doctrine), practice (ritual), and organization (community). In this sense religion has a dimension of objective factuality, the form of something that exists outside of a person as a kind of collection of symbols, meanings, institutionalized behaviors, institutions, and their structures. Lived religion, which is present in society, takes on the form of subjective religiosity.

In my take on religion I wanted in particular to treat this phenomenon in a broader fashion than is usually the case in Poland. By religiosity, I understand the diverse contents and forms of manifestation of the fundamental conviction that the meaning of the life of humans is not exhausted in their biological existence. The contents comprise both those that are culturally inherited and those acquired on the path of individual searches, convictions which can be verbalized on the subject of the nature of humans and the world, the sense and fate, moral rules, usually described by the name of the doctrine, worldview, or ideology. These forms are practical activities resulting from accepted beliefs, expressed by the possession and manifestation of attachment to symbols, by conducting worship and belonging to a community.

These ways of defining religion and religiosity result from premises that are important to me. On the one hand, it is about overcoming that weakness in the sociology of religion of which the fuzzy boundaries of the religious and irreligious are a manifestation. I believe that a broad view of religion, so broad that practically anything is or can be religion, is erroneous. Religion has its own particular characteristics and functions, which allow it to be distinguished from, for example, political ideologies. The second important premise present in my perception of religiosity is the belief that, especially in Poland, we are seeing an excessive concentration on church-based, institutional religiosity. And yet, in Poland too, under the surface of identification with the Catholic Church, rich forms of individualized religiosity are developing. If, however, the concept of religiosity concentrates on institutional orthodoxy, as is the case in some approaches that are still popular in Poland, then sociologists are losing sight of this richness and diversity.

Looking at current sociology of religion as a whole, I feel that the discipline is blooming in comparison to the 1960s and the 1970s when secularization theory in its various versions was formed. Nevertheless, I see this period as extremely important for the development of the sociology of religion. In theories of secularization sociologists made extensive attempts to explain the changes in the position of religion that they had observed. Admittedly, one of the era's most important authors, Peter Berger, claims that – albeit in good company – he was mistaken.[13] At the same time, Thomas Luckmann, another very important author of the period, sticks to his original interpretations – with apparent pride – over 30 years after the first publication of *The Invisible Religion*, saying that he has little to add.[14]

I believe that a certain risk of error is involved in the formation of every theory. The dubious aspects of secularization theory have been demonstrated in numerous debates. Yet the main theses essentially continue to ring true.[15] In addition – and this is particularly important in light of the past 100 years of the development of specialized sociological reflection on religion – theories on secularization are a keystone connecting the classical period with the present. The latest theories of religion, coming thick and fast at the cusp of the 1980s and 1990s, arose to a great degree as the result of criticism and rebuttal of secularization theory. In the same way that the continuation of the ideas of classics such as Max Weber, Emile Durkheim, and Gabriel le Bras was the material of secularization theory, its criticism was also the formative material for the market theory of religion, the concept of deprivatization, and approaches that focus on religion as emotion and memory.

The development of sociological theories of religion constitutes an interesting example of how sociology has struggled with the profound social transformations pin-pointed by the classics at the cusp of the 19th and 20th centuries. It was here that a marked turn towards modernity took place, and with this the structural as well as the functional position of religion changed radically. Trends in the sociology of religion are reflected in the different explanations authors have for this change. Some believe that it is the social system that changes. This option may be observed in the theories of secularization, but also in Durkheim's classical conception. For others, it is the individual who changes, his or her values and needs – and this brings with it religious change. Here we can place theories of the privatization of religion and the market theory of religion. Others still think that it is the change within the religion itself that is crucial – and here the conception of civic religion or deprivatization of religion comes in. An expression of my acknowledgment of the various theoretical perspectives, in consultion with a wide circle of sociologists in Poland and around the world, is *Socjologia religii*, a publishing series in Polish which I started in 1996 with the Polish-language publication of Thomas Luckmann's *Invisible Religion*.[16] Over a dozen books have appeared to date.

Religion and transformation in Central and Eastern Europe

The collapse of communism in Central and Eastern Europe has provided me with a good arena for testing old and new ways of understanding religion and its changes – a kind of sociological laboratory. The 1990s were a very interesting period for sociologists owing to the systemic transformation in Central and Eastern Europe, also encompassing the religious field. There are many contradictions in this sphere. As an example, joining a group of democratic countries requires respect for certain norms, such as recognition of the principle of secularity of the state and equality of religions before the law. At the same time, many countries had a burning need to construct and reconstruct both social and individual identity. It often proved to be an irresistible temptation to favor the dominant religion or church in this construction, especially in the field of influencing politics. These dominant churches often demand state restrictions on other religious groups. On the one hand, there is a tendency to control religion characteristic of the times before 1989. On the other hand, there are contemporary versions of the alliance of "altar and throne," both on the central and local levels.

My reflections in this field are undergoing a kind of evolution. At first I tried to grasp the scope and contents of the transformations taking place both in the institutional order and in the subjective dimension of human religiosity.[17] The institutional changes concern above all the position of churches and other religious organizations in relation to other social sub-systems – politics, culture, academia, and education – as well as encompassing the changing relations between state and Church. The changes in the subjective dimension of religion (i.e., religiosity) are in most post-communist societies a real challenge for sociologists of religion. This is because it is a kind of irony of history awaiting serious analysis and interpretation that, after years of intensive secularism and atheism, religiosity in Eastern Europe has characteristics similar to religiosity in Western Europe: eclecticism, a low level of religious practice and attachment to religious institutions, a changing – one could say "mobile" – subject of faith, and a kind of cult of choice.[18] In this context I am interested in the valorization and revalorization of memory, the way that the past is present in the present in the institutional religious activities of organizations and the biographies of individuals.

Here too a host of questions arise which I will seek to answer in my planned research. For example, what should we make of former atheists, today such devout followers of Orthodoxy, who in the past "believed" (the quotation marks result only from the mental short cut into which I am forced) in communism and today link the metaphorical toothache with punishment for sin? Initial conversations with members of the parish in, for example, the small town of Alushta in Crimea point to questions about religious conversion: the reinterpretation of past events from the perspective of – in this case – a return from atheism to religion, causes, to some extent, an "annihilation" of those past experiences.

I am also interested in comparing various Christian traditions, their similarities and differences, in the context of radical social change. From these comparisons emerge methodological postulates concerning the need to distinguish research methods, their more effective application to important elements of a given religious tradition. In this respect a significant weakness of the sociology of religion is revealed. It is not just that the unequivocally dominant field of its interests and competences is Christianity – we have to note too that it is decidedly Western Christianity (i.e., Latin tradition and Protestant Churches), while Eastern Christianity, the diverse Orthodox Churches, were for many decades neglected, and only on the wave of systemic transformation can it be seen that they found themselves in the sights of sociologists of religion.

Questions related to the role of religion in the process of social transformation are discussed in a series of English-language books I have edited. I believe that this series is important not only for the academic development of reflections on religion, but also for the development of academic communities in Central and Eastern Europe, their presentation to the world, and integration with international academic centers and organizations.[19] These books reveal, on the one hand, the crucial role played by religion in the democratization of social life in post-communist Europe, and on the other hand, the great diversity of processes of religious change taking place in different countries.

Conclusion

I am now sitting in the library of the house to which I moved nine years ago, thinking about the past and future horizons. It is no small irony that I moved to a village in the suburbs of Kraków. My neighbors are villagers. Like so many years ago, I wake up to a rooster's crow early in the morning. Like so many years ago, I feel incredible tenderness while watching a mother washing and grooming her new-born kittens. It seems to me that all the things that I felt were unacceptable and which provoked my protests about life in a rural community in my youth, I see in a different light today. What I perceived as control of the local community over the individual in my youth, appears to me today as civil society in practice. What I saw as unacceptable and irrational pressure on work and an overvaluation of it, I see today as a way of imparting important values to the younger generations. In any case, I expect my PhD students to work hard and to give priority to this value in their life.

I remember my father visiting me in Kraków for the first time years ago. I think he was in his fifties at the time, that is, more or less my present age. Despite many differences between us, we understood each other very well. He had a creative mind and a good imagination. I remember us walking around the famous market square and the medieval part of the city. Of course I expected my father to be impressed and because he kept silent I asked him directly: How do you like it? He looked at me, smiled, and answered: Dirty buildings. You escaped here from us, so far away. My father died 25 years ago and now we can't talk about it. But I wonder: Did I escape? Can we escape from ourselves?

Notes

1 *Vineć* in the dialect possesses several meanings, of which the most important in this case are two – first, wreath, such as those worn by girls on their heads, literally "woven" from flowers. In my childhood this was a common game for young girls – we wove wreaths to be worn as crowns from colourful wildflowers. In this semantic area too are found all other wreaths and ritual bouquets – for example, for mourning. Second, a wedding ceremony, the religious rite conducted in the Orthodox church, lasting for around one-and-a-half hours, was also called *winczannie* (roughly, *weaving*).

2 This expression is used to emphasize the "nobility" of this group's background in order to distinguish them from "postwar intelligentsia," which differed in its social lineage. The postwar version was associated with progress, was ideologically organized, and made it possible for people of worker and peasant origin to advance to the "intelligentsia."

3 She kept diaries containing records of classical – from the perspective of William James and other experts – mystical experiences. I have been promising myself for some time to embark seriously on a biography of Janina, not only because this is a kind of debt, the existence of which I became aware of not so long ago, but also because the materials she left behind are also unique from the perspective of religious studies and the sociology of religion.

4 The Muslim minority in Poland comprises an indigenous group of so-called Polish Tatars, descendants of the Tatars who settled in Poland and Lithuania in several waves starting from the 14th century. They came from the Black Sea, partly to strengthen the Polish-Lithuanian borders and fight as soldiers. In recognition of their services for the defense of the Polish Republic they were given land. In north-eastern Poland they inhabit two villages in which two old mosques may be found. The Pentecostals in north-eastern Poland appeared before World War I as missionaries arriving from Imperial Russia. Catholicism and Orthodox Christianity – religions that appeared here with permanent settlement – have been mentioned above.

5 Irena Borowik, *Charyzma i codzienność. Studium wpływu religii na życie codzienne* (Kraków: Miniatura, 1990).

6 We must remember that the countryside at this time in this part of Poland was poor and relatively backward in comparison to that in western Poland, for example. So bartering one's own products, such as milk or eggs, was a major regular source of income.

7 These were, however, few in number and functioning entirely differently from the Soviet ones, given the existence of a strong individual agricultural economy in Poland.

8 We got to know each other better after the collapse of communism and the disintegration of the Soviet Union, in 1991, when in Krakow I began to organize a series of conferences under the banner "Religions and Churches in Central and Eastern Europe," in which he was a regular participant. Miklós Tomka died unexpectedly on October 25, 2010, at the age of 69.

9 ISORECEA, or International Study of Religion in Eastern and Central Europe Association, was established in the context of the conference series "Religions and Churches in Central and Eastern Europe" which I organized in Krakow, and subsequently, after its foundation, "wandering" through the transforming post-communist Europe. Other than several meetings in Krakow and Budapest, conferences have been held in Zagreb, Lviv, and Brno. Their outcome in publication terms is a series of books and an internet journal. Incidentally, the godmother of the title is Eileen Barker.

10 Irena Borowik, *Procesy instytucjonalizacji i prywatyzacji religii w powojennej Polsce* (Kraków: Wydawnictwo Uniwersytetu Jagoiellońskiego, 1997); Irena Borowik and Tadeusz Doktór, *Pluralizm religijny i moralny w Polsce* (Kraków: Nomos, 2001).

11 Irena Borowik, "Why Has Religiosity in Poland not Changed Since 1989? Five Hypotheses," *Politics and Religion* 3 (2010): 262–275.

12 Irena Borowik, "The Roman Catholic Church in the Process of Democratic Transformation: The Case of Poland," *Social Compass* 49(2) (2002a): 239–252.

13 Peter L. Berger, "The Desecularization of the World: A Global Overview," in *The Desecularization of the World: Resurgent Religion and World Politics*, ed. Peter Berger (Grand Rapids, MI: Eerdmans Publishing, 1999), 1–18.

14 Thomas Luckmann, "Transformation of Religion and Morality in Modern Europe," *Social Compass* 50(3) (2003): 275–285.

15 I am thinking of the analyses by Pippa Norris and Ronald Inglehart which show that hypotheses based on the secularization paradigm are not without foundation. Pippa Norris and Ronald Inglehart, *Sacred and Secular: Religion and Politics Worldwide* (Cambridge: Cambridge University Press, 2005).

16 These books are published by Nomos Publishing House – another activity of mine. This academic publisher was founded by the academic staff of the Institute of Religious Studies of Jagiellonian University in 1991, and since then I have continuously been in charge of its work.

17 Irena Borowik, "Between Orthodoxy and Eclecticism: On the Religious Transformations of Russia, Belarus and Ukraine," *Social Compass* 4 (2002b): 497–508.

18 Borowik, "The Roman Catholic Church."

19 Irena Borowik and Grzegorz Babiński (eds), *New Religious Phenomena in Central and Eastern Europe* (Kraków: Nomos, 1997); Irena Borowik (ed.), *Church–State Relations in Central and Eastern Europe* (Kraków: Nomos, 1999); Irena Borowik, *Religion and Religiosity in Post-Communist Societies* (Kraków: Nomos, 2006); Irena Borowik and Małgorzata Zawiła, *Religions and Identities in Transition* (Kraków: Nomos, 2010).

8

UNINTENDED CONSEQUENCES BIOGRAPHICAL AND SOCIOLOGICAL

Steve Bruce

My ain folk

The Queen Victoria School for the Sons of Scottish Soldiers, Seamen and Airmen in Perthshire was my home for eight years. Being a military institution, it had church parades and, being military church parades, they were compulsory. Thus, from the age of 9, I attended a 15-minute church service every weekday morning with a full hour-long service on a Sunday. I sang the hymns and I heard the lessons from the Bible. The communal singing was fun, the language of the King James translation impressive, the sermons short, and I cannot recall actually believing any of it. Nor was I exceptional. Like that of the soldiers of Chiang Kai-Shek, who were marched under a hose-pipe in a mass baptism, the faith of the Sons of Scottish Soldiers, Seamen and Airmen was communal, social, and nominal. Neither of my parents were Christians. My father was an Aberdeenshire farm loon who in the early 1930s appreciated what the tractor would do to the demand for farm labor and joined the army. Like most people from the rural lowlands, he was a sporadic Presbyterian church attender who was suspicious of anyone who was "awfie religious." My mother, a Bulgarian who was raised in the Orthodox Church, was similarly uninterested in religion.

When I enrolled at the University of Stirling, my original subjects were biology and biochemistry, but I struggled with the maths, and identifying and counting wing shapes on dead drosophila – something to do with genetics – was just too dull for words. I had always been bookish (or at least as bookish as one could be in a military academy). When I first read George Orwell's *1984* description of Winston Smith buying a hard-bound blank notebook and a fountain pen, I recognized my own fetish. Wanting to do something that involved writing rather than counting dead flies, I transferred to English and proved no better at that. I was far too riddled with prejudice against people who liked showing off their erudition (T.S. Eliot) and against fascists (Ezra Pound) to be able to appreciate their poetry. And I could not get away from the sense that literary critics made it up. Provided one was sufficiently florid, one could chunter on about what a text meant without any constraint on the imagination. Norman MacCaig, who was a nice man as well as a great poet, allowed me to pass his course only on the condition that I would not continue with English.

I was saved from a degree-less departure by a bizarre act of administrative pique. In 1972, the Queen visited the University and some students held a well-mannered and ineffectual demonstration. I had become involved in student politics from the highest of motives: I was in love with the president of the Students' Union. She had big, dark eyes, a thick Afghan coat and a rich Glasgow accent. I also became friends with John Reid who later became Tony Blair's go-to-guy for every tough ministerial job. He also had a rich Glasgow accent and a nice coat but not so much the big, dark eyes.

As no one had been arrested during the demonstration, the Principal of the University chose to take out his annoyance on the elected student representatives and expel us all on the grounds of collective responsibility. We had to spend three months touring universities to raise money for our legal defense. Another small Labour history footnote: at Dundee we were strongly supported by "Gorgeous George" Galloway who later became a Labour MP, a thorn in Tony Blair's side, and a star turn on the reality TV show *Big Brother*. Galloway also had the Afghan coat and the rich Scots accent but, like John Reid, he was short in the big eyes department.

As soon as the hearing of the University's disciplinary case against us began it collapsed, and the University admitted that we could not be held responsible for the actions of our fellow students, no matter how much they embarrassed the University. The upshot was that I was permitted to continue my university education but had insufficient credits to take any major. The Sociology Department agreed to share the risk with the Religious Studies Department and I started a joint degree under Roy Wallis, who was then making a name for himself as one of that brilliant generation of students of Bryan Wilson. I also had the good fortune to be taught by Max Marwick, an anthropologist and Africanist who had published extensively on witchcraft and magic. The Religious Studies Department taught me basic Hinduism and Buddhism, Post-Kantian theology, and the rudiments of critical biblical scholarship.

Schleiermacher apart, I found religious studies interesting but I cannot recall it having any personal impact on me beyond stimulating a brief period of faux Eastern asceticism: for a week or two I gave up cigarettes and alcohol, drank green tea, and dispensed with chairs. But with social science I found my calling. The "social" meant that I could study people instead of fruit flies and the "science" meant that there was an objective (or, at least, an inter-subjective) reality that provided some test of one's theories.

Belief systems and social structures

Although my degree was in Sociology and Religious Studies, I was not primarily interested in religion as such. Like many of my generation I was hugely impressed by

Peter Berger and Thomas Luckmann's *The Social Construction of Reality*.[1] What really interested me was which social structures and relationships made particular shared beliefs more or less plausible and, beyond the obvious sociology of religion material, I spent a lot of time reading about the sociology of science, the sociology of knowledge, and the sociology of persuasion. Elihu Katz's work on the two-step flow of communication particularly interested me, as did Robert Merton's early work on persuasion.[2]

For my undergraduate research project I chose to study how the members of the evangelical Christian Union managed to maintain their Christian faith in a setting that was extremely hostile to their beliefs when their requirement to evangelize prevented them from doing the obvious thing, which was to become extremely introverted. Stirling then was sexually permissive and politically radical. As a member of the Communist Party (until I read Marx), I was on the far right of Stirling's student politics: the president who was the object of my puppy-like adoration was a Trotskyite. The conclusion of my research was that the young evangelicals resolved their dilemma by using the language of evangelism as a warrant and a device for group discipline. They advertised their events and meetings in ways that involved little opportunity for painful snubs from the heathen, privately delighted in their minority status, and used the notion of "witnessing" as a way of policing their own behavior. They did not actually witness to the campus – that would have been too embarrassing – but to each other, and more often than not their witness or "walk with the Lord" was concerned with criticizing incipient signs of back-sliding among their own members.

The Christian Union led me into my doctoral research. The national body of student Christian Unions had divided in the 1920s. The conservatives eventually became the Inter-Varsity Fellowship; the liberals operated under the title of the Student Christian Movement. By the 1970s these two bodies provided a perfect quasi-experiment. They operated in the same university and college market, organized the same sorts of activities, had similar structures, and shared a common history. What divided them was the classic rift in Western Protestantism: evangelical (shading into fundamentalist) versus liberal (shading into radical theology). At the time Roy Wallis was working on the social consequences of epistemological assumptions, which was the basis for his improvement of the classic church-sect-denomination-cult treatment of religious organizations and for his theory of factionalism and schism in social movements.[3] My other great inspiration then was David Martin. One single sentence of his – "the logic of Protestantism is clearly in favor of voluntary principle, to a degree that eventually makes it sociologically unrealistic"[4] – fueled my work for two decades as I tried to combine ideas about epistemology, authority, and organizational structure into a historically rooted explanation of secularization that started from the diversity that was an unintended consequence of the Reformation (and subsequent schismatic movements). Crucial to the ideas that I expressed badly in *A House Divided: Protestantism, Schism and Secularization* and better in *Religion in the Modern World* was the Weberian notion of irony: because they lack perfect knowledge and complete control, people set out to do one thing and achieve something very different.[5]

Reform movements that were intended to purify the national church so that its imposition on the people would be justified produced a degree of diversity which made imposition impossible and in turn produced the religiously neutral state. By stressing individual responsibility for salvation, the Reformers also inadvertently laid the foundations for the claim of individual rights independent of religious rectitude and eventually for modern consumerism.

The interest in the links between epistemology, authority, and social cohesion started in a contrast between conservative and liberal Protestantism at a time when sociologists of religion were arguing about the structural merits (or otherwise) of what Dean Kelley called "strong religion"[6] but it continued into arguments with Paul Heelas and others about the nature of, and likely prospects for, what is variously called New Age, contemporary, or holistic spirituality.[7] My focus on the individualism of contemporary spirituality has often been misunderstood: first, as being concerned with substantive individualism (that is, what you would call selfishness, if you did not like it); second, as suggesting that spirituality is not really religious; and third, as denigrating women's religiosity.[8]

That third, literally *ad hominem*, criticism is dealt with below under the general topic of the relationship between interests and scientific advance. The second is easily answered. For reasons explained at length elsewhere, I have always thought a substantive definition of religion more useful to social scientists than a functional one; whether or not any expression of spirituality is religious depends on it involving the existence of supernatural entities with the power of moral judgment.[9] The first criticism is the most deflating because it shows that I have failed to interest the profession in Roy Wallis's work. Belief systems differ in the nature of authority they posit, and in particular in the range of people who are thought to have access to the core truths. In his revision of the church-sect-denomination-cult typology, Wallis showed that much of what interests us about ideological movements and structured belief systems – structure, cohesion, levels of commitment and much more – can be derived socio-"logically" from its practical epistemology. What explains the failure of the New Age (in comparison, say, to Victorian evangelicalism) to produce alternative schools, colleges, universities, prisons, alcohol and drug reform programs is not individualism in the sense of selfishness but the *epistemological* individualism that allows each New Ager to decide what is true for him or her and what degree of commitment he or she will make.

Long before I realized that I was intellectually closer to Martin than to Wilson, Wallis nominated Martin as the examiner of my doctoral thesis. I was always persuaded of Wilson's essential secularization account but, I now realize, felt uncomfortable with the functionalist language he used to explain the process. As I was finally able to articulate in *Secularization*, the language of social functions has to be translated (or at least be translatable) into the language of plausibility; otherwise one misleadingly implies that people were either cynical (pretending to believe in order to achieve some latent function) or easily duped.[10] That some belief or ritual practice serves some latent or secondary function can explain its persistence only through the mechanism of making it seem more plausible than alternatives. My disagreements with Martin were small and largely concern guesses about the future rather than explanations of the past. I have never been guilty of a linear view of secularization (indeed, I cannot think of any modern sociologist who is); Martin is clearly right that the religiosity of societies ebbs and flows. Periods of decline provoke revivals, and revivals are followed by institutionalization and then by stagnation. We only disagree about the height of the high tides. Where he sees a relative steady state of religiosity underlying his cycles of growth and decline, I see each high tide reaching less far up the beach.

Politics and religion

In 1976 Roy Wallis was appointed to the Chair of Sociology at the Queen's University of Belfast and two years later I joined him. Living in Northern Ireland caused my interest in the political causes and consequences of Protestantism. For my first year in Belfast, I shared a house with David Taylor, an American doctoral student who was studying Ian Paisley's religion and politics, and I chummed him along to Paisley's services. I also fell in with the staff of the Religion Department of the BBC in Northern Ireland and was commissioned to write a documentary film about Paisley. That eventually led to *God Save Ulster: The Religion and Politics of Paisleyism*.[11] Contacts on the fringe of Paisley's party introduced me to the loyalist paramilitaries of the Ulster Defence Association and the Ulster Volunteer Force, and to a line of political sociology research that produced *No Pope of Rome: Militant Protestantism in Modern Scotland*, *The Red Hand: Loyalist Paramilitaries in Northern Ireland*, and *The Edge of the Union: the Ulster Loyalist Political Vision*.[12] Paisley was also responsible for my interest in the New Christian Right in America. Despite being thoroughly involved in Ulster politics, Paisley took the Bob Jones line on Jerry Falwell and the Moral Majority: that pietistic retreat from the world was preferable to potentially compromising entanglement in electoral politics. That was enough to stimulate the research that led to *Pray TV: Televangelism in America* and *The Rise and Fall of the New Christian Right*.[13] My interest in Paisley also led to an invitation to be part of the Fundamentalism project organized by Martin Marty and R. Scott Appleby, which in turn got me interested in non-Protestant forms of fundamentalism.[14]

Working with Roy Wallis was educational. We never conducted any original research together. He was fully occupied with new religious movements. Whether I was reading the history of Protestant factionalism and schism or listening to Paisley preach, I was deep in the 18th and 19th centuries. But we fell into a highly enjoyable habit of combining our very different research interests in joint papers on theoretical topics, usually inspired by one of us having a bad-tempered reaction to something we had read. Our working method was simple. At the end of a long day Roy would fish out a bottle of gin and a tape-recorder and we would spend a couple of hours arguing over some new provocation while getting mildly addled. The next day I would listen to the tape, type up the notes, and pass them to Roy, who would add and edit and pass them back for me to do the same, until something sensible and worth reading emerged. The word-processor had just been invented and we all worked on Amstrad machines with identical dot-matrix printers. Even now, 25 years later, I sometimes come across pages of text and, although prose style is sometimes a clue, I cannot be sure if they are Roy's work or mine.

Secularization and rational choice

When people talk about their intellectual influences, they are usually thinking of positive inspiration. It probably says nothing good about our personalities that both Roy and I seemed to be driven mainly by irritation. Gin apart, what fueled our joint work was articulating disagreements with others. My career certainly owed a great deal to the tall, domineering, and opinionated figure of the Reverend Ian Paisley. But it also owed much to the tall, domineering, and opinionated figure of Rodney Stark.

I have no idea how their quarrel began but Roy seemed to feel obliged to challenge Rodney at every turn and, as Robin to Roy's Batman, I got drawn into their arguments to such an extent that when Roy died, I inherited his feud along with his books. For a young sociologist to be repeatedly singled out for ritual denunciation by Stark and his associates was an enormous career boost because it created publishing opportunities and a clear profile. To a generation of American sociologists I was regularly held up as the last defender of a patently false theory, but at least Stark ensured that I was well known for my errors.

One of the lessons I had learnt at Stirling was that all characterization is at least implicitly comparative. Inspired by Ernest Gellner and W.G. Runciman – both of whom I had the good fortune to hear speak a number of times – I probably read more history than most sociologists of my generation and any serious acquaintance with religion in the Middle Ages makes laughable the argument of the secularization-deniers that modern Western Europe is really as religious as ever it was. And as I regularly traveled between the English Midlands (where my parents had retired), Scotland, and Northern Ireland, I was made constantly aware of secularization. In England religion hardly mattered. In Northern Ireland it mattered a great deal. And my homeland was a complex middle ground: parts of the industrial West of Scotland echoed Ulster's religious divide; Calvinist sabbatarians still ruled the roost in the Western Isles; and the farming folk of the rural North-East were as indifferent to religion as most of the English.

My location in Northern Ireland also played a role in my decision to devote a year of my life to a detailed critique of Stark's second theory of religion: the rational choice or supply-side alternative to secularization.[15] It seemed glaringly obvious that, whatever evidence Stark, Roger Finke, and Laurence Iannaccone could find to support their claim that diversity increased the take-up of religion, the bigger picture refuted their theory. The most religious societies in Europe (Ireland and Poland, for example) were the least religiously diverse. If we took comparison over time, Britain in 1990 was patently more religiously diverse than it had been in 1890 and equally patently less religious. The foundation of my rejection of the rational choice approach had an intellectual and a biographical element. The key weaknesses of the economist's version of rational choice became clear when I read Gary Becker, the Chicago economist who inspired the extension of economics to all spheres of social behavior. The biographical element was my location in Belfast. When people were routinely murdered for marrying across the religious divide, it was very difficult to see religion as a sphere in which individual consumers sought to maximize their utility.

Surveys and statistics

My most recent concern – promoting the use of surveys and the statistical analysis of large-scale datasets – has been, to me anyway, the least expected. Before the new British sociology departments founded in the 1960s could be staffed by their own graduates, they depended on anthropologists and, for a wide variety of other reasons (including some vague sense that statistical analysis is "right-wing"), British sociology has generally concentrated on detailed ethnographic studies of small groups.[16] This was particularly true in the sociology of religion. This was partly an accidental outcome of Wilson's influence peaking at the same time as the plethora of 1970s new religious movements was providing topics for a generation of his graduate students. It was also partly a result of the small scale of the British academy. In the USA there were sufficient sociologists of religion to support narrowly discipline-based journals and annual conferences. In the UK, the sociological study of religion has always attracted students from arts and humanities backgrounds.[17]

In one sense, sociologists should be flattered that much of the work that is now done in theology, divinity, and religious studies departments has sociological overtones, and there have been clear benefits for sociologists of religion in mixing with experts in the history and ideological content of the phenomena they study. But two general problems arise from the undisciplined borrowing by arts students of elements of the social sciences.

The first is that many of the outsiders who engage with sociological ideas do so from a position of relative ignorance. The secularization thesis, for example, is routinely denounced by people whose acquaintance with it is largely second-hand and whose acquaintance with the deeper sociological background is nil. There is no reason why scholars of religion in the arts and humanities should be familiar with Talcott Parsons or Robert Merton, but that they are not makes their confident critiques of the sociological secularization paradigm somewhat presumptuous.

The second problem is a general lack of interest in the theory and practice of social research and a particular blind spot about appropriate evidence. Almost invariably, whenever I speak on secularization, someone in the audience will rebut my arguments by telling me that his or her church or spiritual movement is growing. It should be obvious that a national decline in the total levels of religiosity is quite compatible with small pockets of growth: the declining number of the faithful reorganize around the most popular outlets. What matters are the totals. There is little or no value in vague assertions about "the re-enchantment" of Britain if they are not supported by evidence that the total amount of enchantment (the conventionally religious plus those interested in alternative forms of spirituality) is now greater than the same figure for 1950 or 1850. When I offer that response, I am confronted with the ineffability trump card: I am told that we cannot "really" measure religiosity. Such capitulation might be acceptable if scholars confined themselves to description or exposition, but they frequently make unsupported claims about the relative popularity or influence of some religious or spiritual beliefs, or they present some grand, sweeping claim about the change in the Zeitgeist as an explanation for the apparent rise of whatever interests them.

But even if such reticence was consistently sustained, the foundation for it seems unwarranted. Although it has taken a very long time for this to become clear to me, I now realize that I have always rejected the idea that religion is so unlike other social phenomena that it cannot be studied in the same way that we might study a political ideology such as nationalism. That believers think their religion is unique is no reason why we as analysts should shrink from treating it like any other cultural production. We can ask why nationalism becomes popular in certain times and places, what purposes it served, for whom, and the like. We can study why one language loses out to another and we can examine the structural conditions necessary for the reproduction of a minority language. Complex social phenomena are not easy to study but, provided we are clear that we are not in the business of judging their truth claims, I see no reason why we should not study religions in the same ways that we study anything else. That is, the sociology of religion is in principle no different from the sociology of sport, of politics, or of anything else.

Counting things (and multi-variate analysis is just clever counting) is not the only method of understanding, but it is unavoidable for any exercise other than pure description, and even then it is hard to imagine how one would, for example, comprehend the importance of something for a certain group of people (patriarchy for conservative Catholics, for example) without implicitly counting evidences of patriarchy and evidences of matriarchy and finding more of the former than the latter. And it is impossible to move beyond the description of some group to making any claim about its importance without implicitly making statistical claims. Without appropriate statistical evidence, vague assertions of religious revival or re-enchantment or a post-secular Europe are mere gossip. Of course a good grounding in the philosophy and methods of large-scale social research is no guarantee of worthwhile outputs, but that so much of what appears from a distance to be the social scientific study of religion is the work of people who do not, for example, understand tests of significance, is a handicap rarely acknowledged.

Not my ain folk

In 1967 Howard Becker published a controversial paper on the sociology of deviance entitled "Whose Side Are We On?"[18] Although it was an exaggeration of Becker's less contentious case that research has political consequences, it was widely taken at the time as a call for partisanship: the sociologist of deviance should not just study deviants but should stand up for them. Feminists later made the same case and I can recall two of my teachers from Stirling, Russell and Rebecca Dobash (who were among the first people to study domestic violence), arguing that value-neutral research was bad form: we should give something back to the people we studied by helping to improve their circumstances. The notion of the committed researcher had a certain romantic appeal, but as a prescription for the profession it was clearly wrong-headed. While working on *The Red Hand* I was interviewing people who murdered others for political gain. Far from wanting to aid my subjects, I was struggling with the moral imperative to prevent further serious crime by shopping my informants. Taken seriously, the requirement for sociologists to become "engaged" could only mean that we would be confined to studying either people we liked or Snow White and the Seven Dwarfs.

Although it was never a conscious choice (utility-maximizing or otherwise), I have spent my entire career studying people whose views I do not share. In retrospect, this seems a wise choice, and it is one I would now recommend to any young scholar for this reason: personal indifference balances professional sympathy and thus reduces the dangers of going native. Among my original sociological heroes were the symbolic interactionists of the Chicago School. I was raised to believe that before you can explain the actions of a certain group of people it is important to understand them, and understanding requires close acquaintance. Hence the hours spent in prayer meetings, bible studies, and interminable conversations with Christians. I suspect that, had I been a believing Christian, I would have found it remarkably difficult to research and write about my subjects without taking sides.

In saying this, I am not accepting the relativist argument that we cannot transcend our own prejudices and biases. I remain committed to the pursuit of a value-neutral social science in which the key question is not "What are the personal preferences which cause this scholar to see the world in a particular light?" but "To what extent does the evidence support this or that explanation?" Although it may seem like an inhospitable rejection of the underlying purpose of this edited collection, I do not accept that our biographies are of any value in evaluating our research. That Grace Davie, David Martin, and Peter Berger are Christians may explain why they see more religion in modern societies than I do, but whether Davie is right that Britons are "believing but not belonging" depends on scientific testing of the claim.[19] I have benefitted enormously from 20 years of friendly argument with Paul Heelas about the significance of New Age or holistic spirituality. As he acknowledges in the introduction to *The Spiritualities of Life*, he is partisan: his biography is typical of the New Agers he studies and he shares their values.[20] That he is an insider and I am very much an outsider may explain our differing projections for the future of contemporary spirituality, but in the final analysis what matters is a critical internal examination of our theories and social scientific testing of those theories against the best available evidence.

My point about distance from one's subjects is not a methodological claim. I am not asserting that indifference guarantees valid observation. It is the narrower and more pragmatic claim that, as the professional requirement to understand will often cause us to sympathize with our subjects, a personal orientation that pulls in the other direction may help to maintain a sense of balance and perspective. In the end the production of sociological truth is, as Karl Popper argued for science in general, a collective activity which rests, not on the attitudes or personalities of individual researchers, but on the role of competition between researchers.[21] Nonetheless, it helps the enterprise along if the professionally required closeness to our subjects and subject matter is balanced by personal indifference.

Conclusion

Reflecting on one's intellectual career is somewhat embarrassing because, although one can introduce a note of humility by confessing to a few glaring errors, one has to assume that one has been rather successful – or else why the invitation? – when really that is something for others to decide. I certainly do not think of myself as having been a great innovator: while Rodney Stark has formulated two theories of religion, I have not managed one. The best I can claim is to have contributed something to our understanding of religious phenomena in the modern world by applying the basic sociological tools I acquired during a good undergraduate and postgraduate education. How much of this preference is temperament and how much the example of scholars such as Wilson, Martin, and Wallis I do not know, but I have always preferred historically and geographically grounded studies which test (and hopefully extend) theories of the "middle range" to grand, sweeping depictions of the Zeitgeist. Looking back on 35 years of studying religion sociologically, I cannot see that my own religious beliefs (or lack of them) have made any difference to my sociology of religion. What has made a difference is a commitment to sociology as a social science and a concomitant interest in the testing of manageable propositions through systematic comparison. Perhaps those dreary weeks of counting drosophila melanogaster did leave their mark after all.

Notes

1 Peter. L. Berger and Thomas Luckmann, *The Social Construction of Reality* (Harmondsworth: Penguin, 1970).
2 Elihu Katz, "The Two-Step Flow of Communication: An Up-To-Date Report on a Hypothesis," *The Public Opinion Quarterly* 21(1) (1957): 61–78; Robert K. Merton, *Mass Persuasion: The Social Psychology of a War Bond Drive* (New York: Harper & Brothers, 1946).
3 Roy Wallis, "Ideology, Authority and the Development of Cultic Movements," *Social Research* 41 (1974): 299–327; *The Road to Total Freedom: A Sociological Analysis of Scientology* (London: Heinemann, 1976), 13.
4 David Martin, *The Dilemmas of Contemporary Religion* (Oxford: Blackwell, 1978), 9.
5 Steve Bruce, *A House Divided: Protestantism, Schism and Secularization* (London: Routledge, 1990); Steve Bruce, *Religion in the Modern World: From Cathedrals to Cults* (Oxford: Oxford University Press, 1996).
6 Dean Kelley, *Why the Conservative Churches Are Growing* (New York: Harper & Row, 1972).
7 Paul Heelas and Linda Woodhead, *The Spiritual Revolution: Why Religion is Giving Way to Spirituality* (Oxford: Blackwell, 2005).

8 Linda Woodhead, "Why so Many Women in Holistic Spirituality?," in Kieran Flanagan and Peter C. Jupp, *A Sociology of Spirituality* (Aldershot: Ashgate, 2007), 124, says "The holistic milieu … is inhospitable to many forms of male identity based upon the negation of the female. The way in which both academic and popular discourses often dismiss such spirituality as 'pseudoscientific,' 'pampering,' 'trivial,' 'diverting' … is a sign of this unease."

9 Steve Bruce, "Defining Religion: A Practical Response," *International Review of Sociology* 21 (2010): 105–118.

10 Steve Bruce, *Secularization: In Defence of an Unfashionable Theory* (Oxford: Oxford University Press, 2010).

11 Steve Bruce, *God Save Ulster: the Religion and Politics of Paisleyism* (Oxford: Oxford University Press, 1986).

12 Steve Bruce, *No Pope of Rome: Militant Protestantism in Modern Scotland* (Edinburgh: Mainstream, 1985); *The Red Hand: Loyalist Paramilitaries in Northern Ireland* (Oxford: Oxford University Press, 1992); *The Edge of the Union: The Ulster Loyalist Political Vision* (Oxford: Oxford University Press, 1994).

13 Steve Bruce, *Pray TV: Televangelism in America* (London: Routledge, 1990); *The Rise and Fall of the New Christian Right* (Oxford: Oxford University Press, 1988).

14 Steve Bruce, *Fundamentalism* (Cambridge: Polity Press, 2001).

15 Steve Bruce, *Religion and Choice: a Critique of Rational Choice Theory* (Oxford: Oxford University Press, 1999).

16 When, in 2002, I became head of a school of social science with 60 members of staff, I discovered that only three were competent to teach a statistics course. That gap was filled by recruiting Germans, Austrians, Americans, and Canadians, all of whom were numerate.

17 For example, probably a majority of those who attend the annual conference of the British Sociological Association's study group of religion are not sociologists. There is no UK sociology of religion journal. Although much of what is published in the excellent *Journal of Contemporary Religion* reads like sociology, many of its authors have been trained in the arts and humanities.

18 Howard Becker, "Whose Side Are We On?," *Social Problems* 14 (1967): 239–247.

19 Grace Davie, *Religion in Britain Since 1945: Believing Without Belonging* (Oxford: Blackwell, 1994). For an empirical test, see David Voas and Alasdair Crockett, "Religion in Britain: Neither Believing nor Belonging," *Sociology* 39 (2005): 11–28.

20 Paul Heelas, *Spiritualities of Life: New Age Romanticism and Consumptive Capitalism* (Oxford: Blackwell, 2008).

21 Karl Popper, *Conjectures and Refutations* (London: Routledge & Kegan Paul, 1963).

9

SERENDIPITY IN THE STUDY OF RELIGION AND SOCIETY[1]

Mark Chaves

> This discovery, indeed, is almost of that kind which I call *Serendipity*, a very expressive word, which, as I have nothing better to tell you, I shall endeavor to explain to you: you will understand it better by the derivation than by the definition. I once read a silly fairy tale, called *The Three Princes of Serendip*: as their Highnesses travelled, they were always making discoveries, by accidents and sagacity, of things which they were not in quest of.
>
> (Horace Walpole, in a letter to Horace Mann, January 28, 1754)[2]

Observers of scientific research as it actually is pursued rather than as standard research articles represent it have long known that serendipity – the happy accident – often plays a central role. The surprising result, the chance conversation with a friend or colleague, the offhand observation, the unanticipated event: the history of science is filled with discoveries that would not have happened or, at least, would not have happened when and where they did, without occurrences like these.[3]

I am struck by the extent to which serendipity has shaped my own research, so I will take the opportunity offered by the invitation to contribute to this volume to describe three instances of serendipity in my research. I will then offer several reflections about what these experiences might suggest more generally about serendipity's influence on research, and what it might mean in practice to take that influence seriously.

Serendipity and over-reporting church attendance

In 1993, C. Kirk Hadaway, Penny Long Marler, and I published an article documenting for the first time substantial over-reporting of church attendance in surveys of Americans.[4] This article would not exist were it not for several happy accidents.

From my point of view, the story begins with Kirk Hadaway's visit to Loyola University Chicago in the spring of 1992.[5] Kirk came to Loyola to conduct a workshop on the sociology of religion. The workshop was intended for graduate students, but as a brand-new assistant professor who specialized in the sociology of religion and who had admired Kirk's work since I was an undergraduate, I was eager to participate.

At this workshop Kirk told us about the research he and Penny had recently completed in Ashtabula County, Ohio. They had identified every Protestant church in the county, gathered worship service attendance counts from each church, and conducted a survey in the county that asked respondents about their church attendance. They discovered that the conventional survey massively overstated actual weekly church attendance in Ashtabula: 36 percent in their survey, 20 percent in their counts. Kirk and Penny had written a paper that reported this result along with results from other research they had done on church attendance trends, but they had not yet published this finding.

I do not remember anything else about this Loyola workshop, but I remember being tremendously impressed by this Ashtabula discovery. I was impressed by the sheer shoe-leather-burning energy that Kirk and Penny had put into this research: they drove down every road in the county to make sure they found all the Protestant churches, and for churches that did not provide attendance counts they estimated attendance by visiting on Sunday mornings and counting the cars parked outside. And I was impressed by the striking result, which, despite being based on only Protestants in only one county in the country, seemed to me to provide indisputable evidence that weekly church attendance in the United States was much lower than it was commonly believed to be.

I was so impressed by this Ashtabula result that I often mentioned it in conversation over the weeks and months following Kirk's visit to Loyola. One of those conversations was with Ruth Doyle, who worked in the research office of the Roman Catholic Archdiocese of New York. I happened to sit next to Ruth in the audience of a session at the 1992 annual meetings of the Society for the Scientific Study of Religion and the Religious Research Association. I do not remember what the session was about or who presented at it, and I do not remember exactly how the subject came up, but I distinctly recall chatting with Ruth as we waited for the session to begin. I was telling her about Kirk's and Penny's Ashtabula result, and I said something like, "It's too bad we don't have count data from other places that we could use to corroborate the Ashtabula result." Ruth said something like, "Well, you know, many Catholic dioceses do something called the 'October Count,' an effort to count every person who attends mass on a given weekend or weekends in October." I had never heard of the October Count, but I was excited to learn about it. How many dioceses conducted an October Count? Would dioceses which conducted them share their data with a researcher interested in church attendance rates? Ruth wasn't sure.

Back at the office after the conference, I made a lot of phone calls, starting with members of the Catholic Research Forum, a group of researchers who worked in diocesan offices doing research on and for their dioceses. The upshot was that I relatively quickly identified 18 Catholic dioceses which conducted high-quality October Counts and which would share their data with me.

Having these count data from 18 Catholic dioceses was very exciting, but there was a piece missing. These counts gave excellent estimates of how many people attended Catholic mass in these dioceses on an average weekend in October, but they provided only the numerator of a count-based church attendance rate for Catholics. How could we get the denominator? Diocesan researchers could tell us how many registered Catholics there were in each diocese, but the number of registered Catholics clearly was not the right denominator. We needed a count-based Catholic attendance rate analogous to the Catholic attendance rate produced by conventional surveys, which meant that we needed an estimate of the number of self-identified Catholics in each diocese. How could that be obtained?

Here enters the last serendipitous part of this story. It just so happened that in 1990 Barry Kosmin and Ariela Keysar had conducted the first wave of what was then called the National Survey of Religious Identification (NSRI). This survey of a nationally representative sample of Americans gathered data from 113,000 respondents, which meant that there would be enough respondents within each Catholic diocese to calculate, in conjunction with total population data from the 1990 US census, a reasonably reliable estimate of the percentage of self-identified Catholics in each diocese.[6] Since Catholic diocese boundaries are coterminous with county boundaries, and since the NSRI data contained county identifiers for each respondent, aggregating the NSRI data up to the level of the diocese would provide, within a reasonable margin of error, the percentage of self-identified Catholics within each diocese for which I had October Counts. I gave Barry and Ariela a list of the 18 dioceses and the counties that composed them, and they graciously sent me a green-and-white-striped computer printout of a table containing, for each diocese, the number of NSRI respondents and the percentage of self-identified Catholics. Bringing in the 1990 US census population data, it was a short step from the percentage of self-identified Catholics in a diocese to an estimated number of self-identified Catholics in the diocese. Here was the denominator of a count-based attendance rate for Catholics in these 18 dioceses, *circa* 1990.[7]

I do not have the literary skill to convey the drama of the evening in my office when I had in front of me all of these pieces of information – the counts from 18 dioceses, the percent Catholic in each diocese from the NSRI data, and the total population of each diocese from the 1990 US census – and set about using my hand calculator to calculate a count-based church attendance rate for Catholics in these dioceses. Nor do I have the literary skill to convey the excitement I felt when, after a couple of hours, I pushed the " = " button on the calculator for the final time and saw the result: 28 percent weekly attendance rate, compared to a 50 percent Catholic attendance rate produced by conventional surveys at that time. Wow. I was staring at the same result – massive over-reporting – that Kirk and Penny had found for Protestants in Ashtabula. I have never felt more like a scientist making a discovery than at that moment.

I called Kirk and suggested that we combine my Catholic results with his and Penny's Ashtabula result, and send the paper to the *American Sociological Review*. We did that, the reviewers liked the paper, and the editor accepted it quickly, without requiring any revisions. But that article would not exist if any one of these things had not happened: Kirk's visit to Loyola, a casual conversation with Ruth Doyle at a SSSR session, or the 1990 NSRI survey. There are, of course, many other things that had to happen for this article to exist. Catholic dioceses had to conduct October Counts, and Kirk and Penny had to have done their Ashtabula research, for example. Yet, what stands out for me are the parts of the story that seem most serendipitous, by which I mean the parts that seem the least intentionally related to the knowledge that emerged at the end of the story.[8]

Serendipity and women's ordination

I published my first book, *Ordaining Women: Culture and Conflict in a Religious Institution*, in 1997. But neither that book nor the research it reports would exist were it not for a happy accident of a different sort than the happy accidents behind the attendance over-reporting research and discoveries.

I no longer remember why I was browsing the 1989 edition of the *Yearbook of American and Canadian Churches* one day in 1991. I often use the *Yearbook* as a handy reference source for various kinds of contemporary and historical information about Protestant denominations. Its statistical tables provide the latest numerical information about denominational (self-reported) size. Its brief descriptions of each denomination help when one needs to recall some detail from American Protestantism's complex history of mergers and schisms. And even its list of denominations comes in handy when you need to confirm a denomination's official name. But, much as I love the *Yearbook* and appreciate the information it provides, I do not think I have ever turned to it expecting to find intellectual inspiration.

On this particular day, however, I stumbled upon a short list of denominations and the years in which they began to ordain women to full clergy status.[9] Skimming the list, I noticed a peculiar fact: the Methodist Church and the Presbyterian Church in the USA granted full clergy rights to women in the same year, 1956. This seemed strange in two ways. First, it seemed odd that two major denominations would have taken this step in the exact same year. Second, and more important, was the year itself: 1956. Indeed, I don't think a common year for both Methodists and Presbyterians beginning to ordain women would have seemed at all puzzling had that year been, say, 1976. But how did it come to pass that two major denominations institutionalized gender equality in 1956, in the middle of a decade commonly portrayed as the doldrums of the movement for gender equality, long after the first wave of the movement had climaxed in female suffrage and a decade before its second wave would begin in earnest?

This seemed a question worth answering, and I set out to answer it. Several initial hunches proved to be incorrect and, in the end, answering this question required historical and sociological research that occupied me for the next six years. A key part of the answer was the discovery that formal rules about women's ordination were often only loosely coupled with the day-to-day, practical realities of women's involvement in churches. When the Methodists and Presbyterians began ordaining women in 1956, they were doing something other than responding to the practical leadership needs of churches or the political pressure of large numbers of women wanting to enter the ordained ministry. Denominations' formal policies about women's ordination are about something more than the need to regulate or respond to what women are actually doing inside religious organizations. The curious will have to read my book to learn what the Methodists and Presbyterians were accomplishing by opening the leadership doors to women in the 1950s. Here, the point is that this research, and the discoveries and publications to which it led, would not have happened were it not for my stumbling quite accidentally upon a puzzling fact in the pages of the *Yearbook of American and Canadian Churches.*

Serendipity and the National Congregations Study

The National Congregations Study (NCS) is a survey of a nationally representative sample of religious congregations from across the religious spectrum. It gathers data about a wide range of congregational characteristics by interviewing a key informant, usually a clergyperson, from each sampled congregation. The NCS was first conducted in 1998. A second wave was conducted in 2006–2007, and a third wave is underway in 2012. The 1998 NCS broke new ground by surveying the first truly representative national sample of religious congregations. Even though social scientists had known for decades how to draw high-quality national samples of individuals, and even though there had been good national samples of some types of organizations at least since the 1980s, as of the late 1990s there was no high-quality national survey of congregations. The reason is straightforward: there is no comprehensive list of American congregations, so there was no good way to draw a random sample that would constitute a nationally representative sample of congregations.

The NCS overcame this obstacle by using a methodological innovation developed by sociologists who study other kinds of organizations. The key insight is that the set of organizations attached to a representative sample of individuals constitutes a representative sample of organizations. It is therefore possible to generate a representative sample of organizations even in the absence of a comprehensive list of units in the organizational population. One simply starts with a random sample of individuals and asks them to name the organization(s) to which they are attached.

Other scholars had used this strategy – called hypernetwork or multiplicity sampling – to sample voluntary associations and employing organizations. The 1998 NCS implemented this strategy for congregations. It did so with the help of the 1998 General Social Survey (GSS), an in-person interview of a representative sample of English-speaking adults in the United States, conducted since 1972 by the National Opinion Research Center at the University of Chicago. The 1998 GSS asked respondents who say they attend religious services at least once a year to report the name and location of their religious congregation. The congregations named by these respondents constituted the 1998 NCS congregational sample. The sample for the 2006–2007 NCS was generated in the same way, and the 2012 NCS-III sample will follow suit.[10]

But the NCS would not have happened were it not for several happy accidents.

The first piece of serendipity involved the General Social Survey. The GSS's Board of Overseers had decided to develop a 15-minute module of questions about religion for the 1998 GSS. Michael Hout, then GSS Board Chair, convened a small committee to develop this module. I was invited to join that committee, an invitation I was happy to accept. I recall lively conversation when some members of the committee met at a Chicago hotel in 1996 to discuss potential content for this module.

Not long after the GSS religion module committee had met, I was at home reading *Organizations in America: Analysing Their Structures and Human Resource Practices*.[11] I was not reading this book for any specific reason except that I tried to keep up on the sociology of organizations literature as well as the sociology of religion literature, and this was an important new book in the sociology of organizations. It reported results from the 1991 National Organizations Study (NOS), a survey of a nationally representative sample of employing organizations that was generated by asking respondents to the 1991 General Social Survey to tell investigators where they worked.

I do not remember if that evening was the first time I had opened that book. Nor do I recall whether or not I knew about the NOS before that evening. But that evening, as I was reading the book, it suddenly struck me: we could do this for congregations!

I immediately called Michael Hout, who liked the idea of using a few minutes of the GSS's 1998 religion module to ask respondents who attend religious services to tell us where they attend. Both the religion module committee and, eventually, the GSS Board supported using some survey time this way.

But generating the congregational sample using the 1998 GSS would be a waste of time unless we had the resources to gather data directly from the named congregations with a follow-up survey. So I also immediately called Chris Coble, a Program Officer in the Lilly Endowment's Religion Division, and here the last major serendipitous piece of the puzzle fell into place. The Lilly Endowment is well known as a significant source of support for much historical and sociological research about American religion. That was, of course, why I called Chris to see if the Endowment might be interested in funding a National Congregations Study. The serendipitous piece is that, unbeknownst to me, the Endowment had recently launched an initiative precisely on *congregations*, and so a national survey of congregations fitted the Endowment's funding priorities unusually well at that particular moment. Chris encouraged me to submit a proposal, and within a few months the first wave of the National Congregations Study was launched.

Perhaps something like the NCS would eventually have been developed, by me or by someone else, but it would certainly not have happened in 1998 without this conjunction of events: the GSS Board's interest in a religion module for the 1998 GSS, my participation in the committee to develop that module, my reading of

Organizations in America soon after that committee met, and the Lilly Endowment's congregations initiative. I do not think it would have been possible to anticipate or predict this conjunction of events that produced the NCS.

Conclusion

These three examples contain different kinds of happy accidents. In the church attendance example, social interactions with people who knew different kinds of things, along with the coincidental existence of a key data source, led to a new discovery. In the women's ordination example, stumbling upon a peculiar fact in a non-scholarly source prompted historical and sociological research aimed at solving the puzzle presented by that fact. In the NCS example, being part of the GSS religion module committee while reading a scholarly book on a subject unrelated to anything on which I was directly working produced an idea that would not otherwise have occurred to me – an idea that also happened to be in sync with a key funder's priorities.

Let me close with several reflections about these events.

First, serendipity played an important role in all of these projects, but there came a point in each project where intentional action took over. After learning about the October Counts and the NSRI data, I set about trying to establish a count-based weekly attendance rate for Catholics. After seeing the *Yearbook*'s list of dates at which certain denominations first ordained women, I developed a systematic research project aimed at explaining why denominations began ordaining women when they did, and why some still have not done so. After it occurred to me through a serendipitous set of circumstances that one could apply hypernetwork sampling to congregations, and after it became clear that the Lilly Endowment was interested in funding a survey of such a sample, I devoted myself to designing and executing a National Congregations Study that would add to basic knowledge about American religious congregations. In the development of each of these projects there came a point when intentional action took up where serendipity left off. Such a point probably must come in every process of scientific activity and discovery. Moreover, there are research projects I have pursued and discoveries I have made in which serendipity played no role. Some projects proceed from start to finish more or less as planned. Sometimes we discover things by looking for them.

So I do not mean to imply that serendipity rather than intentionality produced these projects, or that serendipity was the most important causal factor behind these projects. Even less do I mean to imply that serendipity is the most important generator of scientific discoveries in general. Indeed, serendipity can be recognized as serendipity only in retrospect, after intentional action has turned a chance occurrence into the source of something that turned out well. The beginnings of the three stories I have told may be understood as serendipity only because we know how they end.

The correct lesson to draw from these stories is a more modest one: serendipity sometimes helps move social science along and sometimes helps us find significant work to do. Even this modest conclusion, however, suggests that researchers will find more opportunities to make important contributions than they otherwise would if they can figure out how to harness serendipity. But how are we to do that? To put this another way: if serendipity amounts to being in the right place at the right time, the obvious question is how to maximize our chances of being in the right place at the right time. The following reflections concern this question.

It seems to me – and this is my second reflection – that these experiences reinforce Robert Merton's emphasis on the sociological rather than the psychological sources of serendipity in science. Some discussions of serendipity focus on the personal characteristics of people who seem to have benefitted from it, asking what it is that apparently makes some people better able than others to turn coincidence or accident into opportunity or discovery. But I agree with Merton that, rather than ask what type of person is more likely to take advantage of serendipity, it is better to ask what type of situation is more likely to produce productive serendipity. Merton mentions Harvard's Society of Fellows and Stanford's Center for Advanced Study in the Behavioral Sciences as two examples of what he calls "serendipitous socio-cognitive microenvironments." The key feature of these particular settings seems to be that, on the one hand, they do not require people to do anything except be present, presumably enabling them to focus better on important problems, and, on the other hand, they provide opportunities for smart people to interact with other smart people with whom they would not ordinarily interact. It makes sense that such places would help people make intellectual connections they would not otherwise have made.[12]

My third reflection, however, is that one does not have to be a Fellow at Harvard or Stanford to experience a serendipitious sociocognitive micro environment. The serendipity-producing social settings featured in my own experience include a visiting scholar's workshop at Loyola University, the annual meetings of the Society for the Scientific Study of Religion and the Religious Research Association (with its special mix of academics and denomination-based researchers), a library containing a run of *Yearbooks*, and a committee meeting convened to construct part of a survey. These settings are relatively mundane, but it is important to recognize that even these are not equally accessible to all scholars and researchers. Colleges and universities vary in their inclination and capacity to sponsor workshops and host visiting scholars, academics may not have the time or the money to attend professional meetings, libraries vary in the richness of their holdings, and committee meetings focused on survey construction are often attended by invitation only. And access to all of these settings is further restricted in tight economic times that affect the budgets of universities, libraries, and survey funders. Still, these examples illustrate that many researchers have opportunities to put themselves in situations in which they interact with people with whom they do not usually interact, and which encourage new kinds of reflection, even if, for most of us, these opportunities last for a few hours, or maybe a weekend, rather than for a semester or a year. My point here is that the routine infrastructure of academic life – colloquia, workshops, professional meetings, libraries – can be serendipitious sociocognitive micro environments. Such environments are more common than we might recognize. They exist to varying degrees in our everyday professional lives.

Fourth, while the right kinds of interactional micro environments are important for serendipity, my experiences suggest that social interaction by itself is not sufficient for productive serendipity. Without a norm that encourages both academic and denominational researchers to share data even with another researcher they have never met, the Catholic Church attendance discoveries could not have been made. Without a traditional reference publication like the *Yearbook*, held in a traditional university library, my research on women's ordination would not have come to be. Without reading a traditional scholarly monograph like *Organizations in America*, or without the infrastructure and resources provided by institutions like the Lilly Endowment and the General Social Survey, the NCS would not have been born. The point here is that we should not reduce "serendipitious sociocognitive micro environments" to smart people mingling with one another. That mingling is important, but the right kinds of norms (like sharing data), practices (like reading books somewhat outside one's area of specialization), and institutions (like the Lilly Endowment) also increase the chances of productive serendipity.

Fifth, the probability that productive serendipity will strike at any given moment is very low. It doesn't happen as often as we would like it to. I have attended many, many SSSR/RRA sessions over the years, and I have talked with many, many people at these meetings. But only once – that conversation with Ruth Doyle – did a specific conversation lead in an entirely unanticipated way to a specific research project. I have browsed many, many reference books and looked at many, many tables or lists of interesting facts, but only once – that *Yearbook* list of several denominations and the years they began ordaining women – did coming across such a list send me down a road to discovery. I have read many scholarly monographs while simultaneously serving on a committee of some sort (indeed, there have probably been very few days in my life since 1990 when I was not serving on some committee while also reading some book!), but only once – reading *Organizations in America* while serving on the GSS religion module committee – did such a conjunction light a bulb over my head.

I hesitate to try to calculate the odds of productive serendipity striking on any given day, but I think the action implications of this reflection are clear enough. Beyond the intrinsic value of attending SSSR (and other) conferences, reading widely, and even serving on (some kinds of) committees, the chances, however small, that one will stumble into a happy accident while pursuing these activities should increase our motivation to engage in them as often as we can. The long odds mean that, unless we are very lucky, we will have to do a lot of this sort of thing to experience serendipity even a very few times.

Sixth, if there is a personal characteristic that makes people better able to take advantage of serendipitous sociocognitive micro environments, I think it is a feel for questions and data that people will care about. Such feel is developed mainly, I think, by being embedded in networks within which ideas and resources circulate. This is what good graduate education provides: immersion in literatures and networks and experiences that develop students' ability to recognize the questions that are worth trying to answer and the data that people will find valuable. I do not think this capacity can be developed only by reading the literature. It is developed by listening closely to how people introduce their work when they only have five minutes to do so at the beginning of a conference presentation, to the questions people ask others about their work, to the things that people in a field talk about over drinks and meals, and to the things that people outside of academia are curious about. It is also developed by watching closely how active and productive researchers actually find, develop, and execute their research, which of course is often, perhaps always, entirely different from how they write about their research and its results in standard scientific articles and monographs. Any graduate program can require students to read journal articles and learn technical skills. The best graduate programs also provide the socialization, micro environments, and meaningful research experiences that develop students' capacity to recognize questions and data that people will care about.

My seventh, and final reflection is that serendipity's influence on research makes it difficult to predict what our most important work will be. We often ask candidates for academic jobs, "What's your next project?" I suppose it's good to have a compelling answer to that question, but both the asker and asked should recognize that an exchange like that should not be taken too literally. What we really want to know when assessing a young researcher's potential is, I think, something like this: Do you have a feel for what the important questions are, and are you putting yourself in situations and doing the things that are likely to present you with opportunities, as yet unknown, to make important contributions? I foresaw none of the three projects described in this chapter before I became immersed in them, and I would venture to say that a research career filled only with projects that were completely foreseen and executed as planned – a research career without any serendipity – is not the ideal kind of research career. It is, in any case, not the kind of career I have had.

Notes

1 Brad Fulton and Andrew Miles offered helpful comments on an earlier version of this chapter.
2 Quoted on page 2 of *The Travels and Adventures of Serendipity: A Study in Sociological Semantics and the Sociology of Science*, by Robert K. Merton and Elinor Barber (Princeton, NJ: Princeton University Press, 2004).
3 Many examples are given in Royston M. Roberts, *Serendipity: Accidental Discoveries in Science* (New York: Wiley, 1989).
4 C. Kirk Hadaway, Penny Long Marler and Mark Chaves, "What the Polls Don't Show: A Closer Look at U.S. Church Attendance," *American Sociological Review* 58 (1993): 741–752.
5 I am reconstructing from memory this and the other two stories I will relate in this chapter. I have not tried to verify all the dates and other details. I believe these stories to be accurate in every respect, but I also know, and readers should keep in mind, that memory is fallible.
6 The 1990 NSRI was repeated in 2001 and 2008. It is now called the American Religious Identity Survey. Details about this survey may be found at http://commons. trincoll.edu/aris/.

7 Later, Jim Cavendish and I eventually gathered October Count data from 48 dioceses, containing 38 percent of all US Catholics, which I believe was every Catholic diocese that did a high-quality count at that time. The result was the same. See Mark Chaves and James C. Cavendish, "More Evidence on U.S. Catholic Church Attendance," *Journal for the Scientific Study of Religion* 33 (1994): 376–381.

8 Perhaps I should note for the historical record that there are two parts of this story, both about timing, that I am aware of not remembering clearly. The first is that I do not remember the exact point in the sequence of events when I contacted Barry Kosmin about using the NSRI data. Did I do that after gathering all the October Count data? Before gathering it? In the midst of gathering it? I don't recall. The other is that I do not remember the exact point at which I called Kirk and suggested that we join forces on a single article reporting both their Ashtabula results and my October Count results. Did I call before I knew what the October Count data would show, perhaps because the Ashtabula and October Count results would be interesting to put together whether they told the same story or different stories? Or did I call only after I knew that the October Counts gave the same result that Kirk and Penny found in Ashtabula? I believe it's the latter, and that sequence is more dramatic, so that's how I told the story. I hope I'm not remembering it this way only because it's more dramatic, but the truth is that I don't clearly recall when in the sequence of events I called Kirk to propose joining forces.

9 The list was in Constant H. Jacquet, "Women Ministers in 1986 and 1977: A Ten Year View," in *Yearbook of American and Canadian Churches* (New York: Office of Research and Evaluation, National Council of Churches, 1989), 261–266.

10 For more about the National Congregations Study and some of what we have learned from it, see Mark Chaves, *Congregations in America* (Cambridge, MA: Harvard University Press, 2004), and Mark Chaves, *American Religion: Contemporary Trends* (Princeton, NJ: Princeton University Press, 2011). See also the NCS website: http://www.soc.duke.edu/natcong/.

11 Arne L. Kalleberg, David Knoke, Peter V. Marsden, and Joe L. Spaeth, *Organizations in America: Analysing Their Structures and Human Resource Practices* (Thousand Oaks, CA: Sage, 1996).

12 Merton discusses serendipitous sociocultural micro-environments, and the ways in which Harvard's Society of Fellows and Stanford's Institute were important for Thomas Kuhn's work on scientific revolutions, in the Afterword to his book with Elinor Barber, *The Travels and Adventures of Serendipity*. See esp. pp. 260–266.

10

THINKING SOCIOLOGICALLY ABOUT RELIGION

Discerning and explaining pattern

Grace Davie

I am a baby-boomer: that is to say I was born immediately after the war, was educated at public expense and am now retiring with a final salary pension. I take none of this for granted but I am not altogether nostalgic for what is frequently termed a "golden age." For a start, relatively few of my generation had the privilege of a university education and even fewer of these were women. In this sense things have most certainly improved.[1] In my own case, the lack of opportunity for most women was largely offset by the encouragement of an academic family, the opportunity to travel at an early age, and a high-flying girls' school where the bar was set unusually high, though in a limited range of subjects. Only later did I realize how exceptional all this was and the significance of both gender and generation for my career. The paragraphs that follow expand on this story and its implications for my engagement in the sociology of religion.

Education and early career

I prospered in a school which demanded high academic standards and went to the University of Exeter to read sociology (well away from Cambridge where the subject did not exist). Why Exeter? To be honest I don't know, but it was there that I encountered the formidable Margaret Hewitt, the author of *Wives and Mothers in Victorian Industry*, first published in 1958.[2] In the 1960s and 1970s Margaret Hewitt was engaged, with Ivy Pinchbeck, in an impressive two-volume study on the social concern for children in Britain, ranging from Tudor paternalism in the 16th century to the establishment of the welfare state in the mid-20th century. In the second volume, the authors reveal how a deep unease about the abuses suffered by industrially exploited children prompted new legislation and a degree of community support.[3] Nowadays, this very significant contribution to social history is recalled less often than Hewitt's conservative, at times reactionary, views expressed in the General

Synod of the Church of England where she was popularly known as "Hewitt the hat." I do not agree with Margaret Hewitt's resistance to change in the church, but I do appreciate the fact that she introduced me to the sociology of religion in lectures that sparkled with interesting, not to say acerbic, asides.

Graduating in 1967, I wanted initially to develop my interests in sociological theory, making use of the fact that I was a moderately competent French speaker. I went to the London School of Economics with this in mind. As so often happened in those more leisurely days (completion rates were not an issue), my topic morphed after a while into a study of the French Protestant community in the inter-war period – focusing on an atypical political movement know as the "Association Sully."[4] The group was tiny (a minority within a minority), but allowed me to grasp the contradictory pressures of French politics in the 1920s and 1930s. It was here, most importantly, that I first understood how historical, political, and cultural contexts impinge upon religious ideas and the people and organizations that carry them. I needed to know why the French Protestant community as a whole leant to the left politically well into the post-war period; I also needed to know what encouraged a fraction of this group to move in the other direction.

Central to this discovery was the influence of David Martin, who – though never formally my supervisor – encouraged my progress as a doctoral student more than anyone else. In retrospect, I realize that out paths crossed at the precise moment that David was working out the argument for the *General Theory of Secularization*.[5] The French Protestants were simply one case among many in the path-breaking account of secularization that became the "general theory." David's influence was formative – in more ways than one. It was at this point that I grasped that the primary task of sociology was to discern and to explain pattern – in other words, to establish and to reflect on the non-random nature of human living, including the religious dimensions of this. It was also David Martin who set me on my way in the sociology of religion. But, as I indicated in the preface to *Religion in Britain since 1945*, he then had the patience to do the whole thing over again some ten years later, after what is best described as prolonged maternity leave.[6]

By the time that I had finished my doctorate I was living in Liverpool and had two small children, who were joined very soon by a third. My decision to take substantial time out from my career to raise a family was entirely typical of my generation – second wave feminism was barely off the ground. Much more positively, I recall this stage in my life with real pleasure. I was busy, not least because I committed significant amounts of time to voluntary activities in the city and diocese of Liverpool. The fact that this coincided with a turbulent period in the political life of Merseyside was in some ways a plus (I learnt a lot about local politics); equally interesting was the transformation of Liverpool from a city of sectarian animosity into a striking example of ecumenical endeavor. The interconnections of religion and urban life were played out in front of my eyes.

A phone call from David Martin in the early 1980s offered me an opportunity to reflect sociologically upon these activities. My first commission took the form of two reports on the Bishops of the Church of England (both Diocesans and Suffragans), which had limited circulation but taught me a lot about the church;[7] the second was a background study for the Archbishops' Commission on Urban Priority Areas, the body which produced the much-discussed *Faith in the City*.[8] My own contribution was published separately a year or so later in a book co-authored with Geoffrey Ahern, entitled *Inner City God: The Nature of Belief in the Inner City*.[9] One thing had led to another and would – I hoped – continue to do so.

Returning to work

In a sense this was true, but not as I had expected. In 1987, we moved again – as the result of my husband's career – this time back to Exeter. Given my incipient interest in the urban church, this did not feel propitious; I was on the other hand moving back to my old university, though to a very different department from the one that I had left. My colleagues, however, were welcoming in the sense that I was encouraged to "join in"; I also undertook some hourly rate tutoring. It was several years before anything resembling a job became available – for which I had to apply like everyone else. For all these reasons I remain deeply sympathetic both to women who have taken a career break in order to raise a family, and to those (in later generations) who are so fearful of not being able to get back into their careers that they continue to work under huge pressure at the same time as raising a family. Neither situation is easy to manage, a state of affairs that has little to do with gender as such, and everything to do with the gendered nature of care – something that I was to reflect on professionally much later in my career (see below). In the meantime, I found myself finally with a full-time permanent post in 1994 – when I was not far short of my fiftieth birthday. That said, I had already been teaching the sociology of religion for a number of years, due largely to the untimely death of Margaret Hewitt when she was acting Head of Department. How the wheel turns.

The books

The date of my appointment turned out to be significant in another sense. It was then that I published *Religion in Britain since 1945*, a book that made a difference – not only to me. Its subtitle, "Believing without belonging," became a touchstone for debate about religion in British society, and indeed beyond. It is difficult to remember how this phrase arose, but it was first used in public in a paper presented in 1989 at the Helsinki meeting of the International Society for the Sociology of Religion, and was published a year later.[10] Believing without belonging became the *fil conducteur* of the 1994 book. Given its continuing significance, it is important to underline how I understood my work:

> The terms "believing" and "belonging" are not to be considered too rigidly. The disjunction between the variables is intended to capture a mood, to suggest an area of enquiry, a way of looking at the problem, not to describe a detailed set of characteristics. Operationalizing either or both of the variables too severely is bound to distort the picture.[11]

Operationalized they were, however – constantly, as a wide variety of scholars and practitioners tried to prove or disprove what I had said. But as I indicated from the start, "the question very quickly becomes semantic, for it is clear that we need some way, if not this one, of describing the persistence of the sacred in contemporary society despite the undeniable decline in churchgoing."[12] The issue remains whatever the terminology deployed. Whatever the case, the publication of *Religion in Britain* opened a huge variety of doors – a growing number of invitations to speak at conferences (academic and other) and ever more opportunities to participate in the ongoing debate about religion in modern Britain. I enjoyed this immensely.

The next step was a double one. My interest in the relationship between religion and modernity continued, but on a wider canvas. Specifically, I was invited to explore the place of religion in modern Europe within a series on European Societies edited by Colin Crouch, published by Oxford University Press. The title of my book was entirely descriptive – *Religion in Modern Europe* does not excite – and this time the subtitle "A memory mutates" did not capture the imagination in the same way as believing without belonging.[13] It did however illustrate my growing connections with the sociologists of religion in France, among them Danièle Hervieu-Léger, whose work on religion as a form of collective memory was formative for my thinking.[14] The French connection will be examined in more detail below. At this point it is important to recall that *Religion in Modern Europe* also introduced a second concept which, in my view, is more helpful than believing without belonging in understanding the religious situation in both Britain and Europe, despite the continued popularity of the latter.

"Vicarious religion" is differently nuanced. The separating out of belief from belonging undoubtedly offered fruitful ways in which to understand and to organize the material about religion in modern Europe. Up to a point it also captured the space between the hard and soft variables concerning religious attachments: belief normally gathers a wider constituency than belonging. Ongoing reflection about the present situation, however, has encouraged me to reflect more deeply about this relationship. It is quite clear, for example, that "belief" can be both hard and soft, as indeed can "belonging." It was in thinking about the latter that the notion of vicarious religion began to emerge. It was a way of describing the continuing attachment of large sections of the European population to their historic churches, whether or not they attended these institutions on a regular basis. I concluded that the idea of vicarious religion, as *the notion of religion performed by an active minority but on behalf of a much larger number, who (implicitly at least) not only understand, but, quite clearly, approve of what the minority is doing* was a helpful contribution to the sociological debate. I began to explore this notion in the book concerned with religion in Europe and have refined it in subsequent publications.[15]

Large numbers of people (scholars, journalists, practitioners, and commentators of various kinds) agree with me. But not everyone is equally positive. It is unwise to generalize, but on the whole those who resist the idea of vicarious religion fall into the same category as those who resist the notion of believing without belonging, and for the same reasons. They operationalize both too severely. Over-rigorous attempts at clarity destroy the subtlety not only of the concept under scrutiny but of the reality that lies beneath. In retrospect I realize that something more serious was at stake in these debates: they reveal different philosophies of science which have profound implications for methodology. Social life is not merely an aggregate of individual attitudes and behaviors, amenable to quantitative assessment, valuable though this may be. It is a subtle, many-layered, and constantly evolving entity which requires imaginative thinking in order to be properly understood. Vicarious religion is an attempt to respond creatively to this challenge.

In the meantime, my own writing moved on, but at this point the narrative takes a rather different turn. No longer could I simply enlarge the scope of what I was doing – from inner city, to modern Britain, to Western Europe. It is simply not the case that the patterns of religious activity discovered in this relatively limited corner of the globe are those of the modern world more generally. *Europe: the Exceptional Case*, published in 2002, deals with these issues by reversing the "normal" question: instead of asking what Europe *is* in terms of its religious existence, it asks what Europe is not. It is not (yet) a vibrant religious market such as that found in the United States; it is not a part of the world where Christianity is growing exponentially, very often in Pentecostal forms, as is the case in the southern hemisphere (Latin America, Sub-Saharan Africa, and the Pacific Rim); it is not a part of the world dominated by faiths other than Christian, but is increasingly penetrated by these; and it is not for the most part subject to the violence often associated with religion and religious difference in other parts of the globe – the more so if religion becomes entangled in political conflict. Hence the inevitable, if at times disturbing conclusion: that the patterns of religion in modern Europe, notably its relative secularity, may be an exceptional case in global terms.[16]

Jumping ahead, rather similar ideas have been explored further in a more recent publication, this time co-authored with Peter Berger and Effie Fokas. *Religious America, Secular Europe* appeared in 2008.[17] It emerged from a series of meetings in Berlin concerned initially with European secularity. Its eventual publication, coinciding with Barack Obama's election as President, was nothing if not timely. The book is made up of a theme and variations, each of which explores in some detail why the religious scene in America is so different from that in Europe. In a nutshell, a series of factors come together in the United States to form an upward spiral: "nation building, economic expansion, rapid urbanization, and an influx of new people interact positively to promote growth rather than decline in the religious sector."[18] Each of these factors supports the others, leading, for better or for worse, to a continuing religious vitality – a far cry from the vicissitudes of Europe's state churches in the same period.

An article that brings much of the above together was published in 2006 – I am particularly proud of this summary and have used it as the basis of countless presentations to a very wide range of audiences.[19] Its title – "Religion in Modern Europe: The Factors to Take into Account" – is self-explanatory. The crucial point to grasp is that the factors in question push and pull in different directions. As old models decline, new forms of religious activity emerge, some of them encouraged by newly arrived populations. The current, somewhat paradoxical, situation may be summarized as follows. There is without doubt a continuing (if uneven) process of secularization in most European societies, offset by growth in some areas. Most worrying of all is a pervasive loss of religious literacy. At the same time, however, few would deny the increasing salience of religion in *public* life, a tendency encouraged by the ever more obvious presence of religion in the modern world order. What follows, predictably enough, is a debate of poor quality about religious issues, punctuated by moments of moral panic. Neither constitutes a sound basis for policy making.

My current thinking reflects this situation and has developed in two rather different directions. In the first instance, it has found expression in a book commissioned by Sage for their Millennium Series, which reflects on why the subject matter of the sociology of religion has developed in the way that it has.[20] Why, in other words, have certain aspects of the research agenda received disproportionate attention and what are the consequences for sociological understanding? The text becomes in fact a critical appraisal of both content and method within the sociology of religion, underlining the importance of contextual factors for the development of the discipline in different parts of the world (the comparative element is central). It was published in May 2007 and has been widely translated.[21] A new edition is in progress which, among other things, asks what has happened since 2007. More specifically it reflects on the multiple research programs currently focused on religion in many parts of the world, the reasons for this unprecedented activity, and the implications for mainstream social science. An essay in the ARDA Guiding Paper Series offers an overview of my reflections.[22]

A second strand of research is very different. It has developed out of my links with Swedish colleagues at Uppsala University (see below), which have led in turn to a series of European-wide collaborative projects on religion and welfare. The first of these, "Welfare and Religion in a European Perspective" (WREP, 2003–2006), was funded by the Tercentenary Foundation of the Bank of Sweden; the second, "Welfare and Values in Europe" (WaVE, 2006–2009), was financed by the European Commission, under the Framework 6 program. Both are central to the understanding of modern European societies and bring together – empirically as well as theoretically – two distinct fields of enquiry: the sociology of religion and social policy. So far, two co-edited books are the fruit of these endeavors.[23] Once again they have appeared when the issues at stake were repeatedly rehearsed in public debate. They concern the place of religion in the public sphere, the anxieties on the part of all Europeans regarding the future of the welfare state, and the centrality of gender to both issues.

It was for this reason that I began to reflect in new ways on the significance of gender both for the understanding of religion itself *and* for those who study it. From the north to the south of Europe, it is women who are disproportionately present in the day-to-day delivery of welfare, as they are in the activities of the church. Both spheres, conversely, are very largely managed by men. More profoundly, this situation was entirely taken for granted; from Finland to Greece, the answer to our enquiries was always the same: women do the caring because they are better at it, just as women do the praying – on behalf of everyone else (an interesting echo of vicarious religion).

An excursus on methodological atheism

As I made clear in *The Sociology of Religion*, the primary task of sociology is the discernment and explanation of pattern. The sociology of religion, it follows, unpacks the patterns of social living associated with religion in all its diverse forms, and attempts to establish explanations for the data that emerge. It is not, conversely, concerned with the competing truth claims of the great variety of belief systems that are present in human societies. That does not mean that sociologists themselves have no (religious) beliefs of their own: some do and some don't. It does mean, more often than not, that – following Peter Berger – they approach their work as "methodological atheists," suspending personal judgments about religion (their own included) while they are engaged in their academic work.[24]

I do not dissent from this position, but over the years I have come to think about it in new ways. Effective sociology involves understanding as fully as possible the individuals, groups, organizations, and institutions under review – and this surely must start with the sociologist him- or herself. Rather than suspending personal judgments or beliefs, I think that these should be much more carefully articulated in order that they may be taken into account. All of us, social scientists included, bring something to the table – pretending that we don't is simply disingenuous. Worse still is the implication that "religious" baggage is in some way a problem whereas secular views are not. I am an atheist, therefore I can study religion without bias, is not a helpful approach. I warm much more to those who are acutely aware of their own "formation" (national, social, intellectual, religious or whatever) and appreciate that this can deployed both positively and negatively. Those who "know themselves" are much more likely to understand the views of others.

I, for example, am acutely aware that I approach my work as a moderately active member of the Church of England, a position that brings with it a multitude of contacts (Anglicans are good at that) and a capacity to understand this particular institution, and its equivalents, in ways that an outsider cannot. I am equally aware of the downside: that my judgments may be coloured by this situation – just like the opinions of those who come from a different ideological position but in a different way. A second point follows from this: establishing one's own "standpoint" is not a once-and-for-all action; it is an ongoing process of self-scrutiny, making sure that in every piece of research or writing "positionality" is properly dealt with. And what I do myself, I expect of others. For instance, I always look for this capacity when examining a MPhil or PhD thesis and, more often than not, probe further in the viva – some fascinating discussions ensue.

People, places, and professional organizations

A cursory look at my CV indicates a prolonged connection with the University of Exeter (in various capacities) and not much else in terms of regular employment. In a sense this is true, for the reasons stated above. I am more than grateful to the Department of Sociology in Exeter for setting me on my way in the sociology of religion, and for offering me the chance to relaunch my career some 20 years later. I have benefitted in countless ways. It was here, for example, that I did most of my teaching – both to undergraduates and Masters students, across a wide range of subjects (including European Studies). More recently I have had the privilege of working with some outstanding doctoral students. On the threshold of retirement, I am sure of one thing: that I will miss the classroom very much, glad as I will be to escape the marking. I have also appreciated warm friendships with some very distinctive colleagues in a department which places a strong emphasis on culture. All that said, there are a number of other people, places, and organizations to take into account.

The French connection

I have had the good fortune to be able to speak French for most of my adult life, a facility which has enabled particular possibilities. These presented themselves initially in an invitation to take an active part in the bilingual International Society for the Sociology of Religion (SISR).[25] Prompted by Eileen Barker, I had already been convenor of the British Sociological Association's Sociology of Religion Study Group – a group that, among other things, did much for my confidence as I returned to the profession after a decade or so away. It has been a pleasure to see the group grow, year on year. And it was Eileen, once again, who suggested that I might stand for election as secretary general of the SISR. Standing for election was a euphemism; it was more a question of twisting someone's arm. I was very glad to accept however and despite some tricky moments before and during the two major conferences for which I was responsible, I gained far more than I lost during my four years in post. I also acquired congenial colleagues all over Europe and beyond, not least a distinguished group of French sociologists.

My initial return to things French had in fact happened rather earlier, triggered by the celebrations surrounding the Revocation of the Edict of Nantes in 1985 – an iconic moment for the French Protestant community. In the 1990s, however, I began to formalize these connections as a visiting scholar first at the Ecole Pratique des Hautes Etudes as the guest of Jean-Paul Willaime (in 1996), and then at the Ecole des Hautes Etudes en Sciences Sociales as the guest of Danièle Hervieu-Léger (in 1998). I returned to the latter for a further visit in 2003. Each visit lasted a month and focused on the (large) graduate seminars that were a feature of each institution. More broadly, my repeated visits to Paris enabled me to get to know not only my hosts and their work, but a wide range of French scholars interested in the place of religion in modern societies, including some excellent doctoral students. Crucially, I learned to appreciate not only that their approaches to the field were very different from my own, but why this was so. If the French are inclined to look for principles to guide both their intellectual reflections and their policy making, the British approach is rather more geared to problem solving. Both can be done well, or less well.

Interestingly, disproportionate numbers of French sociologists of religion are associated with Protestantism. For this reason, I had an immediate affinity with the work of Jean Baubérot and Jean-Paul Willaime and much enjoyed the discussions that I had with both of them. The latter's increasing interest in religion in Europe as a whole ran parallel to my own. In the 1990s, however, it was the work of Danièle Hervieu-Léger that influenced me most, notably her approach to religion as a form of collective memory, which (as already indicated) provided the theoretical framework for *Religion in Modern Europe*.[26] In the fullness of time, Danièle became President of the Ecole des Hautes Etudes en Sciences Sociales, a prestigious position which diminished the time that she was able to give to the sociology of religion.

Transatlantic links

My first invitation to visit the United States in a professional capacity came at much the same time – I attended the New York meeting of the Association for the Sociology of Religion (ASR) in 1996. I was immediately made welcome – not least by the then President, Nancy Ammerman – and became steadily more involved in the ASR Council. I was therefore delighted to stand for election myself and became President for the 2003 meeting in Atlanta. Working with American scholars enabled me once again to see things from a different perspective – I began to appreciate how far my European assumptions had colored my work. Explaining vicarious religion to American colleagues was, for example, a challenge. In a situation where the state, never mind the state church and its legacy, has little or no resonance, the notion of forms of religion carried out on behalf of others is hard to comprehend. In Europe, conversely, it is rare to find an audience that does not appreciate the notion of vicarious religion and the thinking that lies behind it, even if its translation into the language in question makes demands on the interpreter working with me. It is not an everyday term in most languages.

In 2005, I spent a semester at Hartford Seminary in Hartford, Connecticut, from where I was able to travel relatively easily to Boston, thus cementing a link with The Institute on Culture, Religion, and World Affairs (CURA) at Boston University. Peter Berger was the founder and (until 2010) director of CURA. I was privileged to take part in one of the Institute's summer seminars and in two of their research projects. The first, "Between Relativism and Fundamentalism," resulted in a book edited by Berger himself;[27] the second, on "Eurosecularity," became the inspiration for the co-authored *Religious America, Secular Europe*.

A Nordic adventure

In 2000–2001, I was offered an exceptional opportunity – to spend what was effectively a sabbatical year at Uppsala University in Sweden as the Kerstin Hesselgren Professor. This chair is funded by the Swedish Council for Research in the Humanities and Social Sciences and is offered annually to an "outstanding scholar" in any humanities or social science discipline, from any country in the world and can be held in any Swedish University. It has, however, to be held by a woman (at last, an advantage). My sponsor and host was Anders Bäckström, the then professor of the sociology of religion in Uppsala.[28] In the short term, my year in Uppsala permitted the writing of *Europe: The Exceptional Case*, published in 2002; in the longer term, it has resulted in a lasting and very fruitful collaboration, notably the comparative projects on religion and welfare outlined above. I was co-director of both WREP and WaVE. A direct development of this work may be found in the establishment of a Linnaeus Centre of Excellence in Uppsala entitled "The Impact of Religion: Challenges for Society, Law and Democracy," funded by the Swedish Research Council for ten years (2008–2018).[29] I am a senior advisor to "Impact" which is now well established as a university center. I spent the spring semester of 2010 in Uppsala in order to support this work, and return at regular intervals.

Though differently constructed, the "Impact of Religion" is in many ways similar to the "Religion and Society" program funded jointly by the Arts and Humanities and Economic and Social Research Councils of Britain.[30] Both, moreover, are part of the unprecedented surge in research on religion that has occurred all over Europe (and beyond) in the past five to ten years. It is these programs that I have tried to assess in the essay I wrote for the ARDA Guiding Papers Series.[31]

From these many, diverse, and hugely enjoyable opportunities to work in different places, I have learnt two things. First, that you can only understand your own country, including its religious elements, if you are prepared to move outside it from time to time; and second, that comparative work is both the most rewarding and the most demanding form of sociological activity. Organizationally, these sentiments were expressed most fully in my presidency of the Research Committee 22 (Sociology of Religion) of the (truly) International Sociological Association, a post that I held from 2002 to 2006.[32]

Looking forward

What next? In terms of the sociological study of religion, I am convinced of the following: it is clear that a step change is taking place in the subdiscipline. Unusually large numbers of researchers from many different disciplines are currently engaged in the study of religion – something that I did not expect to see in my professional lifetime. Cinderella has finally been invited to the ball. "Success" on this scale suggests, however, a further step: the need to penetrate the philosophical *core* of the associated disciplines and to enquire what difference the serious study of religion might make to their ways of working. The size of the task should not be underestimated. Most of the disciplines in question have emerged more or less directly from the European Enlightenment, meaning that they are underpinned by a markedly secular philosophy of social science. Interestingly it is precisely this point that Jürgen Habermas appreciates so clearly and addresses in his recent writing.[33] He insists, moreover, that others have a similar responsibility: namely to rethink the foundations of their respective fields of study in order to accommodate fully the implications of religion and religious issues in their analyses of modern societies. If Cinderella is to enjoy herself at the ball, she must have something decent to wear.

Notes

1 Both the overall number and the proportion of women in higher education began to rise in the 1970s. See Carole Dyhouse, *Students: A Gendered History* (London: Routledge, 2005).

2 Margaret Hewitt, *Wives and Mothers in Victorian Industry* (London: Rockliff, 1958).

3 Ivy Pinchbeck and Margaret Hewitt, *Children in English Society: From Tudor Times to the Eighteenth Century*, Vol. 1 (London: Routledge & Kegan Paul, 1969); *Children in English Society: From the Nineteenth Century to the Children Act, 1948*, Vol. 2 (London: Routledge & Kegan Paul, 1973).

4 The full title of my thesis was "Right Wing Politics amongst French Protestants 1900–1945, with special reference to the Association Sully" (University of London, 1975).

5 David Martin, *The General Theory of Secularization* (Oxford: Blackwell, 1978); see also David Martin, "Notes Towards a General Theory of Secularisation," *European Journal of Sociology* 10 (1969): 192–201; and Grace Davie, "French Protestants and the General Theory," in *Restoring the Image: Essays on Religion and Society in Honour of David Martin*, ed. Martyn Percy and Andrew Walker (Sheffield: Sheffield Academic Press, 2001), 69–81.

6 Grace Davie, *Religion in Britain since 1945: Believing without Belonging* (Oxford: Blackwell, 1991), xiii.

7 The reports were commissioned by the Crown Appointments Commission. They were delivered in 1984 (Diocesans) and 1985 (Suffragans), and were for internal circulation only.

8 *Faith in the City – A Call for Action by Church and Nation: Report of the Archbishop of Canterbury's Commission on Urban Priority Areas* (London: Church House Publishing, 1985).

9 Geoffrey Ahern and Grace Davie, *Inner City God: The Nature of Belief in the Inner City* (London: Hodder & Stoughton, 1987).

10 Grace Davie, "Believing without Belonging: Is this the Future of Religion in Britain?" *Social Compass* 37 (1990): 455–469; see also the widely read parallel article, Grace Davie, "'An Ordinary God': The Paradox of Religion in Britain," *British Journal of Sociology* 41 (1990): 395–421.

11 Davie, *Religion in Britain*, 93.

12 Davie, *Religion in Britain*, 93

13 Grace Davie, *Religion in Modern Europe: A Memory Mutates* (Oxford: Oxford University Press, 2000).

14 See Danièle Hervieu-Léger, *Religion as a Chain of Memory* (Cambridge: Polity Press, 2000); the French edition was published by the Editions du Cerf in 1993.

15 See Grace Davie, "Vicarious Religion: A Methodological Challenge," in *Everyday Religion: Observing Modern Religious Lives*, ed. Nancy Ammerman (New York and Oxford: Oxford University Press, 2007), 21–37; and Grace Davie, "Vicarious Religion: A Response," *Journal of Contemporary Religion* 25 (2010): 261–267.

16 Grace Davie, *Europe: The Exceptional Case* (London: Darton, Longman & Todd, 2002).

17 Peter Berger, Grace Davie and Effie Fokas, *Religious America, Secular Europe: A Theme and Variations* (Farnham: Ashgate, 2008).

18 Berger et al., *Religious America*, 31.

19 Grace Davie, "Religion in Europe in the 21st Century: The Factors to take into Account," *European Journal of Sociology* 47 (2006): 271–296. A shorter version of this article may be found in Grace Davie, "Is Europe an Exceptional Case?," *The Hedgehog Review* 8 (2006): 23–34.

20 Grace Davie, *The Sociology of Religion* (London: Sage, 2007).

21 Currently the book has been translated into Spanish, Polish, Hungarian, and Greek.

22 Grace Davie, "Thinking Sociologically about Religion: A Step Change in the Debate?" ARDA Guiding Paper Series, State College, PA: The Association of Religion Data Archives at The Pennsylvania State University, from http://www.thearda.com/rrh/papers/guidingpapers.asp (accessed August 22, 2011).

23 Anders Bäckström and Grace Davie, with Ninna Edgardh and Per Pettersson (eds), *Welfare and Religion in 21st Century Europe: Volume 1. Configuring the Connections* (Farnham: Ashgate, 2010); Anders Bäckström, Grace Davie, Ninna Edgardh and Per Pettersson (eds), *Welfare and Religion in 21st Century Europe: Volume 2. Gendered, Religious and Social Change* (Farnham: Ashgate 2011).

24 Peter Berger, *The Sacred Canopy* (New York: Doubleday, 1967).

25 See http://www.sisr.org/012/en/Home for more details (accessed August 22, 2011).

26 Hervieu-Léger, *Religion as a Chain of Memory*.

27 Peter Berger (ed.), *Between Relativism and Fundamentalism* (Grand Rapids, MI: Eerdmans, 2010).

28 Anders Bäckström's retirement in 2011 coincides almost exactly with my own.

29 See http://www.crs.uu.se/Impact_of_religion/?languageId=1 (accessed August 22, 2011).

30 See http://www.religionandsociety.org.uk/ (accessed August 22, 2011).

31 Grace Davie, "Thinking Sociologically."

32 See http://www.isa-sociology.org/rc22.htm (accessed August 22, 2011).

33 Jürgen Habermas, "Religion in the Public Sphere," *European Journal of Philosophy* 14 (2006):1–25.

11

HURDLING OVER BORDERS

Reflections on my intellectual trajectory

Karel Dobbelaere

Until my 18th year, I lived in a segmented world of the Belgian Catholic pillar.[1] In the Belgian context pillars are religiously or ideologically legitimized structures that strive towards self-sufficiency by providing services for their members (e.g., their own schools, youth and adult organizations, trade unions, sick funds, hospitals, banks, and mass-media–newspapers, magazines, and libraries). Born into a Catholic family, I went to church and to Catholic schools and was a member of Catholic organizations. Pillarized Belgium consisted of a Catholic, a socialist, and a liberal pillar, which created vertical pluralism, and the Catholic pillar, which was the largest, was integrated on the basis of the Catholic collective consciousness. Pillarization was a form of segmental differentiation that was at its highest point in the 1950s. In Nieuwpoort, where I was born and went to primary school, there was, for example, Catholic and liberal music. In the summer they played in turn every other Sunday in the market-place, but we only went to listen when the Catholic music was played. In Bruges, in a boarding-school where I did my secondary education, there was a liberal football club and a Catholic one. The boarders went every other Sunday to watch a match of the national football competition on the field of the Catholic club, never on the field of the liberal one. In other cities, such as Liège, there was a Catholic and a socialist football club. We lived "*en vase clos.*"

This did not mean that we could not be critical of the Catholic Church. My paternal grandfather was an authoritarian, fervent Catholic whom I feared as a child. His arguments were always full of references to the teachings of popes and bishops. Fortunately for me, my father was more critical and clashed quite often with his father. At home he stimulated critical reflection; for example, during meals he stimulated discussions on topics in the news. I also remember quite well a couple of events that made me critical of the Catholic Church as an organization. In my teens, I was struck by a parish priest who refused the last sacraments and a funeral in church to a dying neighbor living in an extramarital relationship because she did not reject her lover. I did not understand how a priest could deny heaven to a person. At about the same time, knowing that children were not brought by a stork, I could not understand that the Church had decreed that Mary was a virgin, since she had given birth to Jesus. A priest explained to me that Jesus was born coming through her abdominal wall. This explanation did not satisfy me; I thought it far-fetched. In the Gospel According to Mark, which is historically the first Gospel to be written, there is no reference to a virgin birth, but a reference to Jesus' mother, brothers, and sisters waiting outside for him (Mark, 3:31–35 and 6:1–6a). The reference to the virgin birth is in the later Gospels (Luke 1: 23–38 and Matthew 1: 18–25). Why did the Church state that Mary was virgin "before, during and after" Jesus' birth, taking the virgin birth as literally true but denying this way the references to his sisters and brothers? I asked myself: What does the reference to a virgin birth mean? Later, reading anthropological studies, I was struck by the fact that the reference to a virgin birth implied that the person was an extraordinary figure. Is that not also the meaning of the term "virgin" in the Gospels like the other stories in the later Gospels about the three Wise Men (Matthew 2:1–12) and the shepherds (Luke 2:8–20) paying tribute to the new-born child? This symbolic language is not historical but is meant to convey the idea that Jesus was an extraordinary person.

In the last year of my secondary school, we had to write essays. I wrote one on culture and the Church. Having lived at the seaside and having watched the dikes, the channels, the locks, and the land regained from the sea, which the Church approved of, I could not understand that – as far as human fertility was concerned – the Church opposed control over it. In Genesis 2:19 it is written that God asked man to name all "beasts and birds" and that "whatever the man called each living creature that was its name." By naming things we create a relationship between the one who does the naming and the ones named. This is creating culture. Thus, my argument was that God created nature but that it is up to men to create culture. And building a family is not a purely natural, but most of all a cultural process, and consequently people can and must control fertility. My professor called me to his room and after discussing my essay he said that I was ready to study social sciences, and he convinced my parents to send me to university. Consequently, I went to the Catholic University of Leuven to study social and political sciences and economy.

There weren't many university students in Nieuwpoort in the early 1950s. Some studied at the State University of Ghent, others at the Catholic University of Leuven. We decided to create a student club, called the *Mistpoeffers*. Bringing Catholic students together with students from another university in one organization was not acceptable for many local Catholics. By doing so, I crossed the border between the pillars. I was immediately ostracized by my family and the Catholic upper-middle class of Nieuwpoort. The saying was: "He does not know what he is doing." Later on, when I started publishing about the changing involvement of Catholics in their Church, it became "He does not know what he writes." They did not object to the content of the publications as such, but to the fact that the results were made public, which could have an influence upon half-hearted Catholics.

From middle range to grand theory

On the Masters level at the university, I took mostly sociology courses and after fin-
ishing my first degree I was recruited by one of my professors to help him analyze
research data on the ACW (General Christian Workers' Association). He encouraged
me to embark on a PhD degree and since research monographs on cities were popular at the time, I was thinking of doing my research on the pillarized structure of
Nieuwpoort. However, one evening my mentor visited me after a meeting with his
colleagues. They wanted to propose me as a candidate for a research position at the
National Fund for Scientific Research, but my mentor asked me to change the topic
of my dissertation and to study the religious situation of a suburb of Leuven. The
dean of this suburb had complained that the professors of the Catholic University
were not very much engaged in services to the Church. That is how I started
working in the sociology of religion.

At that time, counting the attendance at Sunday services with a small questionnaire
distributed during the sermon was common in Belgium, as well as in France. I decided that religiosity was not limited to Sunday church practice and that interviews
assembling data on a broader spectrum of practices, and also on beliefs and ethical
principles, should be the basis of a typology of Catholics, to be analyzed according to
their social and cultural positions. Once the data were assembled (512 interviews), no
one in my department was able to help me to do a multi-variate analysis. I was sent
to the United States and did postgraduate work in methodology, theory, and sociology of religion at the University of California in Berkeley in 1963–1964, where I was
supported in my research by Charles Glock, who found that all published sociological
studies on religion by Catholics were purely descriptive, without causal analysis. That
is why – although not downplaying the value of the descriptive tables in my publications – I, in cooperation with Jaak Billiet, have often utilized multi-variate analysis
that allows us to look for net effect explanatory factors.

That sabbatical year enabled me to do the necessary analysis of my survey data and
to finish my PhD dissertation. The central concept of my approach was the degree of
normative integration in the Church which was explained by gender, social class, age,
and other social positions.[2] In fact, these explanations were fragmented, and if a
broader perspective was taken in similar studies on integration in the Catholic
Church, the explanation was quite often linked to factors typical of this particular
church. A good example is Greeley's explanation that the decline of church
involvement in the Catholic Church was caused by the papal encyclical *Humanae
Vita*: Catholics voted with their feet against this encyclical on birth control by
leaving the church or diminishing their church practice. However, by comparing
data from other churches, I became aware that the involvement in most churches
had also strongly diminished in the 1960s. Consequently, I looked, with my first
PhD student, Jan Lauwers, for a more global theory that could explain the changes in
the religious sub-system. Like so many sociologists of religion, we were influenced
by the writings of Berger and Luckmann. In a paper presented at the 10th Conference of the International Society for the Sociology of Religion (ISSR) in

Rome (1969), we pleaded for taking secularization theory seriously and started working on it.[3]

In 1975, at the 13th Conference of the ISSR in Lloret de Mar (Spain), I was commissioned – by the Council of the ISSR on the proposal of Hans Mol, who was then President of the Research Committee 22: Sociology of Religion of the International Sociological Association (ISA), of which I was also a member – to write a trend report on secularization theories to be published in *Current Sociology*. They knew that I was working on secularization and was able to read Dutch, English, French, and German publications. Since starting my work in the sociology of religion I have been a frequent participant in the conferences organized by the ISA, the ISSR, the American Sociological Association, the Association for the Sociology of Religion, and the Society for the Scientific Study of Religion, which allowed me to meet with leading figures in the sociology of religion, many of whom became my personal friends. Consequently, I got help from colleagues to analyze publications in languages other than those I was able to study; for example, Italian colleagues helped me with Italian works on secularization. I did the basic work for the trend report in 1977 at All Souls College, Oxford, where I was a Research Fellow invited by Bryan Wilson. The report was eventually published in 1981.[4] Since then I have extended my study of secularization, strongly influenced by the theoretical insights of Niklas Luhmann, to whose writings I was introduced by my assistants, Staf Hellemans and Rudi Laermans. Luhmann's notion of functional differentiation allowed me to elaborate a general theory of secularization. Many publications have resulted from this theoretical research that was tested empirically with the help of my colleague Jacques Billiet on data from the successive waves to the European Value Study (EVS) and also from the Religious and Moral Pluralism (RAMP) study.[5] A new synthesis of my theoretical thinking was published in 2002.[6]

My publications have stimulated controversies with, among others, Berger, Davie, Greeley, and Stark. It is strange how certain ideas persist even if they are not supported by empirical data; for example, the so-called high church involvement in the USA. Greeley rejected the data presented on the basis of counting the number of people in Catholic churches in the USA during the weekend services which revealed that survey data give an inflated number of participants. He argued, at the symposium "Modernization and Religious Change" in 2000 at Nuffield College, Oxford, that parish priests do not give the correct number of participants but underestimate them, since they have to transfer a certain amount of money to their bishops on the basis of the number of people attending the weekend services; a simple statement without empirical validation. The discussion with Stark was also disappointing, since he misrepresented my arguments at the meeting of the Religious Research Association in 1997.[7]

I have since tried to integrate Stark's rational choice theory (RCT) and secularization theory, as in my view they are complementary.[8] Indeed, RCT only works in countries that are secularized on the societal level, allowing for free competition between so-called religious firms. Consequently, there is no opposition between secularization theory and RCT. However, in Europe, due to an agreement between Christian Churches renouncing all competitive evangelization[9] and the existing state regulations in many countries concerning sects and new religious movements, there is no fair competition. The RCT hypothesis that competition on the supply side activates a latent religiosity suggests an interesting research question. How to check this theory in Europe? My suggestion is that we have to move to a higher level of abstraction, considering religion as a particular meaning system with a supernatural referent in competition with non- or a-religious meaning systems and to check the impact of such competition on commitments.[10]

Extending geographic and cultural borders

In between my postgraduate work at the University of California, Berkeley, and being a Visiting Fellow in All Souls College, I was invited to teach the sociology of religion at Kent State University (Ohio) in 1969 and in 1989. During the spring and the first summer terms of 1969, I visited several religious services in the Kent-Akron area during the weekends, including Store Front Churches. Some denominations – a Jewish synagogue and Amish meetings, for example – I could only visit with the help of colleagues. These observations put flesh on my readings on religion, so to say. During these visits, I also learned how difficult it is to do participant observation without having an impact on the community. Mistakes are so easily made without being aware of it. In an all-black community, for example, where I was sitting in the back of an aisle, I put a dollar on the collection plate. The collector went to different people in the audience to show the banknote. For sure, these people could not give a dollar. Consequently, I became the one being observed instead of being the observer. And when I tried to slip away after nearly two hours, the minister stopped the service to say goodbye at the door, inviting me to come back when I was downtrodden. Indeed, while singing and dancing in the community and listening to testimonies, the participants got the needed energy to survive "across the Jordan." Later, I nearly made another mistake. A teenage girl sat beside me in church and suddenly she fell on the ground and uttered "noises." I thought that she was ill and wanted to help her up, but this was prevented. The minister came and listened to what she uttered and he said "no." To my astonishment, the girl immediately stood up. There I realized that young members of a Pentecostal church have to "learn" speaking in tongues.

The stimuli for a researcher are his "*collegae proximi*,", whom he encounters at conferences and through exchanges, and mostly his PhD students. I have referred already to four of them. Another was René Devisch who did research in the Democratic Republic of Congo, then Zaire, where he studied the Khita, a healing cult for what the Yaka consider to be abnormal births.[11] It struck me that the cult was in fact a ritual process involving both the members of the family and their life world to heal or re-weave the disturbed social and cosmological weave. I had the great chance to stay in the bush for two weeks in the village where Devisch did his research. This enabled me to understand the social context of his research and to see the ritual objects that were used in the Khita. In the village and during the one-and-a-half-day journey from Kinshasa to the village, I was introduced to some chiefs. One was the Regional Prince-Chief 1 of the Lunda dynasty N-nene, who had eight wives and some 30 children, and the Regional Prince-Chief 3 of the Lunda dynasty N-saka, who had 32 wives and more than 100 children. In the village I met Taanda, the Local Chief of 13 villages, who had three wives and 14 children. This information serves as an introduction to an experience I had there. Devisch did not know how to introduce me to the villagers, since a university is unknown to them. He presented me as a "big" chief, and indeed, during the first week I received different presents when I was there, among them a buttock of an antelope from the local Chief Taanda. During the second week, his youngest daughter, a very beautiful girl, asked me if I wanted her as a wife. I explained that I was already married. But that was no problem for her. How many wives and children do you have, she asked me. I said one wife and two children. That was the end of the proposal: to her this was a very clear indication that I was not a "big" chief, so she was no longer interested in me. Back in Belgium, I had a long exchange with a missionary about the Congo and his experiences. I asked him about the conversions he made. One case was an unfortunate experience for him. He was called by a dying chief who asked to be baptized. The missionary replied that the chief would have to renounce all his wives except for the first one. The chief refused, so the missionary would not baptize him. I told the missionary that his request was impossible for the chief. To renounce his numerous wives except for the first one was the same as abjuring his position as chief. In my eyes, the missionary did not understand the social meaning of polygyny. Why do religious enterprises want to convert people of other cultures if they are unable to understand and to accept the social meanings of their non-religious institutions and want to impose their Western views on them?

The importance of rituals also struck me when I stayed in Japan, in 1984, at the Nanzan Institute for Religion and Culture (Nagoya), invited by Jan Van Braght and Jan Swyngedouw, and at Sophia University (Tokyo), invited by Shin Anzai. I visited with them, and other Japanese colleagues, important Japanese Shinto shrines, Buddhist temples, and New Religious Movements. A typical ritual that I studied on two occasions was the visit to shrines (*hatsu-mode*) on the first three days of the year. Millions of Japanese buy a paper that tells them their fortune for the coming year. They hang these papers at the shrines and "pray" that good prospects may result, and if these prospects are bad they ask the *Kami* (gods) to prevent them from occurring. They also buy an *Ema*, a wooden plate, on which they write their wishes and then leave it at the shrine in the hope that their wishes come true. Many go to the Shinto shrines and combine it with visits to Buddhist temples, to ensure good fortune for the coming year.

Syncretism is typical of Japan. The different "religions" have different functions. Buddhism offers rituals for the dead. Some are linear and occur in the temple and at home before the Buddha altar. They go on until the final ritual when the deceased is incorporated into the body of ancestors. Besides linear there are also cyclic rituals at the graves at the autumn and spring equinox. Shinto is the original "religion" of Japan and, in contrast, it celebrates life and offers "this-worldly" protection by the *Kami*. Typical are the rites of passage: the presentation of the newborns to the

Kami (*Miyamairi*); 3-, 5-, and 7-year-olds visiting the shrines with their parents (*shichi-go-san*); and visiting the shrines at the beginning of their university studies and at coming of age (*seiuin-no-hi*). These rituals are very colorful, especially since the women are often dressed in beautiful kimonos. Through the *matsuri* or Shinto festivals, which combine ritual with festivity, the "life-powers" of the *Kami* and the human beings are renewed and revitalized. At these occasions *Nihonshu* or Japanese Sake flows. On the other hand, marriages are often celebrated with a Christian ceremony. One of my colleagues asked a colleague priest to perform such a ritual for the wedding of his daughter since her future husband was a movie star, from a milieu in which divorces are legion, he argued. As Catholicism does not allow divorce, he thought that such a celebration would secure her marriage.

In fact Shinto is not a "conventional" religion, like Buddhism and Christianity, but an "operative religion," as defined by Will Herberg.[12] It is a system of attitudes, beliefs, feelings, standards, and practices that provide society with an ultimate context of meaning, in terms of how social life is integrated and social activities are validated. In other words, it is possibly the only true civil religion still surviving. But, since Japanese society is changing drastically, for how long? Indeed, the traditional community structure is disintegrating through migration from rural villages to the cities and the local shrines are losing significance. However, Shinto is now "used" also to symbolize the industrial "community." The Shinto shrines, rituals, and festivals must promote "*musubi*," the power which enables things to be produced, reproduced, and united. According to Jan Swyngedouw, "Shinto is increasingly transferring this creative, evolutionary idea of *musubi* from forces of nature to the forces that sustain industrial productivity."[13] However, Shinto as a civil religion emerged in a traditional society within a communal basis: can it survive in urban areas where societalization has set in? And are the core values of *Nihonism*, celebrated by Shinto, not lacking in modern companies? Furthermore, does a modern, differentiated society need a civil religion? Luhmann does not think so, and I agree. According to him, a sub-system belongs to a societal system not because it is guided in its structural choices by requirements, values, and norms that apply to *all* sub-systems – a so-called civil religion. Integration is mediated by the fact that all sub-systems are an inner-societal environment for each other and they have to accept reciprocally each other's functions. But why then do some modern "states," such as France, insist on the "identity" of the "nation"? Does this quest not implicitly refer to core values that integrate society, a "civil religion," or better a "civil ideology" in the case of France, which does not fit a functionally differentiated society?

Redefinition of the religious field: sects and New Religious Movements (NRMs)

Bryan Wilson was on two occasions a visiting professor at my university and both times we conductede an empirical study. The first one, in the framework of a research seminar, was on the Jehovah's Witnesses. They were very cooperative; Wilson had done previous research on them. The problem here was to train our students in empathy and to contain their prejudices. The female students were especially critical. Regularly, the Jehovah's Witnesses had to answer in writing a questionnaire about recent lectures and texts they had studied. The women had to take care of the children while the men were filling in the questionnaire and only when they had finished could the women write their responses. A few of our female students intervened and said to the women that they should not accept this. We had difficulty in making these students accept that they had changed their position from a neutral observer to a political position favoring equality of the genders. This happened before the start of a weekly meeting in which a biblical article from *The Watchtower* was discussed in a question-and-answer session. Those presiding over such meetings never made negative remarks. Instead they said "yes but" and asked the audience to be more specific. The exercise for the students was to locate the elders, those who rephrased the answers to arrive at a reasonably correct answer. Indeed, the hierarchy in the sect was not visible as in the religions the students knew; they had to detect it from the interactions. Our study, based on participant observations and replies to a written questionnaire, was published, and the Jehovah's Witnesses responded positively.[14] For me this was a great example of a religious group with little ritual, in contrast to the previously discussed religions, and a belief based on a correct understanding of the Bible guided by the Watchtower Society in Brooklyn, New York.

This society is the most forthright exponent of biblical prophecy in the Adventist tradition, and when we conducted our research in 1976, they were confronting the fact that the prophecy of the return of Christ in 1975 had not materialized. This created significant "cognitive dissonance" in the minds of members and a loss of nearly 7 percent of the membership worldwide. A rationalization of the failure of the prophecy was needed. In 1976, in one of the weekly Public Meetings, a mandated agent of the Society gave the official explanation. He argued that 6000 years ago God created Adam, but Eve was created out of Adam only after he had given names to all "beasts and birds" (Genesis 2), a task that took much time. Only after her creation did mankind exist. And since this interval of name-giving cannot be asserted, Christ will return in 6000 + X years. Consequently, Armageddon is nearby but cannot be correctly predicted. This is indeed "the solution" for an Adventist tradition; the prophecy is maintained but the correct date is not to be known.

Wilson and I also studied a local group of Belgian "Moonies." They disliked our published study and objected to it.[15] The leaders of the movement, on the contrary, were quite positive. While we were conducting this research, a Korean leader of the movement approached us and invited us to become members, promising us that we would receive a leading function in the organization. Quite often, members of religious organizations cannot imagine that sociologists are doing their research from a strictly scientific point of view, but think that we are on a religious quest. During my stay at All Souls College in 1990–1991, we conducted another study on a New Religious Movement, the Soka Gakkai in Great Britain.[16] This study was later replicated by two colleagues in the USA.

Finally, Liliane Voyé (with whom I have published many articles) and I did a study of Scientology in Belgium. The movement paid our travel and other expenses, and when we finalized our report they wanted to correct some of our conclusions, among others, the one in which we underlined a consequence of the fact that the weekly remuneration of staff members was based on the apportioning among them of one-third of the weekly income of the center. We argued that this explained the widely held criticism of the cost of progressing to reach higher levels of "salvation," since such types of remuneration motivated the staff to make as much money as possible by selling books and high-priced ritual instruments. We refused to adapt our conclusions to their expectations and consequently they objected to the publication of the report. It was our mistake to depend upon a religious group for some costs of the research, since it gave them leeway to object to the conclusions of that research.

Recent extension and some reflections

Religions not only have beliefs and rituals; they also have an ethical code, which has been studied in EVS and RAMP and published in joint publications. However, due partly to the still latently present pillar structure, the non-Catholic world sometimes defines Catholics as monolithically conforming to the ethical norms of the Catholic Church. In 2006, a European interdisciplinary research group for the study of religious change (GERICR) was founded in Madrid (Spain) by researchers from Belgium, France, Italy, Portugal, and Spain. The aim of the group is to study the attitudes of professionals and lay members of the Catholic Church towards bio-ethical issues such as abortion, assisted fertilization, euthanasia, and same-sex marriage. This is relevant, since recently a more liberal legislation on these issues has been adopted or is under discussion in these countries. Liliane Voyé and I represent Belgium, and we focus on euthanasia, since the application of the Belgian law (2002) and speculation about the extension of its application are frequently discussed in the media.

In conclusion, I should state that sociology is an empirical science, not a philosophy. As such, its theoretical insights are based on empirical research. Our data should ideally be comparative and/or longitudinal (EVS, RAMP, and GERICR), in order to detect differences, which help to arrive at an explanation. These should fit into a sociological theory that is based on propositions linking interconnected concepts. This is the manifest function of our work.

However, our studies also have latent functions; they have an impact on our vision of the world and religion. My studies have provoked a critical attitude towards the Catholic Church as an organization. Science advances on the basis of a falsification of working hypotheses. Apparently, some religions have difficulty critically reflecting on their working hypotheses. The Magisterium of the Catholic Church is a good example, as it confirms its positions in reference to revelation and its traditions which can be interpreted only by the Church authorities themselves. This way they can claim the virginity of Mary as a physical fact "before, during, and after" the birth of Jesus.

On May 31, 1994, the media made it known that the Pope, in an apostolic letter of May 22, 1994, had confirmed the Declaration *Inter Insigniores* of the *Congregatio pro*

Doctrina Fidei that excludes women from the priesthood. In his letter, symbolically signed on Pentecost, the Pope made it clear that this decision was definite, refusing all further dialogue on this topic and insisting that all discussion in the Church on the priesthood of women must stop. As a sociologist, I could not accept that. For me, an organization that refuses internal dialogue and forbids further discussion on an important issue is a sterile and dead organization, and I made it clear that I could no longer be a member of such an organization. I decided to become a member of the Anglican Church, which I had encountered during my stays in Oxford, and I was accepted. The priest responsible for the Anglican Church in Belgium approached me and during a friendly dialogue informed me that according to his experience my integration into his church would be very difficult. Indeed, after Sunday service, when coffee and biscuits were offered, I was never spoken to by members of the parish in suburban Brussels, although I had been formally introduced to them by the parish priest, who was a friendly man with whom I had several discussions at lunch. Neither British nor American, I was not one of them and I did not belong to the circles they were part of, as staff of international firms, of the administration of the European Union, and of embassies. I experienced the same ostracism when visiting Mount Athos in Greece in 1997. Coming from one monastery, I had to change jeeps on a parking lot to go to the next monastery. I asked the monks for help, using all the languages I know; they looked at me as if they did not see nor hear me, not even reacting to the name of the monastery I wanted to visit. I became very angry since, one by one, the jeeps were leaving, and I told them in all the languages I know: "You are first of all Greeks and last of all Christians." Indeed, some Christian religions are very nationalistic.[17] At the end, not feeling at home in the Anglican Church, I gave up and became churchless. However, I recently rejoined the Catholic Church, to prevent my wife and children from having difficulties in burying me in church.

It is clear that my scholarly career has been strongly influenced by my professors who selected me for a scholarship and oriented me towards the sociological study of religion. Compared to my predecessor in the sociology of religion at my university, I changed reference groups. He was a priest and his reference group was the Church and its teachings; mine was and is my colleagues. I learned from their critical remarks on the papers I presented and the informal discussions we had at conferences, from the discussions at their and my university during our reciprocal visits, from the references to my works in their publications, from their reviews of my books, and most of all from our cooperation in international research projects. My knowledge of foreign languages also had its effects; I learned from the Anglo-Saxon, the French, and the German sociological worlds by studying their publications. I was also strongly engaged in the International Society for the Sociology of Religion where most of my professional relationships blossomed. I referred above to some of my doctoral students; they and others continually challenged my thinking, as did my students at MA level. Finally, I had the privilege of being married to Liliane Voyé, a sociologist studying religion, culture, and urban society. We not only published together, but she was always the first to read my work and to make critical suggestions for improvement. She also helped me to publish in French, and my late colleague and friend Bryan Wilson and, after his death, my friend Peter Barker did this for my English publications. To all of them I owe so much.

Notes

1 See Karel Dobbelaere, "Secularization, Pillarization, Religious Involvement, and Religious Change in the Low Countries," in World Catholicism in Transition, ed. Thomas M. Gannon, S.J. (New York: Macmillan, 1988), 80–115.
2 Karel Dobbelaere, Sociologische Analyse van de Katholiciteit (Antwerpen: Standaard Wetenschappelijke Uitgeverij, 1966).
3 Karel Dobbelaere and Jan Lauwers, "Involvement in Church Religion: A Sociological Critique," in Types, Dimensions and Measures of Religiosity: Acts of the Xth International Conference on Sociology of Religion, Rome 1969 (Rome: CISR, 1969), 101–129.
4 Karel Dobbelaere, "Trend Report: A Multi-dimensional Concept," Current Sociology 29(2) (1981): 3–153.
5 Karel Dobbelaere, Ole Riis et al., "Survey on Religious and Moral Pluralism," in Research in the Social Study of Religion, Volume 13, ed. Ralph L. Piedmont and David O. Moberg (Leiden, and Boston, MA: Brill, 2002), 159–171; Jaak Billiet et al., "Church Commitment and Some Consequences in Western and Central Europe," in Research in the Social Study of Religion, Volume 14, ed. Ralph L. Piedmont and David O. Moberg (Leiden, and Boston, MA: Brill, 2003), 129–159.
6 Karel Dobbelaere, Secularization: An Analysis at Three Levels (Brussels: Peter Lang, 2002).
7 Rodney Stark, "Secularization, R.I.P.," in The Secularization Debate, ed. William H. Swatos Jr. and Daniel V.A. Olson (New York: Rowman & Littlefield, 2000), 41–66.
8 See, for example, Karel Dobbelaere, "Secularization,": 193–196; Karel Dobbelaere, "Testing Secularization Theory in Comparative Perspective," Nordic Journal of Religion and Society 20 (2007): 144–145.
9 Jean-Paul Willaime, Europe et religions: Les enjeux du XXIe siècle (Paris: Fayard, 2004), 32.
10 Karel Dobbelaere, "The Contextualization of Definitions of Religion," International Review of Sociology – Revue Internationale de Sociologie 21 (2011): 201–202.
11 René Devisch, Weaving the Threads of Life: The Khita Gyn-eco-logical Healing Cult among the Yaka (Chicago, IL: University of Chicago Press, 1993).
12 Will Herberg, "Religion in a Secularized Society: Some Aspects of America's Three Religion Pluralism," The Sociology of Religion: An Anthology, ed. Richard D. Knudten (New York: Appleton-Century Crofts, 1967): 471–472.
13 Quoted in Karel Dobbelaere, "Civil Religion and the Integration of Society: A Theoretical Reflection and an Application," Japanese Journal of Religious Studies 13 (1986): 137–142.
14 Karel Dobbelaere and Bryan Wilson, "Jehovah's Witnesses in a Catholic Country: A Survey of Nine Belgian Congregations," Archives de Sciences Sociales des Religions 50 (1980): 89–110.
15 Bryan R. Wilson and Karel Dobbelaere, "Unificationism: A Study of the Moonies in Belgium," The British Journal of Sociology 38 (1987): 184–198.
16 Bryan R. Wilson and Karel Dobbelaere, A Time to Chant: The Soka Gakkai Buddhists in Britain (Oxford: Clarendon Press, 1994).
17 The worst case I ever witnessed was on the boat to Mount Athos in 1997. A Serbian seminarian, who was accompanying me, talked to the Serbian pilgrims on the boat inciting them to oppose a NATO intervention in their country. For him the situation was simple: some 1000 Muslims had to be killed and, as a result, the remaining Muslims would flee from Serbia.

12

THE EMPIRICIST'S TALE

Academic wanderlust and the comparative imperative

Barry A. Kosmin

Chance does nothing that has not been prepared beforehand.

(Alexis de Tocqueville)

In England's green and pleasant land[1]

I grew up in a semi-detached house in the dreary suburban outskirts of London. Austerity-ridden, bomb-scarred, postwar Britain was a homogeneous, safe, but rather boring and deferential society. My family was British and Jewish, so I was raised with a strong antipathy towards fascism and Germans on both patriotic and ethnic grounds. My parents had both had their educations cut short by war service – my father's in RAF Bomber Command and my mother as a nurse – and they were relieved when I passed the Eleven Plus examination to attend a selective, state secondary school which would ensure my social mobility.

Preston Manor County Grammar School was a version of Harry Potter's Hogwarts without the magic and Gothic architecture (it was red brick). When I entered at age 11 it still had old wartime air-raid shelters in the school yard. The Headmaster was Mr. Bannister, an Oxford graduate and a former World War I officer in a Guards Regiment. He presided over highly orchestrated Anglican morning assemblies wearing his academic gown and mortar-board, on a stage surrounded by his gowned teaching staff. The assemblies consisted of the Lord's Prayer (Catholics, Jews, and a lonely Hindu could if they wished remain silent), a selection from *Hymns Ancient & Modern*, and a reading from the large embossed King James Bible that lay permanently on a lectern in the school hall. And of course sports team announcements – *mens sana in corpore sano*. It was all a little baffling at first but not as much as the custom of being referred to by the teachers and fellow pupils only by one's surname. "Christian" names were banned and I was always "Kosmin" and so long regarded as an exotic or perhaps dangerous foreigner of some kind.

My minority status meant that I inhabited two cultures, since there was no hint then of a common Judeo-Christian civilization. On weekdays I enjoyed the formalism of the Church of England. Weekends were for family and Judaism. On Saturdays I attended services at the Kenton District United Synagogue. There, Victorian formalities and the *minhag Anglia* (English customs), such as wardens in silk hats and a rabbi with a dog collar and clerical robes, were combined with older traditions such as gender-segregated seating and a totally Ashkenazi Hebrew service. I also attended Hebrew classes two or three times a week and was taught by a newly minted young rabbi from Scotland, Cyril Harris. His saving grace in his students' eyes was that he was a keen cricketer. Interestingly, he eventually ended up as Chief Rabbi of South Africa (a nice spot for a cricketer) and a good friend of Nelson Mandela. We met again decades later when I was a Visiting Professor at the University of Cape Town and directing a national survey of Jews in the new South Africa.

I discovered early, in school and *shul,* that I was indifferent to religion, and that prayer and matters of faith and the spirit did not move me. However, no knowledge is ever wasted. My familiarity with the Scriptures has stood me in good stead for discussions with clergy and religionists of all types. I could translate the Pentateuch from Hebrew and even some Aramaic. And as one might expect at a good British grammar school I studied Latin for five years because familiarity with Caesar's Gallic Wars and the poetry of Horace and Virgil was still in the early 1960s a necessary qualification to gain entry into a good university. In retrospect my education was an excellent training in the comparative method as well as in religious skepticism, since I learnt of Elijah's critique of Baal, Paul's critique of the Pharisees, and Julius Caesar's critique of the Celtic Druids.

My strong subjects were geography and history. In geography, my interest was not just in maps but the entry it provided into the culture of countries, languages, vegetation, and physical and human environments. I was also taught the Whig view of history. We concentrated on the Tudors and Stuarts – The English Reformation and Revolution – so I underwent further exposure to religious argumentation and conflict. I was adept at both geomorphology and human geography and obtained an A grade in scholarship-level geography but I failed the interview at Oxford. This setback offered an opportunity to indulge my real interests in life which were travel and adventure.

Adventures in Africa

I became an early entrant into the globalized world of jet-set academia when I won a financially generous Fairbridge Commonwealth Scholarship and made a fateful choice, on academic and economic grounds as well a sense of adventure, to study at the small multiracial University College of Rhodesia and Nyasaland (now the University of Zimbabwe) in Salisbury (now Harare) which awarded University of London degrees. They did not offer geography so I read history and anthropology. I arrived just at the "end of Empire" as the "wind of change" predicted by British

Prime Minister Harold Macmillan was becoming a storm across Africa. However, UCRN was an outpost of British standards and its establishment. It was prestigious enough academically that the College Principal, the historian Dr. (Sir) Walter Adams, O.B.E., C.M.G., a well-connected wartime spook, moved directly up and on to be Director of the London School of Economics (1967–1974).

I sailed out from Britain in comfort on a Union Castle liner to Cape Town. On the morning of our arrival we anchored in beautiful Table Bay. Suddenly, while we awaited the Immigration and Customs Officers to come on board, the returning South Africans began tossing magazines and books over the ship's side. This was the first time I had seen the real effects of censorship and visited a totalitarian society. On the voyage I had spent time in the bar listening to many young English-speaking South Africans denouncing the Dominies of the Dutch Reformed Church (NGK) as the source of the country's problems as the instigators of the Apartheid policy of Hendrik Verwoed's National Party Government. Once on land, even in relatively liberal Cape Town one could not avoid the ubiquitous "Whites only/Slegs vir Blankes" signs on park benches, Post Office counters, and in the train compartment we had on the two-day steam train "journey into the interior," northward into Central Africa. When the train left Mafeking and the Republiek van Suid-Afrika we entered the British Bechuanaland Protectorate (now Botswana), a poverty-stricken and totally undeveloped landscape of Savanna with occasional thatched round huts and cattle kraals. The only brick buildings were the churches, schools, and clinics of the mission stations. Here obviously was a continent where religion had a direct impact on everyday life, both good and bad.

I enjoyed my colonial privilege, especially safaris and climbing expeditions. I had won what the imperialist Cecil Rhodes called "the greatest prize in the lottery of life." I was an "Englishman" – well, at least to Africans. As I traveled around Africa in those carefree years as an undergraduate I found a rural landscape and society largely dominated by Christian missionaries often engaged in bitter competition for souls with rival denominations. Their ubiquity was such that in newly independent Malawi even the mountain hut we used to climb Mount Mulanje was owned by the Church of Scotland mission. In Mozambique, a colony of Portugal, then still ruled by the aged fascist dictator Salazar, the Roman Catholic Church and its dour, Ultramontane priests visibly dominated education and most aspects of life in a conservative and authoritarian, if racially lax, society.

My next academic stop on the "Commonwealth academic gravy train" was Canada, then governed by the popular, secular liberal, Pierre Trudeau. The Canadians wanted foreign graduate students but not Vietnam War draft dodgers from the US, so they quickly introduced a compulsory French entrance examination. This as expected was no barrier to us educated Europeans. So with my B.A. Hons., Upper Second Class degree (London) I was awarded an Ontario Graduate Teaching Fellowship and full tuition to study for a Master's degree at McMaster University in Hamilton, Ontario. It was a former Baptist college but there was little trace of its origin. There were a few sociologists of religion around but I was not interested in the topic and never interacted with them.

I then took a job for a year with an insurance company. In retrospect this again was a useful experience. I refined my quantitative skill set and I discovered that, for me personally, the downsides of North American corporate life outweighed the material rewards. My Rhodesian-born wife missed her family and the thought of a few more years in the sun and the great outdoors was attractive. The political conflict in Rhodesia over its Unilateral Declaration of Independence was deteriorating but not yet life-threatening. The British government wanted to keep the College open as an island of multiracial liberalism but it was having difficulty replacing the overseas staff the illegal Smith regime deported from time to time. Thus as a known quantity – neither a white racist nor a supporter of Marxist revolution and African nationalism – I was offered a Fellowship at the Center for Applied Social Sciences and the History Department, which covered my doctoral fees, research, and living expenses. This completed my academic "trifecta." None of my three degrees cost me or my parents a penny in tuition or living expenses. Since my wife worked as a registered nurse this all made for a very comfortable lifestyle even in a country supposedly under economic sanctions.

Although I was not a revolutionary this was 1970, and I chose a thesis topic related to race and class and rural underdevelopment – "Ethnic and Commercial Relations in Southern Rhodesia: A Study of the Asian, Hellene and Jewish Populations." These were the middleman trading groups that stood between the colonial elite and the African population.[2] It was really interdisciplinary research – sociology, anthropology, history, politics, and economics. I found I had a facility to write up quantitative and qualitative social science research findings fast and easily. In the short run my main research focus led to journal publications[3] which when I returned to Britain with my doctorate in 1974 helped secure research posts, and so mentoring and "on-the-job training" with the prominent sociologists who directed the UK Social Science Research Council's Research Unit on Ethnic Relations at the University of Bristol under Michael Banton; at Aston University under John Rex; and the Resource Options Unit at the LSE under the distinguished social anthropologist Sandra Wallman.

The overarching question I was drawn to in Africa and Britain in those years was the transition from *Gemeinschaft* to *Gesellschaft* that lay at the foundation of the discipline of sociology. How do human beings cope with modernity – the transition from traditional, communitarian, agrarian societies to individualistic, urban industrial and post-industrial societies? So how did I get into religion? Well it was partly a by-product of my thesis research and partly serendipity. Trust and loyalty is important in commercial transactions. I found that my trading groups organized themselves around their particular religious institutions – mosque, temple, synagogue, and Greek Orthodox Church. To understand how they operated as social groups in a plural society and how they regarded the "Other" one needed to know something about their religious practice and beliefs.

Religion was also the main focus at the time of many of my academic colleagues across a range of disciplines. One of my thesis advisors was Marshall Murphree, the Rhodesian-born son of American Methodist missionaries who had gained his

anthropology PhD from the LSE with a thesis on Mashona Christianity.[4] David
Beach in history was another valuable informant.[5] His doctoral work on traditional
religion in pre-colonial Mashonaland had direct political relevance to the Chimur-
enga War as the Smith and later Muzorewa governments battled the African
Nationalist ZANU and ZAPU Parties for the allegiance of the Mwari spirit mediums
in the Tribal Trust Lands. These studies and observations of lived religion in Africa
convinced me that religious ties and beliefs, particularly superstition and witchcraft,
were powerful forces and could and did have an important instrumental role in
political mobilization. I considered this excessive "religionization" unfortunate, particularly as it tended to encourage tribal and racial acrimony which did not bode well
for Africa's future. I discovered in Africa what the philosopher Spinoza had concluded centuries before: that one cannot neatly separate "the theological" from "the
political."

The Jewish connection

In Rhodesia, I gained a surprising patron who was particularly enthusiastic about my
research on the Jewish community. This was the influential Professor of African
Medicine and Dean of the Medical School in Salisbury. Dr. Michael Gelfand was a
brilliant polymath. He was an expert on tropical diseases and a former Chief Medical
Officer of Northern Rhodesia with a string of British government honors, medical,
and honorary degrees. His interests included traditional African religion and healing
and history, and his more than 30 books included *Shona Ritual, The African's Religion,*
Medicine and Custom in Africa, and *Livingstone, the Doctor.* He wanted the Jewish contribution to Africa recorded and he persuaded me to write about the local Jews.[6] In
doing so he changed my career trajectory. He helped me gain a doctoral travel grant
from the Memorial Foundation for Jewish Culture which was funded by German
reparations payments and administered by the World Jewish Congress with the
purpose of re-creating a new post-Holocaust generation of Jewish scholars.

These funds enabled me to research in the Colonial Office archives in London,
and on the return journey to Africa I attended the World Conference of Jewish
Studies in Jerusalem. There I came under the wing of another academic powerhouse,
Professor Roberto Bachi. He was an Italian "Jewish aristocrat." His father had been
Professor of Mathematics at La Sapienza Rome University before World War I. Until
the Axis Pact of 1938 and the adoption of exclusionary Italian racial laws, Roberto
had been Professor of Statistics at the University of Genoa. Forced out of his post he
went to Jerusalem and became a keen Labor Zionist, and in 1948 the first Director of
the Israel Government Bureau of Statistics strategically housed in the office of Prime
Minister David Ben-Gurion.

Bachi's obsessions were the graphical presentation of statistics and the renewal of
Jewish demographic studies in the Diaspora. Bachi had a clear view of the role of
scholarship and science. He informed me that as a trained social scientist I had a duty
and responsibility to the surviving remnant of the Jewish people to research, to write,
to teach, and to speak up against totalitarianism and fanaticism both outside and

within Jewish communities. Scholars are not to be judged purely by the number of books or peer-reviewed articles they produce but how they impact upon society and influence elite and public opinion on the issues they (should) care about. This was the first time in my career I had faced the burden of historical duty. Bachi recommended my paper for publication in the *Jewish Journal of Sociology* whose editor at that time was the formidable Maurice Freedman. A world expert on Malaysia and China, Freedman then held the sole Professorial Chair in Social Anthropology at the University of Oxford and had previously done the same at the London School of Economics.

A few months later a letter arrived for me, which I later discovered was engineered by Bachi, offering me the Directorship of the Statistical and Demographic Research Unit of the Board of Deputies of British Jews, whose Chairman was none other than Professor Maurice Freedman. The Board, founded in 1760, was the representative body of British Jewry. There was an economic crisis, a three-day work week and an Arab oil embargo. Added to this the Jewish community was facing a serious political threat and street violence due the rise of the fascist National Front which had received over 150,000 votes in the local elections in London. I was supposed to know about research, Jews, and fascism, so I became the "intelligence arm" of the Board's Defense Department. My first challenge was that Jews were an un-enumerated population in the British Census but with a combination of local fieldwork, small area Census statistics, and analysis of Jewish distinctive first and surnames on the voters' rolls, my young team produced a useful study of the most vulnerable population: that of the London Borough of Hackney.[7]

The Hackney study got me the job with the SSRC, Research Unit on Ethnic Relations, and for the next few years I happily combined my Jewish communal research post with my academic posts. As the fascist threat diminished my work began to take on a more demographic focus that involved studies of life cycle religious rituals such as marriage, divorce, circumcisions, and interments. Since the Jewish community operated a sophisticated network of welfare, educational, and social services I was asked to carry out local community surveys to assist social planning. The research into social problems demography and political issues all had a religious aspect. For example, divorce involved rabbinic law (Halakhah) as well as civil divorce and the sociological issues common to the whole society. Undoubtedly among modern populations religion is usually an independent variable, an additional rather than an overriding factor. However, I admit that this work had a tendency towards an overreliance on behavioralist indices and metrics such as rates of observance that favored a normative view of Judaism and thus were basically a test of religious orthodoxy. Yet the resilience of Jewish behaviors despite an obvious lack of religious belief needed an explanation which I saw in a series of nested Russian dolls – the individual, the family, and the community. The ties and bonds that link that sequence of units of analysis also subject autonomous and free-thinking human beings to peer and social pressures for conformity.

The spatial aspect of communities still interested me and I had a fruitful collaboration in a number of studies with the geographer Stanley Waterman. His goal was new methods in spatial analysis, while mine was to refine residential patterns for a "sociology of place."[8] We relied as often on surrogate or indirect as surveys, since Jewish communities are invariably ambivalent about the benefits of demographic studies. Censuses of Jewish populations have been fraught with unpleasant consequences for their sponsors since biblical times (see II Samuel 24:1–18). In those times they were unpopular because of the belief that unfair advantages and dangerous unnatural powers were conferred upon the initiators of such projects. However, Jewish social science remains a contested field of study. The passions arising from differences in ideology, theology, and discipline run deep in its community of scholars. People care, believe, and argue at a decibel level that is above that in most areas of the academy but it was good preparation for later exposure to the American culture war.

The key to good, relevant, social science, and especially sociology, is asking the right questions at the right time. One of the reasons advanced for the prominence of Jews, among the leading lights of sociology, has been the notion that as quintessential outsiders Jews could ask the awkward questions in Western society. However, there are other intellectual as well as social psychological reasons for this trend. The fact that many of academic sociology's most prominent figures emerged from the traditional Jewish communities of Europe was no accident. Jewish religious scholarship incorporates a similar ethos and mindset to social science whereby asking questions – *shaalehs* – is *de rigueur*. The ability to frame the correct question is as important as finding the right answer, so we need to be constantly framing and refining our questions about how society works and develops.

I spent my sabbatical in 1980–1981 as a Fellow of the Institute of Advanced Studies at the Hebrew University of Jerusalem under the tutelage of Professor Bachi. I did not realize it at first but I was part of an advanced seminar for a hand-picked group who were expected to carry the torch of Jewish demography in Israel and the diaspora. Bachi assembled some outstanding teachers and lecturers for us such as Shmuel Eisenstadt, the historian Salo Baron, and the leading Italian demographer Livi Bacci. I was assigned an office in the Einstein Building on Mount Scopus above the amphitheater with a magnificent view looking out over the Judean wilderness towards Jordan Valley where I could just make out the Dead Sea in the distance. The black tents of the Bedouin shepherds and their goats below made it a very biblical setting. It was a placid year politically, so in the afternoons I would walk leisurely down on an ecumenical excursion through the Mount of Olives and past the two rival Gardens of Gethsemane (Catholic and Orthodox) to the Lions Gate into the Muslim Quarter of the old city. I then went on and passed the Ecce Homo Arch into the Christian Quarter and joined the pilgrims on the Via Dolorosa. Then I would wander into the Armenian Quarter or go towards the Western Wall and the Jewish Quarter where one could freely walk up the step bridge to the Dome of the Rock and Al-Aksa Mosque. Along the way one saw the faithful and the exotically dressed clergy of all three religions hurrying to and from their devotions. It was a medieval scene, since what appeared common to all three monotheistic religions in the Holy Land was unflinching adherence to orthodoxy. They presented themselves as preserved in aspic and were uncompromising in their conservatism and adherence to tradition. Innovation, novelty, and accommodation to modernity were obviously frowned upon and women were unwelcome except as a segregated docile audience. Yet it was clear that "authentic" and patriarchal religion in museum wrapping had great appeal to the hordes of tourists and pilgrims from across the globe.

New York, New York

In 1985 I was approached to establish a North American Jewish Data Archive for the Council of Jewish Federations in New York. During the 1970s and early 1980s the local Jewish Federations in the US which operated as the philanthropic and social service arm of the Jewish communities began to recognize that their populations were undergoing rapid change as a result of social mobility and migration to the sunbelt. They began to sponsor numerous local studies based on a model developed by the internationally acclaimed sociologist and demographer Professor Sidney Goldstein, the founding Director of the Population Studies Center at Brown University who became my mentor. I decided to locate the Data Bank at the City University of New York Graduate Center where I joined in the PhD Program in Sociology, as it had a nucleus of interested sociologists of the Jews on-site including Paul Ritterband, Sam Heilman, and my close friend Egon Mayer.

In contrast to my own ambivalent attitude towards my native land, I found that my new American colleagues, especially the European émigrés, had respect for the American dream, the free market, and its potential to provide material progress. They subscribed to Lipset's assessment that the New World and the United States, the world's first post-feudal society, was profoundly different to the Old World.[9] Thanks to the influence of Enlightenment thinkers such as John Locke, Thomas Jefferson, James Madison, and Adam Smith, America's modernity offered progress and orderly economic and social development. It promised "life, liberty and the pursuit of happiness" even, and maybe especially, to Jews. There were growing economic opportunities as a result of the introduction of the new information and communication technologies and the emergence of a knowledge-based consumer society. This trend also offered considerable opportunities to innovative religious entrepreneurs in the new mega-churches and the Evangelical church-planter movement. This thesis later became the basis of the book *Religion in a Free Market*, which I authored with my long-time collaborator Ariela Keysar based on the findings of the 2001 American Religious Identification Survey (ARIS).

The emerging "post-industrial" and "postmodern" culture of America offered "pluralistic identity" possibilities. In other words, the "cognitive dissonance" thesis postulated by Emile Durkheim that operated in Europe – the homogenization and integration of a society's minorities at the social and cultural levels as a result of economic forces assisted by an all-powerful Jacobin or welfare state – was invalid in contemporary America. There was evidence of a growing tolerance in American society which could be observed to be in some urban environments such as Brooklyn where there was both the persistence of community and a relative absence of cultural integration. This in turn suggested that the fate of what Peter Berger termed cognitive minorities had to be re-evaluated. The obvious cognitive minorities that had heretofore been overlooked as a "residual category" by the official cognitive system (i.e., government statistics and most sociologists) were religious minorities all across the theological spectrum. Though much was written about fundamentalists and the new Religious Right, I realized that the same social forces that provided space for varieties of expressions of orthodoxy to flourish also provided space for a range of other "cognitive minorities" from cults and New Age beliefs. However, nobody had a good handle on the real numbers involved in what appeared to be a new desecularization process in the United States.

ARIS and American religion

Since legislation prevented the US Census from investigations concerning religion, in the 1980s the main source of information on the national profile of religion was the study of US congregations conducted by the Association of Statisticians of American Religious Bodies (ASARB) and compiled as the *Religious Congregations & Membership in the United States*. This compilation provided data only on the affiliated membership. It was a "top-down," institutionally skewed view of American religion. It was quite unable to measure the size of the New Religious Movements or the sentiments of the 40 percent or so Americans who were not religiously affiliated. Religion was obviously the most important variable missing from the national social accounts and it became my new mission to fill this information void.

The opportunity arose when I was asked to direct the 1990 National Jewish Population Survey (NJPS) for the national Council of Jewish Federations (CJF). In order to gain insights into the dynamics of population and identity change through religious switching, this survey aimed to interview a wide population of not only Jews by religion but also cultural or secular Jews, persons of Jewish parentage, and people who just considered themselves Jewish for any reason. The NJPS operated under a National Technical Advisory Committee chaired by Sidney Goldstein with Joe Waksberg, the former Associate Director of the US Bureau of the Census as Vice-Chair. Technology helped advance survey methodology and Joe was the leading methodologist on random digit dialing (RDD) telephone surveys. The NJPS adopted a multi-stage methodology involving a household roster followed up by a long questionnaire.

In order to locate our goal of 2500 completed interviews with Jews we needed to screen a nationally representative sample of 115,000 American households. Whereas the Jewish data belonged to the CJF the national screening data devolved to CUNY Graduate Center and me as the Principal Investigator for what became the first of the ARIS series. My individual innovation was to dispense with the usual long list of religions and denominations but to instead use an open-ended key question: "What is your religion, if any?" This *vox populi* approach had the advantage of allowing an unprompted response to the question and we gathered both generic and specific answers covering a range of traditions, religious groups, denominations, and theological positions. It was a democratic and respectful approach which allowed us to gather the terms popular among the public rather than just those approved by religionists and academics. "Born Again" would probably not have appeared on a denominational list; nor would the increasingly popular "Non-denominational Christian." It is also very unlikely that a list of choices would have included Santeria or Paganism. Interestingly, all the previous lists I perused were alphabetical by denomination but they place Non-theist options at the bottom, including Atheist! In addition, respect for participants means that survey respondents should be able to admit that they do not know a response. There are cases in which respondents honestly do not have an answer or do not know enough about a subject to provide an answer.

The findings of the National Survey of Religious Identification made front-page news in the *New York Times* and the book offers flowed in from publishers. They recognized immediately that the value of our dataset was that unlike the Gallup Polls or the General Social Survey with their relatively small samples (usually 1000–2000), our results could be generalized for some of the smaller groups in a way that smaller surveys could not. This unique dataset with its large sample offered insights into the nation's religious diversity along with the numbers and the social and demographic composition of interesting and heretofore unenumerated small religious groups. Another attraction was its geographic data at the state and metropolitan levels. It showed that states still differed widely in the religious make-up of their populace. Religion was recognized as contributing as much as any other source to differences in their cultural and political climates. Harmony Press made the best offer but the editor wanted a book that provided a strong historical and political background in order to boost sales. So historian and University Dean Seymour Lachman joined me as co-author of *One Nation under God* which went into a paperback edition and became an editor's choice for the then popular Book of the Month Club.

Surveys have to be approached with caution because they are famously prone to error due to bad or fluctuating design, discrepancies in samples, and poor execution. The essence of science, especially as applied to national baseline data collection, is replicable data with standardized and detailed classification rules applied consistently. So when the opportunity arose for a new ARIS in 2001, our team – my co-principal investigator Egon Mayer with Ariela Keysar as the Study Director – was committed to a replicate methodology of 1990 and the same key questions. Nevertheless, we had become enthusiastic proponents of the view that to do justice to today's reality of a society largely composed of sovereign, autonomous individuals we needed to reject forced-choice questions and limited sets of response alternatives. Instead we needed to adopt open-ended questions and make an allowance for a variety of responses on religious identification questions despite the analytical issues that resulted. It was a response to the realization that the contemporary world was not a neat and tidy place and we had to acknowledge that this makes the formulation of general theoretical statements more difficult than ever. We wanted a more textured portrait and so we experimented with the religious-secular scale which allowed for nuanced contours of religion as a form of self-identification, when further shaded by such dimensions as general outlook or worldview, particular theological beliefs, and institutional affiliation.

Our main finding in 2001 was that there was a significant rise in the number of respondents saying they had no religion. The interest this finding aroused in the Posen Foundation eventually led to the establishment of the Institute for the Study of Secularism in Society and Culture (ISSSC) at Trinity College, Hartford alongside the Greenberg Center for the Study of Religion in Public Life. It was this partnership – between the light and dark forces – that gained the necessary across-the-board support from foundations for the 2008 ARIS. For it is now commonly recognized that in order to measure religious change or stability it is necessary to have comparable data that measure these aspects over time.

Secularism

The accumulated ARIS series findings convinced me that secularization complements "religionization" and that both phenomena may occur simultaneously in a complex society. Religions and their various components become, as Bruce maintains, discretionary products in a marketplace of alternatives – a "pick-and-mix counter" – rather than dominating the environment.[10] Eisenstadt's "multiple modernities"[11] can emerge even in different regions of the US in which economic, social structural, and cultural forces interactively yield different results with varying roles for religion. For amid the range of sociological positions on secularization there is agreement on one point, even among its strongest advocates such as Bruce, and critics like Stark[12]: the world is increasingly becoming a competitive marketplace of worldviews – religious and otherwise. As Tony Stevens-Arroyo has insisted with regard to Latinos, this new situation allows for hitherto suppressed religious expressions to emerge and much more room for the development and acceptance of syncretism.[13]

At ISSSC my recent researches and interactions with scholars from many different countries have convinced me that the economic and societal "modernization" or development of the world is, if anything, making matters more challenging (and interesting) for sociology. Economic and social change is increasingly presenting both individuals and nations with the opportunities and challenges of cultural pluralism and worldview diversity. It is becoming ever more difficult for nations and communities to culturally insulate themselves from such forces. This affords greater opportunity for comparison and selective adoption of ideas by choice rather than the unquestioned inheritance or social requirement of all-encompassing cultural packages or "sacred canopies." Such pluralizing and individualizing forces must have substantial effects on the ways people make sense of life, and polities seek to maintain desirable degrees of cultural coherence and social solidarity. Some will be receptive to non-theistic messages (whether positive or negative; hard or soft) by dint of personal experience and cultural context. Nevertheless, personal, institutional, and societal uses of supernatural constructs remain pervasive and powerful throughout the world. Given apparently cross-cutting trends, it may be more apt to speak of the "granularization" of worldviews – individual and societal – rather than secularization or religionization. These worldviews need not necessarily be rigidly religious or broadly atheistic. The resulting social environments can produce accommodative forms of political secularism that as Stepan suggests may further enable worldview pluralism and individualization.[14]

This chapter has been an exercise in reflexivity, so it should conclude with some personal observations on my career and the state of the art. Most of my research publications, especially those in journals, have been jointly authored, which suggests to me that studies involving religion are multi-faceted and privilege interdisciplinary teams. Indeed, my intellectual development has been enriched by exposure to diverse environments, multiple disciplines, and especially by relationships with senior scholars who found time to converse with and guide a new initiate. These influences were consequential and combined to improve my "sociological imagination." Though I acknowledge that theory, speculation, and argumentation enhance our academic endeavors I would maintain that above all, sociologists must follow the Confucian tradition of "seeking truth from facts" in order to enlighten society.

Notes

1 The hymn "Jerusalem" based on William Blake's poem "And Did Those Feet in Ancient Times" was a particular favorite of our school choir.
2 My original inspiration was the pluralism theory of J.S. Furnivall, *Colonial Policy and Practice* (Cambridge: Cambridge University Press, 1948).
3 My most popular article was the neo-Marxian: "The Inyoka Tobacco Industry of the Shangwe People: A Case Study of the Displacement of a Pre-colonial Economy in Southern Rhodesia," *African Social Research* 17: 554–577, which was republished in R. Palmer and N. Parsons (eds), *The Roots of Rural Poverty in Central and Southern Africa* (Berkeley, Los Angeles and London: University of California Press and Heinemann, 1977), 268–288.
4 Marshall Murphree, *Christianity and the Shona* (London: Athlone, 1969).
5 D.N. Beach, *Zimbabwe before 1900* (Gwelo: Mambo Press, 1984); D.N. Beach, *The Shona and their Neighbours* (Oxford: Blackwell 1994).
6 "A Note on Southern Rhodesian Jewry," *Jewish Journal of Sociology* 15(2) (1973): 23–28; *Majuta: A History of the Jews in Zimbabwe* (Gwelo: Mambo Press, 1981).
7 B.A. Kosmin and N. Grizzard, *Jews in an Inner London Borough* (London: Board of Deputies,1975).
8 B. Kosmin and S. Waterman, "The Distribution of Jews in the United Kingdom, 1984," *Geography* 71 (1986): 60–65; "Mapping an Unenumerated Ethnic Population: Jews in London," *Ethnic and Racial Studies* 9 (1986): 484–501; "Residential Patterns and Processes: A Study of Jews in Three London Boroughs," *Transactions Institute of British Geographers* 13 (1988): 79–95.
9 Seymour Martin Lipset, *The First New Nation* (New York: Norton, 1979).
10 Steve Bruce, *Religion in the Modern World: From Cathedrals to Cults* (Oxford: Oxford University Press, 1996).
11 S.N. Eisenstadt, "Multiple Modernities," *Daedalus* 129(1) (2000): 1–29.
12 Rodney Stark, "Secularization, R.I.P.," *Sociology of Religion* 60(3) (1999): 249–273.
13 I was exposed to these ideas while working as an advisor with the Program for the Analysis of Religion Among Latinos (PARAL), which published a four-book series on various aspects of Latino religious experience in the United States for which Stevens-Arroyo was the editor.
14 Alfred Stepan, "The Multiple Secularisms of Modern Democratic and Non-democratic Regimes," in Craig Calhoun, Mark Juergensmeyer and Jonathan Van Antwerpen (eds), *Rethinking Secularism* (New York: Oxford University Press, 2011), 114–144.

13

MY SPECIFIC FORM OF DISORIENTATION

Robert A. Orsi

Nonna stared at the figurines silhouetted against the wall: Jesus, with his pink right hand catching the Bronx sunlight in the middle of a blessing; Saint Francis, his chipped brown arms in the air ready to receive the landing of the birds; Saint Joseph, holding his staff and staring at Nonna. Upon the bed they had some new life and their own silent language.

(Joseph Papaleo, *Italian Stories*)

To put it paradoxically, what matters most in a human life may in some sense be one's specific form of *disorientation*, the idiosyncratic way in which one's approach to and movement through the world is "distorted."

(Eric L. Santner, *On the Psychotheology of Everyday Life*)

I had gone with some friends from high school to see the preview of an off-Broadway play about a New York City couple struggling with guilt over their son's recent suicide. It was the second day of spring break 1972 in my first year at college in New England. My parents had fought fiercely against my leaving the Bronx. "What can you do in a dorm that you can't do at home?" my father asked me when I was pleading with him and my mother to let me go. My father had dropped out of school in the sixth grade to support his mother and younger brother after his father died suddenly. My visit home had begun poorly. A girl from my dorm who I had a crush on dropped me off in the Bronx on the way down from Connecticut to her family's Park Avenue apartment and, leaning next to her against the car while we waited for my mother to return from the beauty parlor, the old neighborhood suddenly seemed strange, shabby, and abandoned, and my neighbors, whose stories I had been telling this girl for months by way of charming her, shuffled by, much older and frailer now than when I last saw them, not recognizing me. My mother, when she got back, looked waxen to me, her lipstick too red, her hair like a lacquered wig, and her cheeks overly bright with rouge. The girl who drove me down declined my mother's invitation to come in for lunch and soon after departed for Manhattan, leaving me standing on the sidewalk alone beside my mother. At dinner that first night home one of my relatives, furiously crushing out her cigarette, called me a "big shot" after I had made some comment about a psychology class I was taking. She did not mean it as a compliment.

The play was the next day. The couple come on stage lugging their suitcases. Their car has broken down on the highway en route to New England, we learn, and they have taken refuge from the snowstorm raging outside in what seems to be an empty house. They put their luggage down, shivering, and brush snow from their heavy coats. Sniping at each other, veering between rage and grief, they begin to explore, and gradually they realize the house is haunted. A family of ghosts, mother, father, and two small children, move noisily through the rooms and up and down the stairs. I think this is where act one ended. The rest of the play is about the interactions between the ghosts and the living people. But then towards the end there is a surprise: the couple from New York turn out to be the ghosts – they had been killed in a car crash on the highway before the action of the play starts – and the 'ghosts' are actually the living people whose house it is.

This plot twist unsettled me at the time, which is why this otherwise forgettable play has lingered in my memory all these years. The ontological switch – between the living and the dead, the real and the spectral – resonated with my sense already of the world having been turned inside out that first year of college. For the rest of that visit home I felt as I did at my Sicilian grandmother's wake and funeral earlier in the same year. It was as if I had been lifted out of ordinary space and time and was seeing my mother and father, aunts and uncles, suddenly from a great distance. But what especially startled me in those days was that I had begun to see myself from a great distance too. Coming when it did, the play has taken on the status of an augury for me, a presaging of the central existential and intellectual dilemma of my life as a scholar of religion.

The world I had taken unquestioningly as real – as really there as the couple in the play assumed themselves to be, as real as my hands and feet – was the Italian American Catholic working-class north Bronx. Here I recognized and was recognized by almost everyone; everyone's personal qualities were endlessly picked over in rounds of conversation on the streets, in the parish, and at kitchen tables, in Italian or some mix of English and Italian (in its various dialects), and then fixed in nicknames we imposed upon ourselves like curses. Things were accomplished relationally, face-to-face, in an ever-expanding web of favors asked for, favors received, and favors owed, all recorded with precision on the running neighborhood balance sheet. What was not done this way was suspect. Talking was essential and a person's quality was judged on the basis of how well he or she did in conversation on public occasions.

This world was formed as well by the supernatural realism of modern devotional Catholicism, a religious imaginary as material and as intersubjective as our everyday lives. Jesus was really present in the Host (the nuns drilled it into me that if I touched it with my teeth the wafer would bleed in my mouth); the Blessed Mother appeared to children (she had appeared in the Bronx on the Grand Concourse in 1948 to a little Italian American boy and I longed for her to appear to me too); the saints crowded around; and I made space at my kindergarten desk for my guardian angel. Sin was real but its gravity was assessed in relation to family bonds and obligations. That I left for college was much more of a fault in this community than if I had been a criminal.

A dark vein of violence ran through all of this, erupting in families, on the streets against Jews, Puerto Ricans, and African Americans, but among us too, in church and school, between children and priests, nuns and children, and in the minds and souls of my relatives and neighbors. I came out into the school yard alongside the church one afternoon when the sky was the color of dirty water and found six of my classmates urinating on a little boy who was often the victim of the fury that circulated mindlessly through our days. This violence was the product of many things: of changing hierarchies at work and in the family (my Sicilian uncles who worked in sales in Manhattan despised the men ahead of them, nearly always Irish Catholics); alcohol abuse; the prevalent practice of disciplining children by beating and shaming them; and the troubled inheritances of the immigrant past. On Good Fridays I kissed the wounds of Jesus crucified; I knelt alongside my Tuscan grandmother as she prayed to the Neapolitan holy man, Padre (now Santo) Pio da Pietrelcina, who bled from wounds in his body like Christ's on the cross; and every day the saints arrayed around the church in scalloped niches displayed their open wounds for all of us to see.

It is not accurate to call this "pre-modern," because the life courses of my relatives and neighbors had been fundamentally shaped by the social and economic facts of the modern world. "Primitive" will not do either (although it has been proposed: see below). I am attentive to the anti-Catholic origins of almost all the available descriptive terms. But some language is needed to mark the difference between my childhood reality from what I encountered when I left it, and the best I can do here is to call it simply the Italian American Catholic working-class Bronx and leave it at that.

The realness of this world faded the further north I went on I-95 towards New England, and by the time I crossed beneath the great stone archway at the entrance to my college it had disappeared. I had never met a Protestant before, never met anyone who did not have a parent or grandparent from another country, or anyone from the American upper class (as opposed to prosperous local lawyers and doctors), and most of them had never met someone from the working-class Italian Catholic Bronx either. It seemed that my identity thinned out too the further north I went. It was troubling and exciting to find myself in an environment where I was a stranger, nearly as troubling and exciting as it was to find myself a stranger back in the Bronx.

There was little talk about social class in the study of religion in those days (there is not much today either for that matter), no mention of the working class (who were well on their way at this juncture in American social and intellectual history to being mocked and dismissed as "hard-hats"), and little about Catholicism (St. Thomas

Aquinas, certainly, but not kissing the purple wounds on the body of Christ). These two absences, of a way of life (working class) and a way of being religious (devotional Catholicism), reinforced each other in modern American society and in the study of religion alike. They were created together and created each other.

The founding theorists of the science of religion, none of whom were Catholic, established normative hierarchies of religious belief and practice that they said had developed and evolved over time and in different parts of the world. The lower forms of religion were identified by their materialism (the idea that there was power in things like relics and rosaries); ritualism; compulsion (practitioners did not freely choose these religions, but were born into them); pragmatism (or magic, the manipulation of objects to get things done); irrationality and emotionalism; and amorality if not actual immorality.[1] The higher religions (modern liberal Christianity being the highest), on the other hand, were non-materialistic, ethical, a matter of the mind not the body, and addressed to a God who was invisible, absent, and in some theologies, departed once and for all. High and low religions corresponded to certain populations (which is what made this such an effective calculus for social domination): to the lower religions belonged people of color, the poor and working class, women, children, "primitives," and Catholics, who had been the prototype of baser forms of religion since the later 16th century. The higher religions were the province of prosperous, educated, and civilized adult white Protestants. The ideologies of class, race, gender, and age reinforced and were in this way sanctified by religious morphology. Material religion and the sweaty and dark bodies of practitioners were aligned; the gods were present to people whose bodies were figured as overly present in the social world too.[2]

Levels of religion and social class share a relationship with temporality as well in this schema. Modern people are expected to grow out of "primitive" forms of religious practice; indeed, this is one of the key markers of the modern; class, which almost always means "lower class," is meant to be risen up from, succeeded out of. The enervation of familiar realities that I experienced already as a first year college student was actually the point of it all. My former not-middle-class identity was *supposed* to be fading away, which is what my relatives feared, that by leaving the Bronx I was jumping from my social class ("big shot") and abandoning my faith. This is what I could do in a dorm room that I could not do at home.

I went to a secular college, but as it happened, owing to social and religious developments in American Catholicism in these years after the Second Vatican Council (1962–1965), the same evaluative hierarchy of ways of being and ways of being religious had been adopted in Catholic intellectual contexts. I discovered this in my senior year of college when I arranged to take a reading course on contemporary Catholicism in the United States.

According to the standard narrative of late 20th-century American Catholicism, after World War II Catholics in the United States became fully American. Catholic veterans took advantage of the G.I. Bill to enroll in record numbers in Catholic colleges and professional schools (my generation made the further move to secular higher education); many more were marrying outside their ethic communities than before the war; they had moved out of the urban core to the suburbs; and they were becoming more prosperous and securely middle class. Their religious practices kept pace with these changes. The modernizing imperatives of the Second Vatican Council ratified a process already underway in US Catholicism (I am still within the dominant narrative), a slow but steady movement towards a more recognizably modern (see above) religious practice. Protestant America gives way in this era to a tripartite nation of Protestants, Catholics, and Jews. Socially, religiously, politically, and economically, Catholics had at last become indistinguishable from other Americans. Catholics had made it (or at least the men ahead of my uncles on Madison Avenue had made it)! In this way the standard narrative of post-Council Catholicism managed to eliminate the working class and devotional practice from contemporary Catholicism.[3]

A close friend and colleague at Yale University warned me when I was debating among various dissertation possibilities that if I chose to work on Italian Harlem, rather than on Anthony Benezet and 18th-century Quaker abolitionism around the North Atlantic, as I was contemplating, my career would be stillborn. Everyone will assume that a dissertation on Italian Catholics is an act of filial piety, he said. They will accuse you of lacking the objectivity and critical distance required by scholarship, he warned. Instead of history and religious studies I would be writing autobiography in an academic environment in which even the use of "I" was discouraged. I will have revealed myself as having never left the Bronx.

But that was then and this is now. We scholars of religion and society have become much more self-critical of such normative assumptions and teleology. The traditional/modern distinction, in all its variations – primitive/civilized, religious/secular, pre-modern/modern, South/North, fundamentalist/modernist, and so on – has lost much of its theoretical force in the study of religion and culture. The notion of the "modern" itself has been destabilized and pluralized. We speak now of "multiple" and "alternative" modernities; of the modern as "braided" with the other-than-modern; we say that the modern is "out of joint with itself"; or even that "we have never been modern." Modernity is laced through and through with "traditional" worlds and the boundary between traditional and modern has become porous.[4]

It is intriguing to speculate that if I had had access to this language of the multiple modern back in 1972 I might not have been faced with such stark conceptual and personal choices. Destabilizing perspectives on the modern might have enabled me to see working-class devotional Catholicism, in all its material and visual abundance, its practices of the presence of God, the Virgin Mary, and the company of saints, and its disciplining of mind and body, as an alternative modernity. But there are two problems with this suggestion of how the idea of the multiple modern might have helped me with my particular existential and intellectual dilemma.

First, the normative scales of being and knowing that constituted the authority and historical inevitability of the modern persist in all domains of contemporary life and retain their full cultural capital. Intellectual work is still more highly esteemed than manual labor, more valued than "flipping burgers," this era's analogue to the "hardhat." More attention is paid to middle-class than to working-class religious practice, or perhaps it is more accurate to say that in this neoliberal time the assumption is that all religious practitioners, or at least all those who are socially and intellectually relevant, are middle class, aspire to be middle class, or are potentially middle class. Such assumptions erased the differences and inequalities of social class. Neoliberal ideology reauthorized the familiar hierarchies: the cosmopolitan over the local, the individual over the community, and mind (in the global North) over bodies (of workers in the global South and in various sectors of the American economy). In psychological and religious terms, the criteria for maturity, personal growth, and mental well-being remain those of the normative modern. Who is saner, more mature, or more reasonable: a young white-collar worker, whose religion, if any, is soberly mainline, or a young working-class Pentecostal who speaks in tongues, jumps up and down during church service, and looks to the Holy Spirit for guidance in how to live?

So while it is true that there is a "plurality of imaginary worlds" in contemporary global culture, of different ways of being and imagining, these disparate realities are not equal, and moving from one to the other provokes anxiety and disorientation. Which world is emergent and which is disappearing or dead? Whose lives are real in the present moment and whose seemingly real lives have been scoured out by time and are still around only because everyone else has forgotten them? Talk of the multiple modern ought not to obscure the social, psychological, religious, and existential challenges confronted by men and women who move back and forth from the traditional to the modern along various highways, oceans, and borders. I have heard stories like mine from Egyptian graduate students in religious studies, from the children of Korean and Iranian immigrants in my classes, and from colleagues from Pakistan, Mexico, and the Philippines, and I have heard them as well from working-class and rural American students who are the first in their families to go to college, from the children and grandchildren of migrants and immigrants from South and East Asia and the Caribbean, and from Southern Baptists, Pentecostals, Jehovah's Witnesses, and Mormons. Nor is it surprising that the dilemma of being and knowing I have been describing often happens at university, which is the gateway to the normative modern for many people from traditional societies. The modern is, as one theorist puts it, "unevenly experienced," but this unevenness has consequences. Nomic disorientation is a widely shared predicament of the modern world, especially among those (of us) who must "imagine the possibility that they or their children will live and work in places other than where they were born," among those of us who come from the other-than-modern.[5]

The second problem with the idea of a fissured but inclusive modernity of plural ontologies is the obverse of the first. To develop this I have to reverse my position. It has always seemed to me a sleight of nomenclatural hand to gather under the rubric of "modernity," even with the qualifier "multiple," the political and religious cultures from which the project of the modern aimed to liberate human beings and societies. Traditional religions were not partners of the modern, not in any way that "modern" retains its specific history. The various goods of modernity – human rights; freedom of thought and expression; gender equality; the rule of law; the public accountability of political and religious leaders; self-determination in matters of one's body, including reproduction and sexuality; democracy and civic responsibility; critical analytical methods, to name a few – were (and continue to be) hard won against the implacable opposition of religious orthodoxies.

The modern arose on "piles of bones," in Voltaire's grim phrase, ossuaries heaped up by protracted internecine religious violence and by the harassment of critics of traditional religion and culture.[6] The earliest advocates of the modern were exquisitely mindful of the dangers which traditional religion posed to individual freedoms and social peace, especially in alliance with absolute rulers. These thinkers had a robust awareness of the harm religions had done and of which they were capable. This is not to absolve the modern of hypocrisy or of its own horrors. As my first objection to the idea of the "multiple modern" should have made clear, it is certainly not to accept the insistence of European and North American modernity in itself as the singular way of life towards which all human history has been aiming for centuries. The modern is indeed multiply fissured. Religious figures and institutions sometimes stood in courageous and necessary opposition to the excesses of the modern, moreover, and in some cases contributed to its finer achievements. Hybrid forms of religious practice and imagination developed among some individuals and in particular communities (I am thinking here of Solomon Schechter and Conservative Judaism, for example). But I do mean to question the generally positive valence of modernity framed as a dynamic compound of plural ontologies and religious imaginaries and the implicit endorsement of anti-modern religious idioms that goes with it. I also want to recall that the modern was a positive and revolutionary project that advanced a set of particular ideals that remain valuable and worthy, however often moderns themselves betrayed them. To refer to contemporary conservative Catholicism, for example, as an alternative modernity without careful historical qualification, a precise attention to difference, and a lot of irony is to annul a long and contentious history. What is incommensurable between traditional, religiously authorized ways of being in the world and the modern cannot be erased by the insistence on plurality. To insist on this difference, as I am doing, is to keep in view the challenges of mind and heart confronted by those who move from the traditional to the modern.

By the time I was 18, I knew I had to get out of the Bronx. It was my choice to leave. I was finding the place claustrophobic and stultifying. The reliance on face-to-face transactions for social business engendered an indulgent and resigned attitude towards corruption and contempt for due process and the rules of civil society. There was aggressive suspicion towards people from outside the neighborhood, who were treated badly when they appeared on our streets, especially African Americans and Puerto Ricans. A pervasive anti-Semitism existed alongside the necessary toleration of Jews and Italian Catholics for each other in the neighborhood. There was also an ugly meanness towards men and women and children from the neighborhood who diverged from local norms or who stood out from the rest in some way. The parents of the boy being pissed on in the churchyard were divorced, at a time when very few Catholics were because the church absolutely forbade it. Nothing was ever heard about this boy's father. His mother showed up at school in high heels and fashionable clothing to complain about the violence against her son, leaving behind her in the hallways a delicious fragrance of flowers and vanilla, but the nuns, who did not like it that she was divorced or that she was so well-dressed and smelled so voluptuously, were utterly unsympathetic to her, so the tormenting of her son went on and on within plain sight of the nuns and priests. There was little restraint on what adults did or said to children. There was no language to talk about pain and terror other than the religious one of sacrifice, suffering, and grace. My aunt's comment that 90 cents and my doctorate from Yale (received a decade after that first spring away) would get me a ride on the subway gave voice to the smoldering resentments and anxieties in the neighborhood and between generations. The neighborhood reviled ambition and belittled achievement.

My nickname was "king of the road" because my ambition to leave the Bronx was so well known. But like all nicknames this one was an exaggeration. The ways of the working class and the Catholic imaginary were far more profoundly pressed into my flesh and blood than that harsh nickname allowed. "King of the road" failed to comprehend that I was both deeply of this community and at the same time deeply desirous of leaving it. It would have been more accurate to say that I was an odd traveler on a long and winding road that always seemed to circle back to the Bronx, which I could not stop thinking of as home.

I was in danger of becoming anomic, in short, a word I learned just in time in 1972. I feared that spring that I might never be completely successful at maintaining "a meaningful existence" given my "isolation" "from the nomic constructions" of the worlds I traversed along I-95.[7] Several choices were available to me. One was to heighten either my working-class ethnic Catholic origins or my identity as a university student and emergent scholar in order to prove to others and to myself that I was really more one than the other. Another was to keep the worlds separate and behave accordingly in each, walking a schizophrenic tightrope, laughing along with the guys in the old neighborhood at anti-gay jokes, descrying them back in the university, saying the rosary with my grandmother but not thinking about it, critically studying religious practice but not remembering saying the rosary with my grandmother. These options would have made my experience less bearable and would have exacerbated my anomie and homelessness. I wanted to live in a way that was authentic.

Had I been less deeply formed in the devotional imaginary, in the real presence of Christ in the Eucharist and of the Virgin Mary and the saints in everyday life, in the traffic between the living and the dead, it may have been possible for me to leave it all behind once and for all. Then again had I been less deeply formed by working-class devotional Catholicism I might not have fastened as fiercely as I did upon the theoretical language of the sociology of knowledge and religion. (The quotes in the paragraph above are from Berger and Luckmann, who I was reading in the spring semester of my first year in an introductory course in sociology.) *The Social Construction of Reality* struck me as a revelation. The apparently solid, flesh-and-blood world of my childhood became transparent. Ironically, approaching working-class ethnic Catholicism with the tools of critical social analysis had the effect of allowing me to return to that world but in a changed relationship to it, giving me a place to stand when I went "home" that was consciously inside and outside simultaneously.

But the coldly remote (as I found it) and totalizing phrase, "social construction of reality," was not adequate to the real presence of Jesus, Mary, and the saints, or to their relationships with my family and with other men and women in the neighborhood. Just as I could not be either fully in or fully out of the Catholic imaginary, so I discovered that because of my experience and my memories I could not be fully in or out of the methods and theories of the sociologies of knowledge and religion either. It is not quite accurate to say that I existed in between these two mentalities. The structural metaphor suggests a terrain that is too clearly bounded and too static. Rather, the two – social science and the devotional imaginary – came within view of each other as I went about the work of studying religion. I slowly came to the understand that holding the two in tension rendered *each* precarious and unstable, and thus unsettled they were more useful for thinking about religion as it is lived in the social world and in history. The theoretical and the devotional contextualized their respective claims to fully account for the real. I knew too much about the struggles of my family's lives, about the ugliness of the streets, about the miseries people brought to the figures on the altar, and about the relationships that formed between heaven and earth and on earth among people and the saints, not to approach these figures as really real. But I also needed the social scientific to explore the sources of the world I had lived, whose inner workings remained painfully opaque to me.

Anomic disorientation (in some circumstances becoming anomic terror) in this way became a condition for the possibility of theoretical work in religion and society rather than a subjective state needing to be healed or resolved. It opened unanticipated ways of understanding the social and the religious, but it required those in motion between the traditional to the modern to learn to live in suspension, never collapsing either of their imaginaries into the other or eliding the fundamental ontological, political, and epistemological differences between them. Such integration, whatever its political, religious, or existential motivations, deprives the modern and the traditional of their theoretically productive and socially subversive possibilities in relation to each other. To live consciously in suspension entails learning to embrace this specific form of disorientation, trusting that what appear to be distortions at the intersection of incommensurate realities are pointers towards new questions, new grounds for challenging the sufficiency of both theories and theologies of religious experience and practice, and new epistemologies for seeing both the traditional and the modern. "All social realities are precarious," write Berger and Luckmann, and so (I will add) are all religious realities. "The constant possibility of anomic terror," they continue, "is actualized whenever the legitimations that obscure the precariousness are threatened or collapse." I am suggesting that this precariousness is exactly the moment when productive and innovative theoretical work on religion and society becomes possible.[8]

I went back to my old apartment building in the Bronx recently, more than 30 years after that first spring break. My mother and father had moved away from the old neighborhood in the mid-1980s, after their apartment was broken into a third time. By then they were living behind barred windows. Drug dealers worked out of the first-floor windows of the apartment house at the end of my street. Some years before my parents left, during the 1977 World Series, the broadcaster Howard Cosell had called the nation's attention to the greasy funnels of black smoke rising from burning buildings behind the outfield of the old Yankee Stadium. "Ladies and gentlemen," Cosell had intoned, "the Bronx is burning." But there were signs of revival now.[9]

I stepped from the blazing sidewalk into the cool shadows of the building's art deco hallway. Most of the pre-World War II ornamentation had been stripped from the walls to be sold in the burgeoning market created by the furious reno-vation of Brooklyn's brownstones, but apart from these scars on the walls the building was in good shape. Three young African American girls, book bags at their feet, sat chatting and laughing on the big radiator in the main entryway. With me was an old friend, also a scholar of his community's past, from the Jewish working class in Melbourne, Australia, whose father sold dry goods at a stall in an outdoor market.

> "I grew up in this building," I said to the girls by way of explaining our suddenly arriving in the building. "I want to show my friend where I came from."
>
> "Things were better back then, I bet," one of the girls said.
>
> "Oh, I don't know," I said, "there were good people and bad people back then too." I wanted to tell her about the Italian American boy in the building, a few years older than me, who threw a Jewish neighbor's little dog off the roof one summer afternoon. He disappeared right after and then his family went away too. But I did not want to frighten her with this gruesome story.
>
> "Still," she said, "it was better then, right?"

The boy who was urinated on grew up to become a fortune teller, reading the stars for clues to other people's fate. Two Jehovah's Witnesses laden with pamphlets about the end of the world were knocking at the door of my old first-floor apartment, but no one was home.

Notes

Epigraphs: Joseph Papaleo, *Italian Stories* (Chicago, IL: Dalkey Archive Press, 2002), 45; Eric L. Santner, *On the Psychotheology of Everyday Life* (Chicago, IL: University of Chicago Press, 2001), 39.

1 One of the books I had to contend with when I was working on my dissertation was Edward C. Banfield, with the assistance of Laura Fassano Banfield, *The Moral Basis of a Backward People* (Glencoe, IL: Free Press, 1963). The backward people in question were southern Italians; the moral basis of their lives was "amoral familism," in Banfield's phrase, by which he meant that their ethics were based on face-to-face exchanges and family loyalties rather than on universal principles. This limited and unsubtle theory had a long and influential run, unfortunately.

2 This paragraph is based on the large literature that has developed in recent years on the history of the modern study of religion broadly conceived (there is still not one comprehensive volume on the subject), including J. Samuel Preus, *Explaining Religion: Criticism and Theory from Bodin to Freud* (New Haven, CT: Yale University Press, 1987); Talal Asad, *Genealogies of Religion: Discipline and Reasons of Power in Christianity and Islam* (Baltimore, MD: Johns Hopkins University Press, 1993); Donald S. Lopez, *Prisoners of Shangri-La: Tibetan Buddhism and the West* (Chicago, IL: University of Chicago Press, 1998); Leigh Eric Schmidt, *Hearing Things: Religion, Illusion, and the American Enlightenment* (Cambridge, MA: Harvard University Press, 2000); Hans G. Kippenberg, *Discovering Religious History in the Modern Age*, trans. Barbara Harshav (Princeton, NJ: Princeton University Press, 2002); David Abulafia, *The Discovery of Mankind: Atlantic Encounters in the Age of Columbus* (New Haven, CT: Yale University Press, 2008); Suzanne Marchand, *German Orientalism in the Age of Empire* (New York: Cambridge University Press, with the German Historical Institute, 2009); Tisa Wenger, *We Have A Religion: The 1920s Pueblo Dance Controversy and American Religious Freedom* (Chapel Hill: University of North Carolina Press, 2009); Lynn Hunt, Margaret Jacob and Wijnand Mijnhardt, *Bernard Picart and the First Global Vision of Religion* (Los Angeles, CA: Getty Research Institute, 2010); Guy G. Strousma, *A New Science: The Discovery of Religion in the Age of Reason* (Cambridge, MA: Harvard University Press, 2010). The classic text is Eric J. Sharpe, *Comparative Religion: A History* (LaSalle, IL: Open Court, 1986, orig. pub. 1975).

3 The most influential expressions of this narrative were, in history, Jay P. Dolan, *The American Catholic Experience: A History from Colonial Times to the Present* (Garden City, NY: Doubleday & Co., 1985), and, in sociology, Andrew M. Greeley, *The American Catholic: A Social Portrait* (New York: Basic Books, 1977). For the enduring hold of this narrative, see, for example, Jerome P. Baggett, *Sense of the Faithful: How American Catholics Live Their Faith* (New York: Oxford University Press, 2009). I otherwise admire this book, but Baggett uncritically accepts the standard narrative. "John Kennedy's election to the presidency in 1960," he concludes, "left little doubt that Catholics had indeed come of age and taken their place within the American mainstream" (14). On the new historiography of the tripartite nation, see, for example, Wendy L. Wall, *Inventing the "American Way:" The Politics of Consensus from the New Deal to the Civil Rights Movement* (New York: Oxford University Press, 2009).

4 The literature on the splintering of modernity is vast. A short personal reading list for this paragraph includes Shmuel N. Eisenstadt (ed.), *Multiple Modernities* (New Brunswick, NJ: Transaction Publishers, 2002); Charles Taylor, *Modern Social Imaginaries* (Durham, NC: Duke University Press, 2004); Dilip Parameshwar Gaonkar (ed.), *Alternative Modernities* (Durham, NC: Duke University Press, 2004); Dipesh Chakrabarty, *Provincializing Europe: Postcolonial Thought and Historical Difference* (Princeton, NJ: Princeton University Press, 2000), where the reference to the modern being out of joint with itself comes from page 16; Bruno Latour, *We Have Never Been Modern*, trans. Catherine Porter (Cambridge, MA: Harvard University Press, 1993); Talal Asad, *Formations of the Secular: Christianity, Islam, Modernity* (Stanford, CA: Stanford University Press, 2003); Schmidt, *Hearing Things*, where the concept of the braided modern appears; Christian Smith, "On Multiple Modernities: Shifting the Modernity Paradigm," unpublished paper, 2006, University of Notre Dame, available at http://www.nd.edu/~csmith22/documents/MultipleModernities.pdf (accessed June 23, 2011); and James L. Heft (ed.), *A Catholic Modernity? Charles Taylor's Marianist Award Lecture* (New York: Oxford University Press, 1999).

5 Arjun Appadurai, *Modernity at Large: Cultural Dimensions of Globalization*, Public Worlds, Vol. 1 (Minneapolis: University of Minnesota Press, 1996), 6; the phrase "unevenly experienced" is on page 3.

6 Voltaire's phrase is from Isaac Kramnick (ed.), *The Portable Enlightenment Reader* (New York: Penguin Books), 119.

7 The quoted phrases in this sentence are from the discussion of "anomic terror" in Peter L. Berger and Thomas Luckmann, *The Social Construction of Reality: A Treatise in the Sociology of Knowledge* (Garden City, NY: Anchor Books, 1967), 102.

8 Berger and Luckmann, *Social Construction of Reality,* 103.

9 For a lively account of the Bronx at the end of the 1970s, see Jonathan Mahler, *Ladies and Gentlemen. The Bronx is Burning: 1977, Baseball, Politics, and the Battle for the Soul of a City* (New York: Farrar, Straus, & Giroux, 2005).

14

ENGAGED FAITH

My own and that of others

Wade Clark Roof

By engaged faith, I have in mind one that privileges the psychological space between certainty and exploration, even doubt, or an inner dialogue of sorts between a taken-for-granted world of meaning and order and the threat of chaos impinging upon it. Of course this is language from Peter Berger, to whom I am greatly indebted; more than any other religion scholar he shaped my sociological imagination as a young sociologist of religion. But there were earlier influences, family experiences growing up that meshed well with, perhaps predisposed me to, Berger's insights. The two sets of influences are so bound together that it is impossible to sort out my career story apart from the personal story. So here I trace those earlier experiences of conflicted identity and ambivalence towards faith, and reflect on how the two are connected – as best I can – with my own religious inclinations and research agenda as it evolved over time, all of course telescoped into a very brief narrative.

Early years

To start with, I have three birth certificates plus as a child had several nick names that were freighted with family history and conflict. At birth my mother misunderstood, or the nurse incorrectly recorded my father's name, listing me as Wayne when it should have been Wade. So for the first seven years I was Wayne Clark Roof. When I was 2 my parents divorced and I was handed over to my mother's parents – the Clarks; my mother was unprepared for motherhood and struggled throughout her adult life with alcoholism and mental disturbances, and finally took her life. Clearly, I was to be called Clark, but early on that morphed into the cute little boyish name Clarkie. Moreover, living with Clarks it seemed only natural that I should bear the same last name, so I began the first grade and continued throughout elementary school as Clarkie Clark. By now my father was serving in the Navy during World War II and, surprisingly, he liked calling me Clarkie, but became pretty upset seeing my last name listed as Clark on my report cards. Having access to free legal service, he decided to clear up my original birth certificate and to make it clear that I was indeed a Roof. And for some unknown reason he chose also to change Clark to Clarkie and shifted the order of the names: So now I became Clarkie Wade Roof. I went through high school and on to Wofford College with that name; then later on as an adult I had it legally corrected in keeping with what I take to be the original intent: Wade Clark Roof.

Elsewhere I have written in some detail about this mix of names in relation to self-identity, family tensions, and experiences of social marginality,[1] but here I focus on its impact upon my religious sensitivities. Like the stories of many southerners, mine is linked to land. The old Clark family home place had been burned to the ground by Sherman's troops during the Civil War, leaving the family not just bereft, angry, and defensive but convinced that they should became "God-fearing Methodists," which was somewhat different from being simply Methodists. God-fearing Methodists, like many dyed-in-the-wool Southern Baptists, especially those living in rural areas, had strong emotional ties to the land, and by extension to defeat, to Dixie, and to God's soldier-saints including the KKK who would make right the awful wrong dealt upon the South; it was a full-blown religio-mythological reality which remains with some southerners, a few even within my own extended family.

Two realities I grew up with especially shaped my religious outlook. One was that my grandfather, while a God-fearing Methodist in many respects, didn't particularly like going to church. His religion had more to do with showing reverence for the farm God has given us, taking care of his cows, and gratitude for having gotten off the bottle earlier on in life which he credited more to his own efforts than to God, and certainly not to the church. He saw church mostly as a haven for hypocrites, many of whom he was convinced had serious drinking problems like himself, but unlike him had become very pious and moralistic. In contrast, my grandmother was a very conventional believer, attended church regularly, and worried about his eternal salvation. To his annoyance she arranged for a string of preachers to come by our house and pray with Alvin that he might accept Jesus, but that never happened. During the Depression the Clarks lost their land but then regained it, partly as a result of hard work but mainly because Alvin took up bootlegging at night; he also pro-tected other bootleggers who stilled on our land and from whom we reaped a cut of their profit. So he did the behind-the-scene work necessary for the family's survival while my grandmother projected a public image of a religious and respectable family. I grew up caught in between these two very differing worlds. That we all benefitted from bootleg while publicly we were identified with a church that denounced drinking as a sin that could lead you to hell was not lost on me, nor did I fail to pick up on how family tensions were reinforced by religious and moral teachings. My grandmother's moralistic views may well have been a factor contributing to my mother's suicide.

The second reality concerns my biological father whom I seldom saw, at best once a year, and even then we had little in common to talk about and almost no emo-tional connection. Even his name – also thrust upon me – became burdensome at some point. He had been named for Wade Hampton, the Civil War hero and South Carolina governor who led the campaign to restore the state to white rule after Reconstruction and belonged to one of the largest slave-holding families in the state. Thousands of boys were named in honor of this man. Of course, I understood why: Hampton was a hero at a time when southerners felt deeply the wounds of defeat. Problematic for me was less the Hampton connection (although I didn't like it) than the fact that my father remained so proud of this name and the racist heritage with which it was associated. He died in 1976 an unrepentant segregationist and confident that God would yet bring about a triumphal return of the old order. As he dreamed of this I was involved in civil rights activities in the South and then later taught religion and race relations courses trying to undermine that old order. It was a topic we couldn't talk about, and once again the message that came through was clear: religion was deeply embedded in history and a way of life but also subject to various interpretations, and hence a source of worldviews and emotional conflicts, even within families. So alienated was I from my father that in my early publications I listed myself as W. Clark Roof (yet another name!) to block out this aspect of my name, which I continued to do until after his death.

Escape and return

Oddly enough, family experiences did not so much turn me against religion as stirred my interest in studying it. It was clear to me that religion was embedded in the messiness of life, that it ran deep within culture and the individual psyche, and I wanted to explore it further: How is it that religion can take on so many diverse symbolic meanings? Why did it have so strong a hold, and take the shape it did for southerners? How odd was my own family? My big break in exploring these questions came in the spring of my senior year in college when I was awarded a Rockefeller Brothers Foundation "Trial-Year Fellowship" to attend the seminary of my choice. For several years I had considered theological study, even possibly the ministry, in hopes of being a progressive leader. My thought was that I would go to Duke or Emory, the two closest Methodist seminaries, and check it out and then make a decision. But an English professor persuaded me that with the opportunity to go to any theology school in the country, I should consider going outside of the South – a chance, he said, to expand my horizons and view the issues of heritage and identity from afar. Thus, in 1961, I enrolled at Yale Divinity School.

Yale was a mind-blowing experience. Theological reflection as such turned out not to be as much of a draw as I had hoped, but James M. Gustafson's sociology of religion course in my second year captured my imagination more so than any other course I took there. The introductions to Marx, Weber, and Durkheim sparked my interest, as did the empirical analysis of American religion and culture. His newly published *Treasure in Earthen Vessels*[2] provided a fresh perspective on religious institutions as human communities, going so far as to suggest that because religion (he says church) takes on many colors fitting into its varying environments it is like a "chameleon."[3] This gave me a better grasp of religion as a human reality, warts and all, and particularly of the southern religious situation embroiled at the time in the civil rights movement with forces resisting change and others pushing for it; similarly, it shed light on my family as a microcosm of the struggles and emotions that were so intense among blue-collar and farm folk, the southern people I knew best. Gustafson's work and teaching did something much more: It introduced me to "lived religion" before that phrase gained currency. Important, too, was his point that we should be cautious about theological oversimplification, and thus not overlook the impact of non-doctrinal influences. That religion is culturally adaptive, he made clear, was not a sign of its failure or weakness but, to the contrary, only as it is socially and culturally embedded can we know, believe, practice, experience – and by extrapolation, even study – it in everyday context. This was obviously the case, yet for me at the time this was revelatory.

Intellectually, I knew all this to be somehow true, but it took two years as pastor in a South Carolina church in the mid-1960s for me to appreciate it fully. From 1964 to 1966 in a United Methodist Church, I faced what other progressive-minded pastors at the time confronted: whites fearing that blacks might enter their church; condemnations of northern civil rights activists intervening in southern life; and political conservatives alleging that liberals were "mixing religion and politics," not recognizing that they were doing the same in trying to preserve the status quo. To be sure, I knew the challenges would be considerable before I landed at the church but I also believed that as a southerner I could relate to my parishioners, many of whom came from backgrounds not unlike my own. So as lunch counters were desegregated and black–white tensions and sometimes violence erupted across the South, I struggled to find my voice: I affirmed my commitment to the equality of all people and sought to prepare my congregation for the new, desegregated world emerging, yet at the same time I knew that if I got too visibly involved in civil rights protests I would seriously damage my relationship with my working-class, largely uneducated congregation. Arriving at the church just two weeks after receiving a Yale degree where in the same commencement Martin Luther King, Jr. received an honorary degree did not go unnoticed in my congregation; thus from the beginning I was viewed through suspicious eyes. So I knew I had to carefully define my role as a southerner who understood the history and culture of the people, yet as one with a committed Christian perspective on race. It was not easy being pastor and prophet, and it was made even harder given that I was paid weekly, and always from the collection taken up from that week's Sunday worship service! While at Yale I had read Liston Pope's *Millhands and Preachers*,[4] one of the classic sociological studies of southern religion, but now I knew what it was really like for the religious voice to be held captive to the grip of social custom and economic power.

Graduate study in sociology

After two years I decided to do graduate work in sociology at the University of North Carolina at Chapel Hill. To a considerable extent the decision was based upon my personal identity issues; my two areas of study were race and religion, not uncommon for a southern liberal in those years. Gerhard E. Lenski would become my mentor; his book *The Religious Factor*[5] introduced me to empirical analysis in religion, an important balance to Gustafson's earlier theoretical work. But it was Peter Berger's *The Sacred Canopy*[6] more than any other book that excited me about studying religion sociologically. There were other important works of his that were very influential as well.[7] Aside from the social-constructionist perspective advanced in his writings, Berger's attention to modernity and how it pluralizes definitions of social reality broadened my perspective far beyond the southern context. At times framed as secularization but always, and most importantly, as leading to a universe of pluralistic worldviews, it was a perspective that was applicable generally. In the American environment particularly with its history of democracy, separation of church and state, and voluntary faith, religion almost from the beginning was understood in terms of denominationalism (i.e., pluralism internal to religious tradition); but now, in the context of advanced modernity there was an upgrading of religious choice, greater emphasis on personal autonomy in an expanded range of possibilities. Ascription, or the religion one was born into, was losing ground to personal preference and self-actualization as a basis of religious identity. No longer was it enough to know whether one was a Baptist, a Catholic, or a Lutheran, but one needed also to know what particular style of Baptist, Lutheran, or Catholic a person was.

The topic of my dissertation arose right out of my southern experience. With survey data collected from a sample of North Carolina Episcopalians I looked at "locals" and "cosmopolitans," i.e., people's social identities as based upon their orientation, either parochially to the local communities in which they lived or more broadly to society at large. My interest was in how and to what extent these orientations related to measures of religiosity and racial prejudice, and sorting out causal influences. The locals were of course the traditionalists for whom religion and racial prejudice were largely taken for granted, if not ordained of God; and cosmopolitans were the modernists for whom such views and relationships were better understood as products of custom. While the former understood faith and morality defined largely on the basis of rigid and literalistic interpretation of the Bible as filtered through southern experience, the latter were more open to a socially constructed view of reality, and often one in which they understood themselves to be playing a part in formulating. Congregations were arenas of conflict between these two outlooks, much as Gustafson's earlier influence had prepared me to expect and I had experienced in my short career as a minister. After a great deal of revision, this work was published as *Community and Commitment: Religious Plausibility in a Liberal Protestant Church*.[8] It had all the marks of an unreadable quantitative dissertation, too many tables, correlations, and regressions, yet in some ways conceptually was a predecessor to the culture-wars perspective of traditionalists versus modernists that attracted so much attention a decade or so later. The research, writing, and rewriting to make the manuscript publishable amounted to a more disciplined, regionally based analysis and reflection of the tensions and clashes of worldviews I had experienced within my family. Looking back today, I realize even more than I did at the time how much the final product was intertwined with my biography.

Broadening the research

Teaching at the University of Massachusetts, Amherst, my interest in the southern religious context waned somewhat as I came to focus more on American religion. Working with sociologists like Jackson W. Carroll, Dean Hoge, William McKinney, and David Roozen, all of whom were either on, or affiliated with, the faculty at Hartford Seminary, I became involved in the "church growth and decline" project. This was a national study aimed at arriving at a better understanding of why some denominations, particularly the so-called mainline faith communities, were losing members beginning in the mid-1960s while conservative communities were growing. The social, cultural, and theological factors all bearing upon this complex religious pattern had not been systematically studied, and our research documented that the situation was even more complex than even we had thought, and hardly reducible to any single explanation. Edited by Hoge and Roozen, the book resulting from our research, *Understanding Church Growth and Decline: 1950–1978*,[9] was soon regarded as "must reading" for those interested in gaining a more informed, better documented analysis of this shift – indeed, a "seismic shift" as Martin E. Marty[10] put it in the Foreword – in religious trends. Moreover, the trends we identified, while largely institutional in character, were reflective of dramatic moral, political, cultural, and ideological changes, which ignited in the 1960s and would reverberate for the remainder of the 20th century and contribute to a major reconfiguration of American culture and life as we know it today.

This project prepared the way for my collaboration with McKinney on another major research project, out of which came *American Mainline Religion: Its Changing Shape and Future*.[11] What we sought to do was to spell out in greater detail what was happening to the mainline faiths, or perhaps better put the historic, old-line traditions as in the case of Protestants. So much at the time was being written about new religious movements, particularly the Eastern spiritual groups that were birthed, or took on new life during this period. So much too had happened in the 1960s that pointed to a post-WASP culture increasingly in the making: the Kennedy election and the Supreme Court ruling that public school prayer was unconstitutional, both hugely symbolic of a changing normative context. Vatican Council II had opened the way to modernizing influences within Catholicism in keeping with the larger American pattern of increasing individual autonomy in religion. Hence a social profiling of the mainstream faith communities and their new configurations culturally, economically, and politically seemed timely. Using NORC survey data, we looked at patterns of religious switching – into, out of, and across religious communities observing the extent of losses for the liberal groups and gains for the conservative religions plus, increasingly important, for non-religious sectors. We examined birth rates documenting little difference between liberal Protestants and Catholics, and the more telling fact that the new conservative Protestants had much higher rates than either of these more established constituencies. We introduced the term "New Voluntarism" to describe generally this new situation of choice which involved more than the selection of a religious or non-religious identity; instead, there were increased choices in styles of religious belonging and reliance upon subjective criteria of self-authenticity and spiritual well-being in making decisions about faith and practice. Partly due to its breadth of perspective, the book captured something of the mood of the times and sorted out trends affecting religion's location within the culture that continued to evolve for decades, some in fact even to this very day. Of the various books I have authored or co-authored, this one is still the most cited and/or quoted.

One of the important findings reported in *American Mainline Religion* was the extent to which the liberal religious communities were losing their youth. That observation was not headline news nor really all that new historically, but the extent to which young people were dropping out of these groups as conservative faiths were picking them up was surprising to us as well as to many others. Religious liberals brought up their children to think for themselves, particularly so in the white middle-class sector during the 1960s and 1970s; not surprisingly, their youth were at the vanguard of a shift towards a more spiritual questing mood. Because the future of these communities was in question, the Lilly Endowment, Inc. hosted a one-day seminar on the book in New York City for a dozen or so religion scholars, out of which came a call for more research on the changing religious patterns for youth. And out of this conversation soon followed, to my great surprise, an invitation from the Lilly Endowment to submit a proposal for a large national study profiling the religious and spiritual lives of the post-World War II baby-boom generation. This was an important opportunity that just fell my way and marked the beginning of a series of projects focusing on generational trends in religion that would occupy me for many years.

Generational trends

The Lilly-funded project was designed with a random telephone survey in the first stage, followed by a second stage of interviews with selected respondents. Though my first such study of this sort, it proved to be ideal for my purpose, combining survey parameters allowing for generalizations and in-depth accounts of religious and spiritual biographies. *A Generation of Seekers: The Spiritual Journeys of the Baby Boom Generation*[12] emerged from this project, the first of several books aimed at profiling broadly the post-World War II generation. This was followed some years later by my *Spiritual Marketplace: Baby Boomers and the Remaking of American Religion*,[13] which was based on a second round of interviews with a subsample of the same respondents from the first study. A longitudinal research design allowed us to compare the same individuals seven or eight years apart, many of whom were now approaching mid-life, and thus at a critical juncture in their marriages, families, careers, and community activities. This later round of interviews documented again the fluid character of their religious and spiritual lives, how many continued to move in and out of religious communities but did so now with greater maturity and a clearer focus of what they were doing; as was to be expected, many were more settled in their life-situations. They told rich stories about their quests for faith and certainty, yet also stories of spiritual growth within and outside of religious communities. There were stories of hurt and disappointment within organized religion; for many the stories were about living with doubt and uncertainty, echoing what appears to have been better known then than earlier that doubt and faith need not necessarily be mutually exclusive. A growing number understood that doubts and life's challenges not only test conventionally held often unquestioned beliefs, but can deepen personal faith by forcing them to come to terms with hitherto confronted questions. Spiritual growth, especially for those not claiming strong religious identities but also for many who did, was more appreciated than earlier.

Several intellectual developments greatly contributed to how I framed my conceptual approach in these studies. Most importantly, there was the so-called "cultural turn" in sociology giving renewed attention not just to the search for meaning but also and less subjectively to moral codes, practices, textual interpretations, and reflections on taken-for-granted religious notions. Boomers were an ideal constituency for such in-depth study: they were exposed to greater religious diversity than any generation before them; they had experienced a great deal of family breakup, and hence ruptures in patterns of religious socialization while growing up; they were at the center of the widespread changes in the 1960s that eroded trust in institutions and encouraged experimentation with new lifestyles; and they were immersed in a marketing and consumption-based culture that privileged the self as having almost unlimited choices. Religion in virtually every way conceptualized was touched by these engulfing trends; as true for a wide range of life-spheres reflection and greater agency in religious decision-making were enhanced, one had to "work on" whatever inherited religion, or lack of, they had.

Second, and more specifically, there was the growing attention within religious studies to "lived religion," a shift away from focusing so much on official, authoritative religion to how individuals and groups thought about and acted upon their religion in everyday life. Perhaps more accurately, attention turned more to the ways in which people negotiated beliefs and practices in relation to what religious authorities prescribed. This negotiation and re-enactment of religious values in everyday life circumstances is indeed complex and multi-faceted, considering that, as Robert Orsi put it, "particular people, in particular places and times, live in, through, and against the religious idioms, including (often enough) those not explicitly their own."[14] My own summary of these complexities looking just at the widely used self-definitions as being religious, spiritual, religious and spiritual, or claiming neither of these labels was itself a challenge, stated in *Spiritual Marketplace* as follows:

> Drawing off the "cultural toolbox" metaphor, we explore the linkages between individuals and institutions, and the interplay between the "spiritual" and the "religious" as identities: when the spiritual is lost to frozen religious forms, when the religious and the spiritual are creatively fused in lived narrative, when religious rhetoric is rejected in favor of the spiritual, and when even both the religious and the spiritual fail to provide a meaningful language of self-construction [...] the interpretation stresses the role of believers and followers themselves in using symbols, doctrines, experiences, and concerns as "cultural

tools" in defining who they are and for marking themselves as distinct and different from others.[15]

Still another specific intellectual strand was the focus upon the "production of culture." This yielded the important insight that religious institutions, no less than other social institutions, were more open and flexible than many sociologists often presumed. Internally, changes could originate from within organized religion as a result of deliberate efforts by some members to bring about reforms or new adaptations to their environments; and externally, institutions were virtually at all times adjusting to and/or creatively engaged with shifts in values, beliefs, and moods characterizing society at large. Because intentionally minded people make up social institutions and the latter's boundaries are porous, and thus hardly self-contained, the two sources of change blend easily together and are often impossible to separate. The rise of the seeker church is an example: it was deliberately created to appeal to a largely post-Christian sector of the society who had lost touch with older religious styles yet was open to addressing spiritual concerns broadly shared across society. There were innovators who identified a particular audience, drew selectively off tradition and repackaged it in new, more culturally current idioms. Related studies of de-institutionalization and re-institutionalization, or of de-traditionalizing and re-traditionalizing patterns by scholars like Giddens[16] and Beck, Giddens, and Lash[17] underscored the crucial point that religious memory and tradition are always undergoing, to one degree or another, a process of formulation and reformulation. Studies of this sort helped me to link the micro-world of boomers' subjective choices to the larger macro-restructuring of institutions, making them more adaptable to their needs and preferences. It was all very complex: this younger generation was engaged, often deeply and reflexively, in religious reality construction, yet did so consciously or not within a larger context of religious and symbolic formation at the hands of cultural producers.

Further insight into these changing religious patterns came in other generational projects of which I was a part: first, a cross-cultural study of the postwar generation mainly in European countries,[18] and second, a study of generational cultures within the United States.[19] The first brought together distinguished sociologists in Europe including Eileen Barker, Karel Dobbelaere, and Danièle Hervieu-Léger and others documenting a widespread shift after World War II in 11 countries, essentially a transition from religion as a culture passed from generation to generation to religion as a personal matter which people attended to themselves. With this transition came, we observed, related important developments: greater exploration across religions, or a mixing of codes; an emphasis upon experience and life's journey; and multi-layered meaning systems making use of both traditional and popularized religious and spiritual beliefs, scientific teachings, psychology, folk culture, inspirational literature, festive practices, and the like. We observed, in Hervieu-Legér's words, the "deregulation" of the religious world,[20] or the further erosion of the authority of religious establishments to define and control fixed religious definitions. Implications for religious meaning-making in an open market, including increased innovation, product differentiation, and competition for the individual's loyalty, were obvious.

The second project compared three generations: pre-boomers, boomers, and generation Xers. We viewed them as overlapping yet quite distinct cultural waves within religious institutions. More than in my earlier projects, this one focused almost exclusively on the relation of the several generations to congregational life, and how these latter institutions adapted or should adapt to the differing cultures. Carroll and I drew upon personal interviews, case studies, and survey data to describe the generational cultures, looking closely at ways in which religious institutions must, if they are to survive, bridge differing worlds, or as we say, engage in understanding "the various life experiences and outlook of its followers, to negotiate with one another over competing interpretations, and to carry on a larger dialogue with historic tradition."[21] We argued that this task of bridging, if it is to be authentic, must become a more self-conscious undertaking within these institutions, and especially so in a time of rapid social and cultural change. Exercising some degree of agency, institutions – not unlike individuals – have to be cognizant of the cultural waves of which they are a part and recognize the need for ongoing, reflexive interpretations of religious meaning; that is, to re-create tradition by forging a mix of the past with the present. Though not mentioned explicitly in the book, both Carroll and I, having attended theology schools, remembered what Karl Barth once said about Christians: that they should engage in theological reflection holding the Bible in one hand and a newspaper in the other.

Religious Studies and California

For more than 20 years now, my academic home has been in Religious Studies at the University of California, Santa Barbara. Here I am known as an Americanist who "happens to be" trained sociologically. Having suffered through one after another change in name, this relabeling poses no real problem; indeed, it has opened up possibilities for engaging in discussion about the American setting in deeper ways – historically especially, but also greater comparative religious study, broader debates on modernity and postmodernity, and religion globally. Aside from the benefits of a multidisciplinary focus of study within religious studies, the California setting itself offers rich and unusual opportunities for examining religion in a hyper-modern context. As has been observed about California, it "stretches our religious imagination and our conception of what it means to be religious."[22]

Two topics in particular have attracted my attention of late: one, the challenges of religious pluralism; and two, the new progressive religious movement arising in response to the conservative evangelical-fundamentalist mood of the past several decades. Southern California is a good setting for carrying out both of these projects. Few places within the country can boast as much religious diversity as is found here, both historically and currently, and for the presence of a relatively strong culture of pluralism.[23] Lacking a dominant religious establishment (unless we regard secularity as a functioning establishment), the locale is fluid and ever-shifting, and thus allows for exploration of the changing mix of religious and political alliances across faith traditions, and increasingly, with non-faith sectors, with regard to conservative and progressive causes. The public presence of religion is highly contested and disproportionally influenced by low-commitment Catholics, of which there are many, and low-commitment mainline Protestants, who along with non-Christians and secularists occupy a crucial position ideologically. Often this combined constituency is a swing vote, typically leaning to the left on lifestyle and cultural issues, but aligning with more conservative groups on bread-and-butter issues. In a time when the political has expanded and become an even stronger venue for religion's public impact,[24] whatever else religion in California may be, it is highly mobilized and engaged publicly in support of causes and related matters of religious dialogue.

Conclusions

Throughout this outline of research projects and intellectual interests, prominent are themes of fluidity, interpretation, and engagement. The first enhances possibilities that the second and third will be creative and meaningful. Fundamentalist movements in the contemporary world seek to sustain certainty and stable views by means of biblical literalism and reliance upon frozen tradition, yet the dislocations of modernity propel far more of us to engage religious texts, traditions, and ideologies, including even those that are secular, in search of a holistic and sustaining view of life. In this respect my research has looked mainly at the general trends within the United States and elsewhere, trying to discern the broad societal dynamics of religious and spiritual change and how these changes force people to engage religious questions. Hence the large mainstream religious sectors are of more interest to me than new religious movements; the culture and society as a whole more interesting as a context for the study of meaning-making than what occurss just within narrowly defined religious enclaves; social change and its consequences more critical to grasp than to overly assume continuity.

In the end, how much of my – or any religion scholar's – approach to and/or sensitivities about religion arise out of biography or as a result of other, more impersonal intellectual influences is impossible to judge, but I know the two to be closely fused. If the study of religion was an objective, value-free exercise, then this would be a serious deficiency; but we all know that ours is not an objective and value-free area of study, and hence the question becomes: How well does the religious scholar handle his or her past plus and make use of it when defining a research agenda on lived religion? What I know for sure is that over time I moved away from the narrowly defined empiricism of my graduate training towards a greater appreciation for cultural interpretation, for experience, for process and growth of the individual. Rather than simply documenting patterns of church attendance and belief in God as ends in themselves, or using them to spin macro-level theories of religious growth and decline, as some sociologists do, I was drawn more to the question of what is the contextual meaning of religious attendance or belief in God, to what way is the former important religiously, and to varied imageries of God and their social and political correlates. In effect, I have looked for the big picture; at religion in the broadest sense; its shifts in form, meaning, and significance across social contexts and the life span; and sought to offer new mappings of religion and modernity as evolving in our time. In a very real sense, this has been a risky, perhaps even presumptuous undertaking, but more than just an intellectual adventure it has been an exercise of the soul, an engaged quest of my own.

Notes

1 Wade Clark Roof, "That Ain't Your Name," *Southern Cultures*, forthcoming.
2 James M. Gustafson, *Treasure in Earthen Vessels* (New York: Harper & Brothers, 1961).
3 Gustafson, 112.
4 Liston Pope, *Millhands and Preachers* (New Haven, CT: Yale University Press, 1942).
5 Gerhard E. Lenski, *The Religious Factor* (Garden City, NY: Doubleday, 1963).
6 Peter Berger, *The Sacred Canopy* (Garden City, NY: Doubleday, 1967).
7 Earlier I had read Berger's *The Precarious Vision* (Westport, CT: Greenwood Press, 1976) and *The Social Construction of Reality* with Thomas Luckmann (New York: Anchor, 1967), and then later, *The Heretical Imperative* (Garden City, NY: Doubleday, 1980) to mention those that were particularly important to me.
8 Wade Clark Roof, *Community and Commitment: Religious Plausibility in a Liberal Protestant Church* (New York: Elsevier, 1978).
9 Dean Hoge and David Roozen (eds), *Understanding Church Growth and Decline: 1950–1978* (New York: Pilgrim Press, 1979).
10 Foreword, 13.
11 Wade Clark Roof and William McKinney, *American Mainline Religion: Its Changing Shape and Future* (New Brunswick, NJ: Rutgers University Press, 1987).
12 Wade Clark Roof, *A Generation of Seekers: The Spiritual Journeys of the Baby Boom Generation* (New York: Harper SanFrancisco, 1993).
13 Wade Clark Roof, *Spiritual Marketplace: Baby Boomers and the Remaking of American Religion* (Princeton, NJ: Princeton University Press, 1999).
14 Robert Orsi, "Everyday Miracles: The Study of Lived Religion," in *Lived Religion in America*, ed. David D. Hall (Princeton, NJ: Princeton University Press, 1997), 7.
15 Roof, *Spiritual Marketplace,* 13.
16 Anthony Giddens, *Modernity and Self-Identity: Self and Society in the Late Modern Age* (Stanford, CA: Stanford University Press, 1991).
17 Ulrich Beck, Anthony Giddens and Scott Lash, "Living in a Post-Traditional Society," in *Reflexive Modernization: Politics, Tradition and Aesthetics in the Modern Social Order*, ed. Ulrich Beck, Anthony Giddens and Scott Lash (Stanford, CA: Stanford University Press, 1994).
18 Wade Clark Roof, Jackson W. Carroll and David A. Roozen (eds), *The Post-War Generation and Establishment Religion: Cross-Cultural Perspectives* (Boulder, CO: Westview Press, 1995).
19 Jackson W. Carroll and Wade Clark Roof, *Bridging Divided Worlds: Generational Cultures in Congregations* (San Francisco, CA: Jossey-Bass, 2002).
20 Danièle Hervieu-Léger, "The Case of French Catholicism," in *The Post-War Generation and Establishment Religion: Cross-Cultural Perspectives*, ed. Wade Clark Roof et al. (Boulder, CO: Westview Press, 1995), 164–165.
21 Carroll and Roof, *Bridging Divided Worlds*, 13.
22 Elden G. Ernst, "Religion in California," *Pacific Theological Review* 19 (Winter 1986), 48.
23 For further discussion, see Wade Clark Roof, "Pluralism as a Culture: Religion and Civility in Southern California," *The Annals of the American Academy of Political and Social Science* 612 (July 2007): 82–99.
24 James Davison Hunter, *To Change the World: The Irony, Tragedy, and Possibility of Christianity in the Late Modern World* (New York: Oxford University Press, 2010).

15

STUDYING PROTESTANTISM IN A CATHOLIC AND SECULAR CONTEXT

Lessons for a comparative sociology of religion

Jean-Paul Willaime

I will begin my sociological self-portrait by describing the academic path that led me from the University of Strasbourg to the Ecole Pratique des Hautes Etudes in Paris. I will discuss the impact of this career move on the development of my identity as a sociologist of religion, and will mention various research topics that have meant a lot to me. The second part of this chapter focuses on the sociology of Protestantism, and attempts to demonstrate the comparative advantages of studying this particular religious world for a general sociology of religion.

From the University of Strasbourg to the Ecole Pratique des Hautes Etudes in Paris

In the 1970s, still influenced by the protests of 1968 – and all the philosophical, religious, sociological, and political questions they had raised – taking an interest in the sociology of religion in France meant, first of all, familiarizing oneself with the Marxist approaches which analyzed religious phenomena as ideological super-structures that masked the reality of things and invited each individual to liberate him- or herself from a religion that was viewed as alienating and obsolete. I thus devoted my first PhD (1975) to the development of a critical analysis of the Marxist pattern of infrastructure and superstructure.[1] I was subsequently appointed as a lecturer in "religious sociology" at the Faculty of Protestant Theology of the University of Strasbourg where, from 1975 to 1992, I taught sociology of religion to several generations of students of Protestant theology (who, on completion of their studies, chose or did not choose to become ministers).[2] Since 1992, the year when I was appointed as the director of studies at the section of religious sciences at the Ecole Pratique des Hautes Etudes (Sorbonne, Paris)[3] to the Chair of "history and sociology of Protestantisms," I have been teaching the sociology of religion in general and sociology of Protestantisms in particular to a body of auditors and students, diverse both in terms of national origins (in particular European, African, and Asian) and disciplinary background (history, sociology, anthropology, philosophy, theology, law, languages, and civilizations). This double experience gained in Strasbourg and in Paris exercised a major influence on my way of working in the sociology of religion, a way that articulated a specialization in the study of a particular religious world – Protestantisms – and a constant interest in a sociology of religion conceived of as a contribution to general sociology. It very quickly became obvious to me that religion in general did not exist and that, as a social phenomenon, only some special expressions of it could be recognized corresponding to practices, representations, organizations, and determined socializations.

Teaching theology students required being explicit about what could and what could not be expected from the sociology of religion. Asserting my identity as a sociologist within a faculty of theology – in this case a Protestant faculty – I constantly insisted that sociology was not a denominational subject, that it was an empirical and non-normative subject, that it actually described and analyzed religious phenomena as they were and not such as one desired them to be. This fact immediately made me extremely vigilant with regard to axiological neutrality and I am always shocked that some sociologists, not only in the field of sociology of religion, but also in other fields of investigation, step outside the scientific code of conduct of social sciences by bringing a sort of scientific "blessing" to this or that cause. I had to be even more vigilant because, in the 1970s, I had to curb the eagerness of "progressive" students of theology who expected too much from sociology by believing that it was going to provide them with recipes for reforming the Churches. I think that studying the significance of each other's values while maintaining some critical distance with as much respect to "progressive" as well as "conservative" students is the specific contribution that sociology can bring and how it can be useful.

While specializing in the study of the Protestant world, I maintained a constant interest in the history of the sociology of religion and the contribution of the great classics to this field.[4] To me, the discovery of Max Weber's comprehensive sociology of religion was essential. It was facilitated by the fact that the University of Strasbourg, open to the contributions of German sociology, included professors Julian Freund and Freddy Raphaël, who had played a major part in the introduction of Max Weber's work in France. The reference to Weber usefully complemented an initiation into sociological research that I discovered through the sociology of Catholicism that had been developed in France by following the lead of Gabriel Le Bras. Three works were particularly important for me: Jean Séguy's *Les sectes protestantes dans la France contemporaine*[5] introduced me to the historical sociology of Protestant diversity (Jean Séguy also contributed to initiating me to Weber and Troeltsch); Emile Poulat's *Eglise contre bourgeoisie. Introduction au devenir du catholicisme actuel*[6] took me away from the bipolar evidences of the conflict of the two Frances (Catholic right versus republican and secular left); finally, Peter Berger's *The Sacred Canopy: Elements of a Sociological Theory of Religion*[7] made me aware of the deep mutations of the socio-cultural situation of the religious in modern societies.

After my first above-mentioned doctoral thesis which was theoretical, I undertook a second doctoral thesis based on an empirical investigation of ministers who exercised their ministry in the different Protestant Churches of France, an investigation that was subject to a PhD in sociology at the faculty of social sciences of the University of Strasbourg and which gave birth to the work *Profession: pasteur*.[8] While teaching the sociology of religion and Protestantisms at the faculty of Protestant theology of the University of Strasbourg, I undertook research activities in cooperation with the French National Centre for Scientific Research (CNRS). As a member of a faculty of theology, I particularly valued this cooperation with the CNRS and the scientific recognition that it brought. When the CNRS proposed merging the sociology of religion team from the faculty of Protestant theology with the religion and law team from the faculty of Catholic theology within the same research laboratory located in Strasbourg, I deliberately supported this initiative despite the opposition of the faculty of Protestant theology.

This project became a reality with the creation of the laboratory *Société, Droit et Religions en Europe* that I founded with my colleague Francis Messner, Research Director at the CNRS, and a well-known specialist in the study of law and religion. While working with lawyers, I became aware both of the internal laws of religions (canon law, Protestant ecclesiastical disciplines, Jewish law, Muslim law, and so on) and the state laws concerning religion. This had a twofold impact on my understanding of the sociological study of religious groups. On the one hand, the very way in which religious groups understood and instituted each other, according to their self-understanding, was important. On the other hand, we need to examine how this way of understanding and organizing each other as religious organizations was part of – not without tensions and conflicts – the legal frameworks imposed by state laws on religion.

I developed a particular interest in the latter. Ever since, I have been interested in Church–state relations in France, not only in the notorious secularity question and the 1905 law of separation of Church and state,[9] but also in the local law of Alsace and Moselle regarding the specifics of worship. From there on, I developed an interest in a comparative approach to Church–state relations in different European countries and was able to better assess the uniqueness of French secularism within the European context.[10] Harboring a personal distaste for intellectual nationalism, I became more and more critical of approaches that – by considering French secularism as the state-of-the-art separation of the Church and the state – tended to consider it as a normative model which other (European) countries should follow. I took issue on this subject with Jean Baubérot, a French specialist in secularism.[11] The attention paid to the historic and legal arrangements of Church–state relations in other European countries particularly enabled me to note that the respective autonomy between religion and politics – specific to democratic societies – could cope with various national schemes of Church–state relations, including those that had instituted various systems of recognition of religious groups and cooperation with them in different fields (e.g., education, social action, etc.). Although Church–state relations are in line with the political and religious histories specific to each country, and although the schemes that were created to manage these relations are significant elements of the national identity of each country, I decided to take a closer look at features of Europeanization in this field.[12] This European dimension of my research was embellished in 2006–2009 by joining the European program REDCo ("Religion in Education: A Contribution to Dialogue or a Factor of Conflict in Transforming Societies of European Countries?"). Since then, the way in which religious facts and teachings are integrated into school life by the public schools of different countries has remained one of my preferred areas of research.[13]

In 1992, when I arrived in Paris and joined the section of religious sciences at the Ecole Pratique des Hautes Etudes, I found myself in a "great institution of higher education" where approaches to religious phenomena (history, anthropology, philosophy, sociology) were largely multidisciplinary, and very internationally oriented, thanks to both the cultural areas that were studied and the origin of the students. While mixing with colleagues who were studying the religion of ancient Rome (John Scheid), African traditional religions (Michael Houseman), or Siberian shamanism (Roberte Hamayon), I expanded my horizons as a sociologist of Protestantisms. After a seminar dedicated to "belief" organized with anthropologists, I adopted the expression of "relations with invisible entities" to qualify the relation that, in religious activities, people tie up with various forms of otherness (God, gods, spirits, ancestors, forces, etc.). Deploying my sociological activities in such an institution was no longer about defending my sociological identity in front of theologians, but in front of historians and anthropologists who were not all well disposed towards sociologists. Indeed, some people, such as Pierre Legendre, considered that sociology represented some sort of engineering specific to modern societies. Such issues were rather stimulating. In my courses at the EPHE, I continued to teach the sociology of religion in general and sociology of Protestantisms in particular. Joining the laboratory *Groupe Sociétés, Religions et Laïcités*, a joint research unit EPHE-CNRS (I supervised this laboratory from 2002 to 2007) and the *Institut européen en sciences des religions* (which I supervised from 2005 to 2010) in many ways defined my research activities relating to the question of religion in schools.[14]

The contribution of the sociology of Protestantisms to a comprehensive sociology of religion

My academic career as a sociologist of religion has been built on both theoretical and empirical grounds. It is the study of Protestantisms in particular, however, that I want to discuss in the second section of this chapter, with an emphasis on the contribution a sociology of Protestantisms can make to broader sociology of religion. Several works, especially by Jean Séguy,[15] Steve Bruce,[16] and, more recently, the historic analyses of Alister McGrath[17] and Harold Berman,[18] have been formative in my thinking about the field.

Reconsidering the relation between religion and modernity

Studying the Protestant world was for me, first of all, a way of confronting the question of the relation between religion and modernity. I was regularly upset by the radical way in which many of my colleagues, specialists in Catholicism and often themselves of Catholic origin, saw religion and modernity as opposites. It is true that Catholicism and modernity clashed, often severely (in issues like education and in the modernistic dispute). A framework which argued that individuals were able to liber-ate themselves from religious guardianships exclusively thanks to the pressure from secular humanism and philosophies just didn't seem plausible for me. There was more to Western modernity than opposing religion. Influenced by Max Weber, I was sensitive to the contributions of Judaism and Protestantisms to the religious genealogies of Western modernity, but I was also interested in the contribution of Catholicism itself.

As a specialist in the Protestant worlds, and being a Protestant myself, I looked at Germany, Great Britain, Scandinavian societies, and the United States, and discovered configurations where, indeed, tensions and conflicts between religion and modernity could be noted. But there were also all sorts of arrangements and parallel evolutions of religion on the one hand, and political and cultural dimensions on the other. It is no coincidence that I insisted on including Tocqueville among the classics of socio-logical thought relating to religion. The years spent in Strasbourg, the devotion of my academic activity to the study of a religious phenomenon that is a minority in France, and coming from a Protestant culture myself marked my path as a sociologist in a country very deeply influenced by Catholicism, and in which most of the sociologists of religion have a Catholic origin.

The prevailing view in the sociology of religion was marked by a perception of religion through Catholic worship: in this perception, religion was mainly perceived as a clerical power imposed upon individuals and upon society, a clerical power against which one had to fight. As to secularity, this resulted in what, with some others, I have called "catho-secularity," namely a modality of Church–state relation-ships which was very much influenced by the importance of Catholicism in France and which, beyond a de jure equality, showed a de facto inequality in the way in which different religious expressions were treated.[19] Catholicism gave us a good way to measure the decline of clericalism and institutional religion that claimed to impose its standards upon individuals and upon an inclusive society. On the other hand, paying attention to the social-religious Protestant realities, with their anti-clerical dimension, enabled a sociological study of the way in which the Churches revised their self-understanding (their theology and their way of conceiving evangelization) and adapted their strategy to be more in line with certain aspects of modernity.

In this context, I was especially interested in the mutations of the pastorate by noting an evolution from the preacher-teacher to the listener-coordinator. The works of Peter Berger also spurred me to make some incursions into the sociology of theology. However, studying the relations between Protestantism and modernity also turned out to be successful for another reason: the paradoxical observation made by Dean Kelley[20] and Steve Bruce[21] in which the most liberal Protestant churches (the *mainline* churches) were losing members while the conservative *evangelical* Protestant churches were growing.[22] The fact that the mainline Protestant churches did not receive the social dividends from their more accommodating adaptation to modernity was a rich source of education for a sociology of religion that might otherwise have been too inclined to presuppose that the lack of modernity in the churches was the cause of their decline. This boom of Evangelical and Pentecostal churches which I studied with my colleague Sébastien Fath[23] was a perfect example of the recomposition of religion in modern secularized societies: a recomposition through subcultures of identity and resource communities which offered people the opportunity to be in line with a pluralist, inclusive society, and to confront the uncertainties and difficulties of contemporary ultra-modernity.[24]

As I was already aware of the different configurations of religion in the English, Scottish, German, French, and Italian modernities since the Enlightenment, I was increasingly sensitive to the problem of the multiple modernities of Shmuel Eisenstadt.[25] On a more diachronic plan, I joined the debate on postmodernity by analyzing the current system of Western modernity as a globalized ultra-modernity which deconstructed the mythologies of progress that national modernities had generated and abandoned modernistic certainties to the profit of logics of uncertainties.[26] This is an ultra-modernity that represents both a radicalization of secularization with the disenchantment of secular utopias (I speak in that sense of a secularization of secularity), and a return of religion to the public sphere.

Religious authority

The second element of the sociology of the Protestantisms that has proven to be useful for a general sociology of religion concerns religious authority, and the manner in which religious legitimacy is achieved. In my work *Profession: pasteur*, I analyzed the figure of the minister and examined the authority that was or was not recognized in him. I was then led to ask this question: How is legitimacy achieved and how is a religious claim to truth transmitted? Which ways and which vectors are utilized by this claim to truth to gain legitimacy and ensure its sustainability? In other words, how does a division of religious labor manifest itself and which types of social relationships are established between clerics and non-clerics? These were the questions that I focused on in the Protestant sphere.

I have always attached great importance to Max Weber's assertion that people's religious qualifications are unequally distributed. Some claim, more or less successfully, to be more qualified than others to communicate with invisible entities (whether they are shamans, soothsayers, witches, priests, spiritual advisors, sages, monks, and so on). Most striking from a sociological point of view are the various divisions of religious labor between the most skilled and the less skilled – divisions that induce constant discussion and negotiation. In this connection I want to highlight two things: (1) the relation to invisible entities – the key component of religion – shows itself, socially speaking, in social interaction between specialists and other people; and (2) if the question of the origin remains debatable, and we can speak of a foundation only when charisma leads to a process of transmission. Religion therefore involves both foundation and transmission.

The Protestant case is of particular interest in this respect since the Protestant Reformations in the 16th century originated in a questioning of the authority of the institution and its hierarchy in the very name of the message that the Church claimed to transmit. The institution of the Church being no longer legitimate in and of itself, its representatives not being infallible and its authority being relative, the religious truth in Christianity was therefore no longer unquestionable. This revolution in the matter of religious truth turned out to have major consequences because this truth became a hermeneutic issue linked to the way of interpreting the biblical texts, which opened the door to all sorts of debates and conflicts. As Alister McGrath wrote so well:

> The dangerous new idea, firmly embodied at the heart of the Protestant revolution, was that all Christians have the right to interpret the Bible for themselves [...] a dangerous new idea that gave rise to an unparalleled degree of creativity and growth, on the one hand, while on the other causing new tensions and debates that, by their very nature, probably lie beyond resolution. The development of Protestantism as a major religious force in the world has been shaped decisively by the creative tensions emerging from this principle.[27]

Being sensitive to differences relating to religious authority – not only between the different Protestant denominations but also between the various Christian denominations (Catholicism, Orthodoxy and Protestantism) – I was led to distinguish, in an ideal-typical way, different types of religious authorities: priest, prophet, spiritual master, wizard, master (teacher), ancestor, ascendant, and preacher. Each of these different types of religious authority privileges special mediations in implementing communication with God;[28] that is, vectors that could be institutional (the institution as such embodies legitimacy), personal (the charisma of a particular individual), experiential (the apprenticeship of exercises enabling access to one or other form of divinity), magical (the apprenticeship of tools and performative acts), doctrinal (intellectual rationalization), historical (legitimacy by generational heritage), and social (legitimacy produced by the assembly itself).

In this approach, which aimed to report on the diversity of the Protestant assemblies – in other words, to analyze the differences between Lutheran, Reformed, Baptist, Methodist, and Pentecostal worship – I accorded a central role to the devices for worship that were implemented because, in my opinion, these devices show two major dimensions: the social construction of communication with the divine on the one hand, and the associated forms of sociability on the other. With regard to the first dimension, depending on the more or less important role assigned to rites, texts, speeches, songs, exercises, and emotions, the diversity of Protestant spiritualities could be typified according to the mode of communication with the divine which it privileged. As for the second, it dealt with the social links and senses of community generated by the different expressions of religion.

Social links and religion

In fact, the different types of authorities corresponded to forms of variable sociabilities according to the mediations privileged in the communication with the divine: parish, circle of disciples, network of initiated practitioners, network of customers, study circle, militant community, heritage community, emotional group, etc. This typology of modes of mediation of the communication with the divine and forms of religious sociability elaborated from studies concerning Protestantisms enabled me to take account of Protestant diversity such as it is attested in assemblies of worship that differ depending on whether one has to deal with Lutheran, Pentecostal, or Baptist assemblies. At the core of this analysis was the question of the social link, of the elaboration of a "we," of a sense of community built on shared representations and rites relating to invisible entities, but also differentiation in relation to the surrounding society and to other links and allegiances.

A religious system produces a social link not only by creating particular networks and groups (institutions, communities), but also by defining a mental world through which individuals and groups express and live a certain conception of humans and the world in a particular society.

Religions create social links in time and space and act as societies in their different ways – both on institutional and community levels – and the forms of sociability that are manifest are different. You only have to do a bit of ethnographic observation to realize it. But how do different religions act as societies and what kinds of social links do they generate? Are Buddhist, Muslim, Christian, and Jewish social links of the same nature, and do they take on the same forms? And, within each of these religious worlds, is there not a great diversity? Religion is a social link, not only longitudinally in its dimensions of filiation and transmission but also horizontally in its dimensions of sociability and solidarity. In each of these dimensions, it is necessary to study the particularly *religious* part; that is to say, to introduce a way to deal with the sociological specificity of religious matter: the fact that in religion, one fits in *a special way* into filiation and transmission (while referring to publicized foundation by holders of charisma) and one can also form society in an equally *special* way (religious sociability is irreducible to other types of sociability).

Conclusion

I was able to develop these three foci – the relations between religion and modernity, religious authority, and the forms of sociability and communalization – from studies in the sociology of Protestantisms. While having learned a lot from the works of historians and lawyers, I have also increasingly learned from the works of anthropologists. By studying societies that are different from our own, anthropologists have taught me to better integrate into a sociological approach to religion the relationships with "invisible entities" and the ways in which these relationships are implemented. I totally agree with Albert Piette when he says that "there is no reason to truncate the religious fact from its 'invisible' interacting factors, as they are considered important by the actors themselves."[29] In other words, the sociology of religion cannot be reduced to the study of the non-religious aspects of religion, but must also include "invisible entities" and not be satisfied with a curious division of labor that leaves God to theology.

The economic, social, political, and cultural determinations that act on religion do not exhaust it and – even if there is no one essence of religion – I think there is a social reality sui generis for religion that it is important to grasp. It is precisely because religions constitute cultures – that is to say, complex worlds of signs and meanings that are in line with history and passed down from generation to generation – that they have a relative autonomy in comparison with all the social determinants that inform them. Of course a religious culture cannot exist without regulating organizations and individuals who express it, but this is not a reason to reduce the analysis of a religion to that of its organizations or to that of its actors: a religious universe is also a permanent work of reinterpretation and reinvention based on inherited symbolic material. There is therefore symbolic consistency and historical depth in religion.

For sociological analysis, the challenge therefore consists in studying a *unique* social activity that creates *unique* social links and that is manifested by specific forms of *authorities*. Indeed, if there is a specific social phenomenon of religion, the proper task of sociology is to study and understand this specificity from its own point of view, namely a point of view that pays special attention to social links, forms of sociability, and modes of legitimation. That is why I say that religions are manifested (1) through "singular social links," and (2) by "specific forms of authorities." From a sociological perspective, religion can be approached, in my opinion, as *a regular social and symbolic activity related to representations and practices that, while referring to invisible entities, gives meaning to life and death, to happiness and unhappiness, guides behavior, generates filiation and a sense of community, and allows one to be situated in temporality*. In this activity, religion involves the three meanings of the French word "sens": the *meaning*, the *direction*, and *sensitivity*. One could sum up by saying that religion acts as a society (by creating a link) and as truth (by building legitimacy) in its own way and that these historical processes are always evolving. These symbolic layouts of the human condition through representations and rites referring to invisible entities are fully historical phenomena; that is to say, they should be comprehended regardless of any essentialism and should always be situated within space and time – they are evolving realities, even if they are part of distinct traditions and claim loyalty to different heritages.

A more sustained attention to the experience and to the speech of religious actors permits a detachment from a perspective that consists in telling religious individuals, in the name of a critique of its object, "you are not what you claim to be," which amounts to thinking that sociological analysis could help to disperse the "false consciousness" of actors who are alienated in obsolete representations. The secularization of Western modernity itself and of the mythologies of progress it has produced on the one hand, and, on the other hand, the globalization and the transnationalization of religion itself, are not unfamiliar to these more comprehensive approaches of symbolic layouts of the human existence that are religions.

Notes

1 Jean-Paul Willaime, "L'Opposition des Infrastructures et des Superstructures: Une Critique," *Cahiers Internationaux de Sociologie*, Vol. 61, Nouvelle Série, 23ème année, juillet–décembre 1976: 309–327.

2 The University of Strasbourg has two state-sponsored faculties of theology: Catholic and Protestant. This constitutes an exception in the French academic sphere. This exception is explained by the special historical background of the Alsace-Moselle area, where religious groups benefit from a special system in which the priests, the ministers, or the rabbis are paid by the state and where denominational religion courses are taught in public schools. In other regions of France, faculties of theology exist only in private further education.

3 The School is named "Pratique" (i.e., "Constructive") because it focuses on research apprenticeship at the level of Masters degrees and PhDs. The department of religious sciences was created in 1886. After suppressing the faculty of (Catholic) theology at the Sorbonne in 1885, the Republic considered that it was important for the French higher education system to continue studying religious phenomena. Yet, they should be studied within a multidisciplinary and non-denominational framework. Great scholars such as Marcel Mauss, Claude Lévi-Strauss, and Gabriel Le Bras made a significant impact on this section of religious sciences that nowadays includes about 60 specialists ranging from Japanese Buddhism and Taoism to contemporary Catholicisms and Protestantisms, and including the religions of ancient Rome and Greece, Sunni and Shiite Islam, and so on.

4 Jean-Paul Willaime, *Sociologie des Religions*, 3rd edn (Paris: PUF, 2005a); Jean-Paul Willaime and Danièle Hervieu-Léger, *Sociologies et religion. Approches classiques* (Paris: PUF, 2001).

5 Jean Séguy, *Les sectes protestantes dans la France contemporaine* (Paris: Beauchesne, 1956).

6 Emile Poulat, *Eglise contre bourgeoisie. Introduction au devenir du catholicisme actuel* (Paris: Casterman, 1977).

7 Peter Berger, *The Sacred Canopy: Elements of a Sociological Theory of Religion* (New York: Doubleday, 1967).

8 Jean-Paul Willaime, *Profession: pasteur. Sociologie de la condition du clerc à la fin du XXe siècle* (Genève: Labor et Fides, 1986).

9 Jean-Paul Willaime, "1905 et la pratique d'une laïcité de reconnaissance sociale des religions," *Archives de Sciences Sociales des Religions* 129 (2005c): 67–82.

10 Jean-Paul Willaime, *Europe et religions. Les enjeux du XXIe siècle* (Paris: Bayard, 2004); Jean-Paul Willaime, "The paradoxes of Laïcité in France," in *The Centrality of Religion in Social Life: Essays in Honour of James A. Beckford*, ed. Eileen Barker (Aldershot: Ashgate, 2008c), 41–54; Jean-Paul Willaime, "European Integration, Laïcité and Religion," *Religion, State & Society* 37(1–2) (2009): 23–35.

11 Jean-Paul Willaime, *Le retour du religieux dans la sphère publique. Vers une laïcité de reconnaissance et de dialogue* (Lyon: Editions Olivétan, 2008a); Jean-Paul Willaime, "For a transnational sociology of secularity in the contemporary Ultra-Modernity," *Archives de Sciences Sociales des Religions* 146 (2009): 201–218.

12 Along the same lines, see Philippe Portier's analyses that distinguish between different recognition models of religion and emphasize the effects of a "legal globalization": Philippe Portier, "L'essence religieuse de la modernité politique. Éléments pour un renouvellement de la théorie de la laïcité," in *La modernité contre la religion? Pour une nouvelle approche de la laïcité*, ed. Jacqueline Lagrée and Philippe Portier (Rennes: Presses Universitaires de Rennes, 2010a), 7–23; Philippe Portier, "Modernités plurielles? Une analyse longitudinale de régimes de régulation du croire dans les démocraties stabilisées," in *Pluralisme religieux et citoyenneté,* ed. Micheline Milot, Philippe Portier and Jean-Paul Willaime (Rennes: Presses Universitaires de Rennes, 2010b): 241–271.

13 Jean-Paul Willaime, "Different Models for Religion and Education in Europe", in *Religion and Education in Europe: Developments, Contexts and Debates*, ed. Robert Jackson,

Siebren Miedema, Wolfram Weisse and Jean-Paul Willaime (Münster: Waxmann), 57–66.

14 Jean-Paul Willaime and Céline Béraud (eds), *Les jeunes, l'école et la religion* (Paris: Bayard, 2009b).

15 Séguy, *Les sectes protestantes.*

16 Steve Bruce, *A House Divided: Protestantism, Schism and Secularization* (London and New York: Routledge, 1990).

17 Alister E. McGrath, *Christianity's Dangerous Idea. The Protestant Revolution – A History from the Sixteenth Century to the Twenty-First* (New York: HarperOne, 2007).

18 Harold J. Berman, *The Impact of the Protestant Reformations on the Western Legal Tradition* (Cambridge, MA: The Belknap Press of Harvard University Press, 2003).

19 Willaime, "1905 et la pratique d'une laïcité de reconnaissance"; Willaime, *Le retour du religieux.*

20 Dean Kelley, *Why Conservative Churches Are Growing* (New York: Harper & Row, 1972).

21 Bruce, *A House Divided.*

22 Jean-Paul Willaime, *La précarité protestante. Sociologie du protestantisme contemporain* (Genève: Labor et Fides, 1992).

23 Sébastien Fath and Jean-Paul Willaime (eds), *La nouvelle France protestante. Essor et recomposition au XXIe siècle* (Genève: Labor et Fides, 2011).

24 Jean-Paul Willaime, "Protestantism in France: A Minority Defining its Place in Catholic Culture," in *Religious Newcomers and the Nation State*, ed. Erik Sengers and Thijl Sunier (Delft: Eburon Academic Publishers, 2010), 99–114.

25 Shmuel N. Eisenstadt (ed.), *Multiple Modernities* (New Brusnwick, NJ: Transaction, 2002).

26 Jean-Paul Willaime, "Religion in Ultra-modernity," in *Theorising Religion: Classical and Contemporary Debates*, ed. James A. Beckford and John Walliss (Aldershot: Ashgate, 2006), 77–89; Jean-Paul Willaime, *Le retour du religieux.*

27 McGrath, *Christianity's Dangerous Idea*, 2.

28 Jean-Paul Willaime, "La construction des liens socio-religieux: essai de typologie à partir des modes de médiation du charisma," in *Le religieux des sociologies. Trajectoires personnelles et débats scientifiques*, ed. Yves Lambert, Guy Michelat and Albert Piette (Paris: L'Harmattan, 1997), 97–108; Jean-Paul Willaime, *Sociologie du Protestantisme* (Paris: PUF, 2005b).

29 Albert Piette, *La religion de près. L'activité religieuse en train de se faire* (Paris: Métailié, 1999), 24.

16

SIDE ROADS AND DETOURS

A narrative reconstruction about studying religion

Robert Wuthnow

Long story short: I fell into the study of religion quite by accident. Or perhaps I should say through an unending series of accidents.

Yes, like many who study it, I was raised by parents who took their church-going quite seriously – so seriously that my Presbyterian mother never saw eye to eye with my Baptist father. We often had "roast preacher" for lunch on Sundays. Those heated discussions undoubtedly struck a chord in me somewhere deep down. At least, in retrospect I can say that.

But I never imagined growing up to study religion. Not for anything other than my personal edification. As a child, my first vocational aspiration, once it dawned on me that adults needed somehow to earn a living, was to become a yard man. A yard man was a person who tended people's yards. I aspired to live in a tarpaper shack out near the dump, mow lawns, and rake leaves. Setting my sights low, I must have somehow figured at that early age, would prevent disappointments.

For a very brief time I abandoned that early wisdom and allowed myself the fantasy of becoming a professional basketball player. I gave up that ambition when I was cut from the sixth-grade team. There were six boys in my class.

An epiphany of sorts finally came in the fall of my junior year in college. Sitting in class one day, watching the professor pacing back and forth reading from his notes, it dawned on me: I could do *that*. Surely I could! I would just have to retool enough to get into a graduate school. But in what? Psychology? Economics? Sociology?

Not having the prerequisites to do psychology or an aptitude for economics, I chose sociology. I had little sense of what it was about, other than having struggled through a terrible introductory sociology course as a freshman, but I figured it would certainly be more interesting than economics. I dropped all the practical courses I had planned on taking during my final three semesters of college, took as many statistics courses as I could, and read sociology on the side. The year after I graduated I spent my entire life savings (about $2,000) taking classes and reading about sociology.

My forays into the underbrush of Emile Durkheim and Talcott Parsons left me completely discouraged. Oscar Lewis' *Five Families* and Nathan Glazer and Daniel Patrick Moynihan's *Beyond the Melting Pot* were like visits to another planet.[1] What fascinated me most were complex organizations. A sociologist at Berkeley named Arthur Stinchcombe was said to be the leader in that field.

I trundled off to Berkeley in hopes of learning about organizations from this man Stinchcombe. When I got there, I learned he was on leave. That proved to be the case the following year and the year after that. Meanwhile, a friendly man with a beard introduced himself one day going up in the elevator as Charles Glock. I knew he had done some work on religion and was teaching a seminar on the topic. Not much else was being offered at Berkeley that fall, so I took it. A paper was required. Glock suggested I interview students at the Graduate Theological Union seminaries in Berkeley to find out what was happening. A little later that fall he found me a vacant desk at the Survey Research Center and showed me a large stack of green-and-white IBM computer printouts.

Glock's main interest at the time was racial prejudice. Having decided that he was a good mentor, I went to work developing a dissertation proposal on that topic. I had barely started when the Ford Foundation gave Glock a grant to study new religious movements. Glock's collaborator was Robert Bellah, who was going to oversee some ethnographic studies as part of the project. There was to be a survey, too. Glock asked me to help with that survey. My dissertation, published in 1976 as *The Consciousness Reformation*, was the result.[2]

Survey research in the study of religion

With polls and downloadable datasets now instantly available, it is worth reconsidering the profound effect that survey technology had on the study of religion. Gallup polls tracked church attendance, starting in 1939, and included questions about religious beliefs in the 1950s. A few other surveys in the 1950s tapped beliefs and practices among Roman Catholics, Episcopalians, and Presbyterians, and in scattered geographic locations. Early scholarly studies of religion based on surveys included Joseph Fichter's *Southern Parish*, Gerhard Lenski's *Religious Factor*, Glock and Stark's *Christian Beliefs and Anti-Semitism*, and a few others.[3] Surveys were of practical interest to church leaders, who saw ways to examine whether parishioners believed in church teachings. They also fed social scientists' aspirations to be scientific. It was now possible to see if Max Weber's hypothesis about the Protestant ethic held water and to test H. Richard Niebuhr's assertions about social class and sectarian beliefs.

It was of considerable value to appear scientific in those days, even if accomplishments often fell short of aspirations. In *Durable Inequality*, Charles Tilly argues that status, whether in academia or in real life, is attained through opportunity hoarding.[4] What he means is that gatekeeping – union cards, professional credentials, schooling, membership in a majority race or gender – is always used to keep out wannabes. The study of religion had plenty of wannabes. Not only the usual crowd of journalists and pundits that social scientists worried about, but also the devout, the preachers, the theologians, and the armchair philosophers all had something to say about religion.

Survey research was not hard to learn, but it was a closely controlled commodity. It took an exorbitant amount of money to conduct a survey – special funding at that, since the US Census Bureau did not collect information about religion. Few scholars had surveys at their disposal and those who did carefully guarded who gained access to it. Computing was still insufficiently developed that statistical analysis was tedious and time consuming. Even with access to an IBM mainframe, the typical process involved laborious hours at a keypunch machine, overnight waits at the computer center, stacks of printouts, and endless repetition to correct errors.

But surveys had their scholarly advantages. It was now possible to make systematic comparisons that resembled quasi-experimental techniques. It was possible to draw inferences from samples about the characteristics of populations and to make generalizations about patterns in those populations. Rigorous tests of significance could be calculated, descriptive statistics published, and statistical associations among variables examined. I suppose what intrigued me about that stack of IBM printouts that Glock handed me one day was something akin to voyeurism. What did those people you saw going to church on Sundays really think about God, the Bible, Jesus, or, for that matter, sex?

As we know, surveys came to be used increasingly to study religion during the 1970s and 1980s. Software for statistical processing became more readily available and computing gradually evolved from mainframes to desktops. The prestige associated with large-scale surveys prompted more numerous small-scale and specialized studies. Foundation funding was available more often, and standardized national projects, such as the General Social Surveys, increasingly incorporated questions about religion.

Surveys by no means replaced interest in ethnographic studies, which continued and produced important inquiries into established congregations and new religious movements. But surveys did shape the content of sociological research about religion. Studies emphasized participation in organized religion and creedal assent to the teachings of these organizations. Believing and belonging were the shorthand rubrics under which much of the research was done. Common topics included belief in God, beliefs about the Bible, agreement with church teachings about moral issues, attendance at worship services, and participation in private devotional activities, such as prayer. Although the study of religion was increasingly taking place in religious studies departments and in anthropology, literature, and history, the one distinguishing mark of sociological researchers was their ability to count.

On the surface, the most serious division *within* the sociology of religion in those years was between quantitative and qualitative research. Survey researchers drew on ever larger and more abundant datasets and more sophisticated statistical techniques, while qualitative researchers conducted studies that often more subtly examined the nuances of meaning, power, gender, symbolism, history, and conversion. The differences could be interpreted as a function of training and personal style as much as anything else.

There was a second division, though, that was harder to identify or to pin down precisely. This division turned on views about positivism. It was long-standing, and, for anyone interested in tracing it, could be found even in comparisons of Emile Durkheim and Max Weber. Durkheim's interest in studying suicide and in the rules of sociological method that he put forth as a guidebook for the discipline was oriented towards producing timeless sociological generalizations. Sociological *facts* interested him and it was his belief that lawful generalizations about these facts could be found – whether from statistics about suicide or from anthropological studies of primitive beliefs. In contrast, Weber took on big problems – accounting for the rise of Western capitalism was hardly a modest task – but with a keener eye towards their historical specificity. Ideal types and concepts of bureaucracy and rationality were not ends in themselves, but tools with which to examine the varying meanings in different religions and in different cultures and periods.

The epistemological divergence evident in Durkheim and Weber applied profoundly to the interpretation of survey results. On the positivist side lay hopes for an accumulation of scientific generalizations through the cumulative conclusions of one survey after another, just as social psychologists – and natural scientists – aspired to achieve by adding the results of each new laboratory experiment. On the other side, what might be termed a more hermeneutic approach viewed survey data more like the results of ethnographic and historical research. Surveys were a fine addition to the scholarly portfolio for investigating meanings and practices within specific historical and cultural contexts, but the chances of finding law-like scientific generalizations were arguably slim.

To return to my own narrative for a moment, my initial inclination was strongly on the positivist side. I spent days and days combing through journals and abstracts looking for all the cumulative science I could find. But having gone down that side road for a while, and having found it filled with contradictory results that offered little in the way of cumulative scientific generalizations, I detoured towards the interpretive path. That was easy to do at Berkeley through a searching methodology course taught by symbolic interactionist Norman Denzin, by immersion in the work of Herbert Blumer and Robert Bellah, and by my growing frustration with the empirical results themselves. That stack of printouts Glock confronted me with at the Survey Research Center was supposed to be the makings of a volume he and Rodney Stark were planning that would demonstrate the merits of deprivation theory as a scientific explanation of religion. That volume was never written.

Cultural theory and historical sociology

If research results are affected by their contexts, research interests are too. American sociological studies of religion were shaped by the fact that American religion was predominantly Christian, which meant that nationally representative surveys necessarily found it easier to examine church-going and beliefs about God and the Bible than anything else. Studies of Judaism and of specific traditions within Christianity, such as African American churches and Latter-Day Saints, took place alongside the dominant interests of survey researchers. The most important alternative in the 1970s and early 1980s, though, were studies of new religious movements. These were largely qualitative studies that opened new questions at the micro-sociological level about conversion, experience, ritual, and alternative beliefs. My involvement with the Glock and Bellah project on new religious movements took me in that direction to a small extent, but my interests largely turned towards other considerations. These were interests influenced by the cultural and social ferment of the time as well as by theoretical developments in the wider discipline.

Cultural theory was a factor in the study of religion (for me at least) most obviously through the work of Robert Bellah, under whom I studied directly, and Peter Berger, whose books I consumed as soon as they appeared, and to some extent of Clifford Geertz and Mary Douglas. Other than having tried to incorporate some ideas about meaning systems into *The Consciousness Reformation*, I was unable to think very clearly about how cultural theory might be useful in survey research. It was, however, a way of connecting with literatures that went beyond the sociology of religion, and in my teaching I found that students were increasingly interested in these broader questions: How did language work? How were cultural meanings produced and instantiated in organizations? Could they be examined systematically? What roles in public life were played by discourse, rhetoric, and collective memory?

These were questions that had been asked to some extent by Bellah and Berger and by Geertz and Douglas, but they were also of interest to scholars whose work had little direct connection with the study of religion. Michel Foucault and Jürgen Habermas were two of the most prominent examples. Others included Frederic Jameson and Paul DeMan in literature, Noam Chomsky and George Lakoff in linguistics, Claude Lévi-Strauss in anthropology, Jacques Derrida and François Lyotard in cultural studies, and Louis Althusser and Terry Eagleton among neo-Marxists. An important theme that runs through these works is the de-centering of the person to a sufficient extent to bring language more clearly into view, rather than, as it were, "seeing through" language to identify underlying beliefs, values, and worldviews. "Looking at" language forces attention towards the form, structure, style, and content of discourse, but also necessitates asking sociological questions about who can speak about what to whom under which conditions.

The sociological questions that interested me were also increasingly ones about historical change. Some of these questions of course were driven by new religious movements and by discussions in the popular media about shifts of consciousness. The sociological literature, however, was asking more interesting questions about political and economic change. Important questions were being raised especially in Charles Tilly's work on labor history and rebellion, Theda Skocpol's writing about states and social revolutions, and Immanuel Wallerstein's inquiries into the development of the modern world system. Much of this work combined insights from both Marx and Weber, but also benefitted from newer primary research done by historians. Common themes that emerged emphasized the interplay among class fractions, competition among social movements, and the production and mobilization of public discourse.

My attempt to bring together ideas from cultural theory with work in historical sociology resulted in *Communities of Discourse*, which drew on hundreds of historical studies to examine and compare the social conditions surrounding the Protestant Reformation in the 16th century, the Enlightenment in the 18th century, and the rise of European socialism in the late 19th and early 20th century.[5] Other than the not insignificant fact of examining in considerable detail the Reformation, my work during these years was largely unconcerned with religion.

Whether in retrospect the metaphor of side road or detour applies best, working extensively in cultural theory and historical sociology was much like spending time in the wilderness. Only the wilderness involved months on end buried in library stacks and wading hip-deep through materials that were difficult to converse about. A few colleagues and graduate students provided the necessary intellectual sustenance. It was thus with some ambivalence that I returned to a topic more conventionally within the sociology of religion and, as I noted in the Preface to *The Restructuring of American Religion*, would likely not have written it without the patient encouragement of historian John Wilson and sociologist Jay Demerath.[6]

Restructuring was hardly an attempt to capitalize on the work that had interested me in cultural theory and historical sociology, but did to some extent benefit from and reflect those interests. Although the central storyline that drew reviewers' attention was the emergence of the fracture between conservatives and liberals in American religion in the 1980s, the theoretical underpinnings of the argument derived from several sources that I had found useful in previous work over the past decade. One is that religion as an institution is guided by its collective memory of itself and its leaders' efforts to engage actively with public life. That idea is Weberian in essence but also draws on Habermas' discussion of how public spheres develop, on Michael Schudson and others who have written about collective memory, and on my own inquiry into the development of a bourgeois public sphere in the 18th century. A second idea is that religious movements emerge in relation to class fractions from which they derive resources and in turn compete with one another for legitimacy and attention. The declining significance of denominationalism cleared a space for that to happen, and resources from the media and the state facilitated it. The book's argument about competing interpretations of American civil religion is an attempt to look closely at public discourse and cultural meanings.

Restructuring was also, in retrospect, an attempt to bridge several methodological styles. It depended heavily upon reading primary and secondary source materials about the early to mid-20th-century history of mainline Protestants, evangelical Protestants, and Roman Catholics. It benefitted considerably from my various ethnographic forays into various religious organizations. Though downplayed in terms of statistical presentation, it was also built on an edifice of quantitative data from several major national surveys.

The favorable response to *Restructuring* took me by surprise and, along with a growing interest in the topic among graduate students at Princeton, was one of the reasons my research interests returned as much as they did to the study of religion.

Studies of practices

The next accident in the series of accidents that have shaped my views about the sociology of religion occurred as a result of funding that became available (largely from the Lilly Endowment) to engage in research that could not have been done, as I had been doing, alone in the library. A big project that takes more than a decade to complete and rummages across several centuries of European history is, I suppose, something that takes more endurance than most of us (certainly me) are able to muster more than once in a lifetime. I was ready to follow the advice I routinely give to graduate students writing dissertations, which is to chew on a small bone. I was also eager to see if some of the ideas I had gleaned from cultural theory could be put to use in small ways with information from qualitative interviews and surveys.

The series of projects I worked on in the 1990s that resulted in *Acts of Compassion*, *Sharing the Journey*, *God and Mammon in America*, *Poor Richard's Principle*, and *After Heaven* reflected a conviction that religion needs to be studied in relation to the cultural tensions in which it is embedded, and that these tensions can be examined in multi-method projects that combine quantitative data from surveys with qualitative data from interviews, field observations, and archival materials.[7] If there is a theoretical strand running through these inquiries, it is the idea that cultural tensions (contradictions, if one prefers) engage us as the inhabitants of a society in cultural work, and that this work is accomplished through narratives, accounts, code shifting, metaphor, and heteroglossia. We are, in short, cultural creatures, and we create, sustain, legitimate, and enact meanings through the words we use and the gestures that accompany those words.

These are emphases that have become widely evident in the sociology of religion and have become one of the key linkages between the study of religion and cultural sociology. They represent a loosely related repertoire of ideas, rather than a theory in the normal usage of that term. From Peter Berger comes the idea that through conversation we legitimate the plausibility of taken-for-granted realities and divide these realities into finite spheres of meaning. Bellah and his colleagues in *Habits of the Heart* explored the ways in which surface accounts of work, love, spirituality, and service reflect a cultural unity of utilitarian individualism.[8] Mikhail Bakhtin, the Russian formalist, suggests that contending cultural values are strung together in heteroglossic discourse that permits multiple voices to be registered. Lakoff points to the ways in which coherence and meaning are achieved through the arrangement and repetition of metaphors. C. Wright Mills developed an idea about motives that viewed them as accounts or justifications. Empirical studies of discourse suggest the importance of code switching, intensifiers, and register shifts. And of course narrative structure is central in studies of spiritual journeys and conversion.

In developing these ideas in several books and articles in the 1980s, and in further developing them in the early 1990s, I was fortunate to be working in an academic context that made it easy to absorb and tinker with ideas both from within sociology and beyond. Geertz's continuing work and the disciples he collected around him at the Institute for Advanced Study were among these sources of inspiration.

Comparative literature scholar Caryl Emerson made it easy to learn about Bakhtin. Historians Robert Darnton and Natalie Zemon Davis demonstrated how to think about discourse and ritual in historical settings in innovative ways. As is so often the case, it is also from brilliant creative graduate students that a faculty member is able to learn new approaches. Marsha Witten, who brought an exceptional understanding of discourse analysis to her work in sociology and who produced *All Is Forgiven* as the published version of her dissertation, was one such student.[9] Another was Courtney Bender, who combined brilliant ethnographic fieldwork with a rich understanding of Bakhtin's work in *Heaven's Kitchen*.[10]

Although it is possible to think of language purely as an entity separate from its use in social interaction, sociological inquiry is naturally more interested in relating the two. Thinking of discourse as a social practice is helpful, especially as the idea has been developed in the work of philosopher of religion Jeffrey Stout in *Ethics After Babel*.[11] Practices are sets of interrelated activities that are purposive, involve a certain degree of repetition and skill (which means that they are learned), and follow socially prescribed scripts or repertoires. Practices are observable but are also situation-specific and are interlaced with other practices. Playing chess or tennis is a practice. So is cooking a meal, saying a prayer, participating in a worship experience, or describing a religious conversion. Practices can also be evaluated normatively in relation to such criteria as human flourishing and the instantiation of virtue.

An emphasis on practice has been increasingly attractive in studies of religion because practices are the ways in which underlying beliefs and values are expressed and thus become observable. Practices are organized by and often occur in settings orchestrated by religious institutions, but may just as well be studied outside of these institutions, either in private settings such as homes or in public venues such as restaurants and volunteer centers or through interviews with individuals. The interlacing of practices points to the likelihood that a religious practice may be influenced by the work a person does or the music that person enjoys. While practices suggest a certain degree of internal coherence (such as knowing the rules of chess), they also occur within diverse spaces that may challenge this coherence and require creativity.

In the divide I mentioned earlier between positivist and hermeneutic perspectives, an emphasis on practices falls clearly on the more interpretive side. The contrast is perhaps most evident in relation to the so-called religious economies perspective that aims to be a positivist science by reducing everything it possibly can about religion to the preferences of rational actors in a religious market. This is a fine idea as long as it is understood as a hypothesis that illuminates certain aspects of religious behavior, but it is otherwise quite limited. My point is not that a practices approach is the alternative, but that market-oriented religious behavior may be viewed as a practice governed in part by principles of rational market behavior and in part by other considerations. To suggest that people go more often to church on rainy days because the opportunity cost of not being able to play golf or wash the car is lower, for example, may be an interesting idea. But a more satisfactory approach would be to ask in addition how a person talks about going out in the rain, why golf or washing the car provides a preferential frame of reference, what one says upon meeting a fellow parishioner at the golf-course, and how one interacts with the priest the following Sunday.

It was largely this interest in practices, and in related ideas about cultural work and lived religion, that provided the theoretical scaffolding in the 1990s for my work on religion and acts of compassion, religion and ways of accounting for work and money, the spiritualities of dwelling and seeking, devotional practices, and the narrative reconstruction of selves in small fellowship groups. In this and in subsequent work, the main sociological concept that interested me continued to be the idea of community. Communities are central to sociological questions about belonging, and communities are always discursively constructed.

Cognition and culture

Although the religious economies argument has attracted its share of devotees in the sociology of religion, a more serious challenge posing itself as science stems from recent developments in cognitive neuroscience and in related fields, such as cognitive anthropology and evolutionary psychology, and including cognitive sociology. The principal argument is that certain ways of thinking are natural to the human brain, meaning either that they are somehow hard-wired or are learned very early in life, and thus explain a great deal about religious belief and ritual practice. Indeed, part of what is claimed to be explained is why religion developed in the first place and why it continues to exist at all.

Sociologists are skeptical of such claims, for two reasons. One is that if sociology tells us anything it is that beliefs and behavior are shaped by culture and context, rather than being innately determined. The other is that the evolutionary metaphor was borrowed from biology by sociologists in the late 19th and 20th century and, most spectacularly in the form of Social Darwinism, led nowhere into a kind of vacuous functionalism. Whether the emergence of something like religion eons before recorded history was somehow conducive to the survival of the human species may be an interesting conjecture, but is unlikely to strike many sociologists as a testable proposition.

However, with some looseness of interpretation cognitive theories have begun to be incorporated into the work of sociologists and other scholars in religious studies. Careful and cautious borrowing may be useful. For example, what are variously termed cognitive schemas or cognitive domains reveal that certain aspects of reality are perceived and interpreted similarly in different cultures and places. For example, animals are associated with greater agency and movement than plants. Folk understandings of simple physics suggest that something can be moved by pushing on it but not by just thinking about it.

It remains to be seen, but some of these ideas may be useful for understanding how different images of God lead people to associate different actions with God, or how they think gods are similar to or different from human beings. Some of the research suggests that prayers are structured by anthropomorphic assumptions about God and that memories of religious experiences are influenced by how normal or abnormal these experiences are perceived to be.

In some of my recent work, I have tried to borrow ideas from cognitive anthropology to consider the ways in which we pray or think about prayer and to ask questions about the "reasonableness" of religious beliefs. For example, if we assume that most of us do not want to be regarded as nutcases for thinking that God or heaven exists, then how does our desire to seem reasonable influence what we say and believe about God and heaven?

Another potential contribution of cognitive research is to examine the locations in the brain in which emotions are activated and thus to provide a clearer sense of the emotions people may be dealing with as they describe religious experiences and reactions to events. For example, Ann Taves has suggested a "building blocks" approach to religious experience that begins by treating them as part of a larger category of special events and then examining the particular attributes that make them special.[12] A related possibility would be to follow Randall Collins' suggestion that violence always involves fear and tension to see if this is true, and if so, how situations channel the response.[13] In my recent work on cultural responses to terror, annihilation, environmental devastation, pandemics, and other life-threatening catastrophes, I found evidence in the cognitive science literature refuting the notion that fear and denial are the primary responses and suggesting that an active problem-solving reaction is more common.

Sociology as open space

I conclude with a broader observation about sociology as a discipline in which to study religion. Few who study religion as sociologists have failed to contemplate the feeling that religion is marginal to the discipline. In reality, it is indeed marginal. Sociology departments have standard required and core courses on topics such as theory, methods, and social stratification. Issues of race, class, and gender are usually taught, and bread-and-butter courses with large enrollments may include topics such as deviance, crime, and family. Religion generally is not a required, core, or bread-and-butter course. At many colleges and universities, there may be a fine religious studies department that offers ample courses on the topic. PhD candidates interested in attaining an academic teaching job are wise not to concentrate too exclusively on religion.

Having explained that, I always hasten to point out to PhD candidates that there is widespread recognition in the discipline of the value of studying religion. This recognition is, if anything, increasing. While there may have been a time when modernization theory suggested to sociologists that religion was old-hat and close to extinction, nobody can seriously entertain such thoughts now. Religion is clearly an important part of American politics and international relations, part of the lives of many immigrants, importantly related to questions about race and gender, and a rich arena in which to examine questions about culture and self-identity.

These realities suggest the importance of sociologists of religion not specializing too narrowly. For all the advantages specialization provides, it can also insulate specialists within narrow professional networks, restrict their publishing to a few journals visited only by like-minded specialists, and focus their attention on an overly limited range of research questions. Over the decades, the most interesting sociological writing about religion has seldom been done by scholars who narrowly identified themselves as sociologists of religion. Weber and Durkheim certainly did not. Nor did theorists such as Robert Bellah and Peter Berger, or empiricists such as Charles Glock and Gerhard Lenski.

At present, one sees increasing evidence of sociologists with interests in other subfields writing about religion and contributing creatively to the topic. Douglas Massey's and Alejandro Portes' work on religion and immigration would be examples, as well as Peggy Levitt's and Margarita Mooney's. Michele Lamont's and Katherine Newman's work on low-income working men and women include insightful discussions of religion. Judith Stacey has written about religion and gender, Paul DiMaggio has written about religion and science, and Benjamin Zablocki has written about religious communes.

These broader examples bring us finally to the question of whether a scholar has to believe in religion in order to study it effectively, and the related question of how studying religion may affect a scholar's beliefs. My own beliefs have certainly evolved over the years, but far less from studying religion than from the normal life experiences of raising children, facing illnesses, losing parents, and witnessing the good and evil that exist in our world. At times, I was aware that critics thought I was writing too much for an audience professionally interested in organized religion, and it was evident enough that those readers were indeed paying more attention than anyone in the discipline. Having as short an attention span as I do, though, it was never long before I became bored with those topics and moved on to other ones.

What I do think matters is the connection between one's religious practices, however infrequent or provisional those may be, and the topics one chooses to study. A person who has never darkened the door of a church, synagogue, mosque, or temple is unlikely to understand very well what goes on there or why those institutions are important. Spending time at religious organizations or talking with people who are religious quickly illuminates why the topic is important. Not only that; the experience sparks the sociological imagination. Questions bubble to the surface about leadership, social relations, modes of belonging, and meanings.

Another way of saying this is to view sociology as an open space. It is a discipline, too. No question about that. It has its pecking order, its expectations, its standards of what constitutes good work. But it is an exceptionally open discipline that provides freedom to investigate nearly anything with almost any method. It is the discipline in which Weber's classic work on the Protestant ethic is read alongside texts on Bayesian statistics and structural equation models, and in which a single department may include a scholar studying the Taiping Rebellion down the hall from someone doing research on nongovernmental organizations in Uganda and another studying racial discrimination against convicted felons, and yet another studying low-wage workers in Brazil. It is hard to imagine that studies of religion will not continue to be an important part of work in a discipline such as this.

Notes

1 Oscar Lewis, *Five Families: Mexican Case Studies in the Culture of Poverty* (New York: New American Library, 1965); Nathan Glazer and Daniel Patrick Moynihan, *Beyond the Melting Pot: The Negroes, Puerto Ricans, Jews, Italians, and Irish of New York City* (Cambridge, MA: M.I.T. Press, 1963).

2 Robert Wuthnow, *The Consciousness Reformation* (Berkeley: University of California Press, 1976).

3 Joseph H. Fichter, *Southern Parish: A Sociological Analysis of an American Catholic Parish* (Chicago, IL: University of Chicago Press, 1951); Gerhard E. Lenski, *The Religious Factor: A Sociological Study of Religion's Impact on Politics, Economics, and Family Life* (Garden City, NY: Doubleday, 1961); Charles Y. Glock and Rodney Stark, *Christian Beliefs and Anti-Semitism* (New York: Harper & Row, 1966).

4 Charles Tilly, *Durable Inequality* (Berkeley: University of California Press, 1998).

5 Robert Wuthnow, *Communities of Discourse: Ideology and Social Structure in the Reformation, the Enlightenment, and European Socialism* (Cambridge, MA: Harvard University Press, 1989).

6 Robert Wuthnow, *The Restructuring of American Religion: Society and Faith Since World War II* (Princeton, NJ: Princeton University Press, 1988).

7 Robert Wuthnow, *Acts of Compassion: Caring for Others and Helping Ourselves* (Princeton, NJ: Princeton University Press, 1991); – *Sharing the Journey: Support Groups and America's New Quest for Community* (New York: Free Press, 1994); – *God and Mammon in America* (New York: Free Press, 1994); – *Poor Richard's Principle: Recovering the American Dream through the Moral Dimension of Work, Business, and Money* (Princeton, NJ: Princeton University Press, 1996); – *After Heaven: Spirituality in America Since the 1950s* (Berkeley: University of California Press, 1998).

8 Robert N. Bellah, Richard Madsen, William M. Sullivan, Ann Swidler and Steven M. Tipton, *Habits of the Heart: Individualism and Commitment in American Life* (Berkeley: University of California Press, 1985).

9 Marsha G. Witten, *All Is Forgiven: The Secular Message in American Protestantism* (Princeton, NJ: Princeton University Press, 1993).

10 Courtney Bender, *Heaven's Kitchen: Living Religion at God's Love We Deliver* (Chicago, IL: University of Chicago Press, 2003).

11 Jeffrey Stout, *Ethics After Babel: The Languages of Morals and Their Discontents* (Boston, MA: Beacon, 1988).

12 Ann Taves, *Religious Experience Reconsidered: A Building Block Approach to the Study of Religion and Other Special Things* (Princeton, NJ: Princeton University Press, 2009).

13 Randall Collins, *Violence: A Micro-Sociological Theory* (Princeton, NJ: Princeton University Press, 2008).

INDEX

Please note that page numbers relating to notes will have the letter "n" following the page number.